Praise for *Environmental Health and Racial Equity in the United States*

Dr. Bullard and colleagues have done it again, offering yet another must-read volume for those working in the arena of environmental justice. This book is destined to be both a reference for those already in the field and an important introduction for those just beginning to explore the links between the environment, race, and public health.

Manuel Pastor, *Director, Program for Environmental and Regional Equity*
Co-Director, Center for the Study of Immigrant Integration
University of Southern California, Los Angeles

This book provides both a narrative and a catalogue of history, science, organizations, and people. Together, it tells not only the story of the impact of environmental disparities on health in the United States but also of the importance of charting a future that integrates the environmental justice movement with the green and sustainability movements. It's a great resource.

Howard Hu, *NSF International Endowed Chair, Department of Environmental Health Sciences*
Professor of Environmental Health, Epidemiology and Internal Medicine
University of Michigan Schools of Public Health and Medicine, Ann Arbor

Environmental Health and Racial Equity in the United States is an indispensible resource. The authors emphasize the power and promise of those individuals and organizations working tirelessly to produce the knowledge, science, legal frameworks, and coalitions that move us closer to a world where environmental justice and healthy communities are no longer dreams deferred. This book should be required reading for every elected official in the United States.

David Naguib Pellow, *Don A. Martindale Professor of Sociology, University of Minnesota*
Author of Garbage Wars: The Struggle for Environmental Justice in Chicago
and Resisting Global Toxics: Transnational Movements for Environmental Justice.

Environmental Health and Racial Equity in the United States

Building Environmentally Just, Sustainable, and Livable Communities

Environmental Health and Racial Equity in the United States

Building Environmentally Just, Sustainable, and Livable Communities

AUTHORS

Robert D. Bullard, PhD

Glenn S. Johnson, PhD

Angel O. Torres, MCP

American Public Health Association

www.aphabookstore.org

WASHINGTON, D.C. • 2011

Published by: American Public Health Association
800 I Street, NW
Washington, DC 20001-3710
www.apha.org

DISCLAIMER: Any discussion of medical or legal issues in this publication is being provided for informational purposes only. Nothing in this publication is intended to constitute medical or legal advice, and it should not be construed as such. This book is not intended to be and should not be used as a substitute for specific medical or legal advice, since medical and legal opinions may only be given in response to inquiries regarding specific factual situations. If medical or legal advice is desired by the reader of this book, a medical doctor or attorney should be consulted.

The use of trade names and commercial sources in this book does not imply endorsement by either the APHA, W. K. Kellogg Foundation, or the editorial board of this volume.

While the publisher and author have used their best efforts in preparing this book, they make no representations with respect to the accuracy or completeness of the content.

This manuscript was prepared with support from the W. K. Kellogg Foundation. The opinions, conclusions, and recommendations expressed or implied within are solely those of the authors and do not necessarily represent the views of the W. K. Kellogg Foundation.

An earlier version of Chapter 3 appeared as *Environmental Justice Timeline—Milestones*, by Robert D. Bullard, a report to the Second National People of Color Environmental Leadership Summit in Washington, DC, October 23–26, 2002 (available at http://www.ejrc.cau.edu/summit2/%20EJTimeline.pdf), and as "Environmental Justice Timeline/Milestones 1987–2007," Chapter 2 of *Toxic Wastes and Race at Twenty: 1987–2007, Grassroots Struggles to Dismantle Environmental Racism in the United States, March 2007, A Report Prepared for the United Church of Christ Justice and Witness Ministries*, by Robert D. Bullard, Paul Mohai, Robin Saha, and Beverly Wright, March 2007 (available at http://www.ejrc.cau.edu/ TWART-light.pdf). Reprinted with permission.

Georges C. Benjamin, MD, FACP, FACEP(E), Executive Director
Howard Spivak, MD, Publications Board Liaison

Printed and bound in the United States of America
Typesetting: Originated by The Manila Typesetting Company
Cover and interior design: Jennifer Strass
Printing and Binding: Sheridan Press

Library of Congress Cataloging-in-Publication Data
Bullard, Robert D. (Robert Doyle), 1946–
  Environmental health and racial equity in the United States : strategies for building environmentally just, sustainable, and livable communities / Robert D. Bullard, Glenn S. Johnson, and Angel O. Torres ; foreword by Gail C. Christopher.
    p. ; cm.
  Includes bibliographical references and index.
  ISBN-13: 978-0-87553-007-9 (alk. paper)
  ISBN-10: 0-87553-007-9 (alk. paper)
  1. Environmental health–United States. 2. Poor–Health and hygiene–United States. 3. Minorities–Health and hygiene–United States. I. Johnson, Glenn S. (Glenn Steve) II. Torres, Angel O. III. American Public Health Association. IV. Title.
  [DNLM: 1. Environmental Health–United States. 2. Poverty Areas–United States. 3. Residence Characteristics–United States. 4. Social Justice–United States. 5. Vulnerable Populations–United States. WA 30.5]
  RA566.3.B85 2011
  362.196'9800973–dc22

                                                                                              2010035288

4/2011

Contents

Foreword

THE MISSION OF THE W. K. Kellogg Foundation is to support children, families, and communities as they create and strengthen conditions that propel vulnerable children to achieve success, both as individuals and as contributors to the larger community and society.

Chronic exposure to environmental contaminants from toxic waste contributes to poor health outcomes. These exposures and other conditions must be addressed if vulnerable children are to be propelled to success. Children and families of color bear a disproportionately high burden from these exposures in communities across this nation. As this book documents, people of color make up the majority—56%—of Americans living in neighborhoods within two miles of commercial hazardous waste facilities, nearly double the percentage in areas beyond two miles away (30%). The percentage is much greater, 69%, when considering neighborhoods with clustered facilities.

These disparate exposures are linked to health disparities via multiple biological and biochemical pathways. Scientific insights are now emerging that shed new light on the possible consequences of cumulative exposures to background contaminants. This era of the genome is also providing new insights into the mechanisms of vulnerability and impact during prenatal periods, early infancy, childhood, as well as on birth outcomes. Children, expectant mothers, and the malnourished are particularly vulnerable to the negative impact of pollutants. From excess lead and arsenic levels in groundwater and drinking water, to mercury present in fish and wildlife, to diesel emissions that impact air quality, people of color live in locations across America that force them to live, work, and play in harm's way.

The W. K. Kellogg Foundation recognizes that chronic health disparities among children of color, particularly in low birthweight and childhood asthma, impede the realization of the Foundation's overarching vision of "a Nation that marshals its resources to assure that all children thrive." We must address environmental health inequities if we are to effectively reduce related health disparities. We are pleased to have sponsored this publication written by the true Father of the Environmental Justice movement, Robert D. Bullard, along with his colleagues Glenn S. Johnson and Angel O. Torres. It is our hope that the "story" of the movement and the reminder of the injustices that communities continue to struggle to overcome will help to ignite an even more robust effort nationwide to improve environmental conditions of health for all.

Reading this book provides tremendous inspiration for those working to achieve social change on behalf of vulnerable children and families. But is also a stark reminder of the slow, seemingly glacial pace of meaningful change.

We have not accomplished enough on this critical aspect of health equity. The publication of this summarative work is a call for more concentrated and effective action.

Gail C. Christopher, DN
Vice President - Program Strategy
W.K. Kellogg Foundation

Preface

MUCH OF THE SUCCESS of the work around environmental health and racial equity can be attributed to its community-based grassroots focus. Leaders emerged in part to fill a gap and to advance a health and racial equity agenda to address environmental and health threats in low-income communities and communities of people of color. For the past three decades, they have been the leading national voice for eradicating environmental racism and public health threats facing low-income communities and communities of color. Grassroots leaders and community-based organizations have also been the impetus and driving force behind the call for more inclusive, democratic, and proactive environmental health and racial equity policies in the United States.

The aim of this book is to assist funders, government, and nongovernmental organizations in identifying near- and long-term needs and collaborative opportunities, assess the state of the field, and support decision-making around environmental health using a racial equity lens. Specifically, this book (1) documents the state of environmental health and racial equity over the past three decades; (2) identifies the impact of this work on public health research, health policy, health legislation, health education, and health networking among grassroots, community-based, and national networks and organizations; (3) reviews, summarizes, and synthesizes existing environmental health and racial equity research and resource materials; (4) chronicles important milestones and achievements of the movement over the past three decades; (5) profiles selected groups and leaders who have won national and international awards, honors, and recognition for their environmental health and racial equity work; (6) illustrates how the environmental health and racial equity framework has been applied in broad solution-oriented areas, including quantitative risks analysis, health implications of suburban sprawl, transportation, air pollution and asthma, industrial pollution and schools, childhood lead poisoning, energy and "dirty power" plants, climate change, and transition to "green jobs" and a "green economy"; (7) tracks environmental health and racial equity policies and federal and state laws, executive orders, and ordinances; and (8) profiles environmental health and racial equity work carried out in academia in partnership with communities.

From New York to California, thousands of justice groups and individuals are now part of a growing movement working to address environmental health disparities, differential enforcement of our environmental, discriminatory land-use practices, disparate facility siting, faulty assumptions in risk analysis, single-exposure models that do not assess cumulative and synergistic impacts, and exclusionary practices that limit the participation of people of color and underrepresented stakeholders in decision-making boards, panels, task forces, committees, and staffs.

These groups are also actively pursuing a range of goals from pollution prevention clean energy, "green transportation," "green jobs," and "green chemistry." It is these voices that have kept social equity at the forefront in pre- and post-Hurricane Katrina Louisiana and in the aftermath of the British Petroleum oil spill catastrophe that threatens Gulf Coast states from Louisiana to Florida. They provide the backbone of the struggle to dismantle unfair and unsafe home, school, and work conditions in cities, suburbs, and rural areas all across the United States.

Acknowledgments

WE WOULD LIKE TO acknowledge the many individuals who aided us in completing the research for this book. First, we would like to extend special thanks to the W. K. Kellogg Foundation, whose program supported our work. Numerous other individuals provided us with valuable information on which this book is based.

We want to thank the following persons for taking time out of their busy schedules to respond to our queries, e-mails, faxes, and phone calls soliciting information: Kalila M. Barnett, Alternatives for Community & Environment; Steven Bonorris, University of California Hastings College of Law; Casey China, International District Housing Alliance; Suzie Canales, Citizens for Environmental Justice; Robert William Collin, Willamette University Center for Sustainable Communities; Robin Morris Collin, Willamette University College of Law; Celeste Cooper, Deep South Center for Environmental Justice at Dillard University; David C. Crowley, vice mayor of Cincinnati; Luis Davila, Environmental Grantmakers Association; Gopal Dayaneni, The Ruckus Society; Danielle Deane, The William and Flora Hewlett Foundation; Michelle Dillingham, legislative aide to Vice Mayor David C. Crowley; Linda Fardan, Harambee House Inc/Citizens for Environmental Justice Inc; Caroline Farrell, Center on Race, Poverty & the Environment; Bill Gallegos, Communities for a Better Environment; Cathy Green, Just Transition Alliance; Roger Kim, Asian Pacific Environmental Network; Aaron Mair, Arbor Hill Environmental Justice Corporation; Paul Mohai, University of Michigan School of Natural Resources and Environment; Devon G. Pena, University of Washington Department of Anthropology; Francisca Porchas, The Labor/Community Strategy Center; Dwayne Proctor, Robert Wood Johnson Foundation; Michele Roberts, Advocates for Environmental Human Rights; Mark A. Mitchell, Connecticut Coalition for Environmental Justice; Mike Schade, Center for Health, Environment & Justice; Nicky Sheats, New Jersey Environmental Justice Alliance; Peggy Shepard, WE ACT for Environmental Justice, Inc; Donele Wilkins, Detroiters Working for Environmental Justice; Kathy Sessions, Health and Environmental Funders Network; Elizabeth Tan, Urban Habitat; Justine Thompson, GreenLaw; Kimberly Wasserman, Little Village Environmental Justice Organization; Nsedu Obot Witherspoon, Children's Environmental Health Network; Elizabeth C. Yeampierre, United Puerto Rican Organization of Sunset Park; Miya Yoshitani, Asian Pacific Environmental Network; Sylvia Hood Washington, University of Illinois at Chicago School of Public Health.

Introduction

HISTORICALLY, PEOPLE OF COLOR and poor communities have borne a disproportionate burden of pollution from landfills, garbage dumps, incinerators, smelters, sewage treatment plants, chemical plants, and a host of other polluting facilities. Many high-pollution industries have followed a path of least resistance, allowing low-income communities and neighborhoods of people of color to become environmental "sacrifice zones" and the "dumping grounds" for all kinds of health-threatening operations.[1]

A new framework emerged in the early 1980s to address environmental threats where people live, work, play, and learn, as well as threats in the physical and natural world. Using a racial equity lens, proponents built a movement on the principle that all Americans have a right to equal protection of the nation's environmental, health, housing, transportation, employment, and civil rights laws and regulations.[2] Advocates also emphasized the promotion of healthy communities and prevention of harm before it occurs. They also called for government policymakers to adopt the "Precautionary Principle," allowing them to make discretionary decisions where there is the possibility of harm and when extensive scientific knowledge on the matter is lacking. This principle also emphasizes protecting the public from exposure to harm when scientific investigation has found a plausible risk.[3]

Because all communities are not created equal, and low-income people and people of color are exposed to greater environmental risks than the general population, this new national environmental movement emerged around racial equity and social justice—two areas that were consistently omitted from the agendas and priorities of environmental and conservation organizations and the national environmental movement.

Birth of a New National Movement

Just three decades ago, the concept of environmental justice had not registered on the radar screens of environmental, civil rights, or social justice groups. Nevertheless, it should not be forgotten that Dr. Martin Luther King Jr. went to Memphis Tennessee, in 1968 on an environmental and economic justice mission for striking Black garbage workers. The strikers were demanding equal pay and better work conditions. Dr. King was assassinated before he could complete his mission.

In 1978, another landmark garbage dispute took place in Houston when African American homeowners began a bitter fight to keep a sanitary landfill out of their suburban middle-income neighborhood.[4] Northwood Manor residents' attorney, Linda McKeever Bullard, filed a class-action lawsuit to block the waste facility from being built. The 1979 lawsuit, *Bean v. Southwestern Waste Management Corp.*, was the first of its kind to challenge the siting of a waste facility under civil rights law.

The landmark Houston case occurred 4 years before the environmental justice movement was catapulted into the national limelight in the rural and mostly African American Warren County, North Carolina. In 1982, the siting of a 142-acre PCB (polychlorinated biphenyls) dump in rural and mostly Black Warren County ignited the national movement.[5] The decision sparked protests and over 500 arrests. The protests also provided the impetus for a U.S. General Accounting Office (1983) study, *Siting of Hazardous Waste Landfills and Their Correlation With Racial and Economic Status of Surrounding Communities*. The study revealed that three out of the four off-site, commercial hazardous waste landfills in Region 4 (which includes Alabama, Florida, Georgia, Kentucky, Mississippi, North Carolina, South Carolina, and Tennessee) happen to be located in predominantly African American communities, although African Americans made up only 20% of the region's population. More importantly, the protesters put "environmental racism" on the map.

The protests also led the Commission for Racial Justice to produce *Toxic Wastes and Race in the United States* (1987), the first national study to correlate waste facility sites and demographic characteristics. The *Toxic Wastes and Race* study was revisited in 1994 using 1990 census data. The 1994 study found that people of color are 47% more likely to live near a hazardous waste facility than are White Americans.[6]

Although the "midnight dumpers" paid by the Ward Transformer Company to dump contaminated waste oils along rural roads were fined and jailed, the innocent Warren County community was handed a 21-year sentence of living in a toxic-waste prison.[7] The PCB landfill later became the most recognized symbol of environmental racism in the county. Despite the stigma, Warren County also became a symbol of environmental justice. By 1993, the facility was leaking, with 13 feet of water trapped in the landfill.[8]

In December 2003, after living with toxic wastes for more than two decades, an environmental justice victory finally came to the residents of Warren County. State and federal funding sources spent $18 million to detoxify or neutralize contaminated soil stored at the PCB landfill.[9] A private contractor hired by the state dug up and burned 81,500 tons of oil-laced soil in a kiln that reached more than 800°F to remove the PCBs. The soil was put back in a football field–sized pit, re-covered to form a mound, graded, and seeded with grass.

Toward an Environmental Justice Framework

The nation's environmental laws, regulations, and policies are not applied uniformly—resulting in some individuals, neighborhoods, and communities being exposed to elevated health risks. In 1992, staff writers from the *National Law Journal* uncovered glaring inequities in the way the federal Environmental Protection Agency (EPA) enforces the nation's environmental laws and regulations.[10] In their article, the authors wrote, "There is a racial divide in the way the U.S. government cleans up toxic waste sites and punishes polluters. White communities see faster action, better results and stiffer penalties than communities where Blacks, Hispanics and other minorities live. This unequal protection often occurs whether the community is wealthy or poor."[11]

These findings suggest that unequal protection is placing communities of color at special risk. The *National Law Journal* study supplements the findings of earlier studies and reinforces what many grassroots leaders have been saying all along: Not only are people of color differentially affected by industrial pollution, they also can expect different treatment from the government. Environmental decision-making operates at the juncture of science, economics, politics, special interests, and ethics.

The dominant environmental protection model places communities of color at special risk. It also reinforces rather than challenges the stratification of people (race, ethnicity, status, power), place (central cities, suburbs, rural areas, unincorporated areas, Native American reservations), and work (i.e., office workers are afforded greater protection than are farmworkers). The dominant paradigm exists to manage, regulate, and distribute risks. As a result, the current system has institutionalized unequal enforcement, traded human health for profit, placed the burden of proof on the "victims" and not the polluting industry, legitimated human exposure to harmful chemicals, pesticides, and hazardous substances, promoted risky technologies such as incinerators, exploited the vulnerability of economically and politically disenfranchised communities, subsidized ecological destruction, created an industry around risk assessment, delayed cleanup actions, and failed to develop pollution prevention as the overarching and dominant strategy.[12]

The environmental justice framework incorporates other social movements that seek to eliminate harmful and discriminatory practices in housing, land use, industrial planning, health care, and sanitation services.[13] The framework includes the following elements:

- Attempts to uncover the underlying assumptions that may contribute to and produce unequal protection.
- Incorporates the principle of the right of all individuals to be protected from environmental degradation.
- Adopts a public health model of prevention (elimination of the threat before harm occurs) as the preferred strategy.
- Rests on the Precautionary Principle for protecting workers, communities, and ecosystems. Shifts the burden of proof to polluters/dischargers who do harm, discriminate, or who do not give equal protection to racial and ethnic minorities and other "protected" classes.
- Redresses disproportionate impact through targeted action and resources.

The right to health is a basic human right. Environmental and public health threats are not randomly distributed. Healthy places and healthy people are highly correlated. The poorest of the poor within the United States and around the world have the worst health and live in the most degraded environments. Although access to insurance and health care is important, social conditions are also major determinants of health. Social forces acting at a collective level help shape an individual's biology, individual risk behaviors, environmental exposures, and access to resources that promote health.

Applying a Racial Equity Lens to Health and the Environment

One of the most important indicators of an individual's health is one's street address or neighborhood. Where you live affects your health and chance of leading a flourishing life. Today, numerous researchers are now looking at individual health outcomes through an ecological lens, recognizing that *place* (or *space*) matters. They are using geographic information system (GIS) analysis to map relationships between the availability of fast foods, neighborhood racial and income composition, nutrient intake, and body mass index (BMI). Researchers are also examining links between the built environment, walking, and pedestrian accidents; outdoor alcohol advertisement and youth attitudes about drinking; recreation facilities and physical activity; park acreage, green access, and ethnicity; distribution of transportation dollars, transit access and alternatives to driving, air quality, and asthma; pollution "hot spots," industrial facility siting and permitting, and health impact assessment (HIA).

One of the Centers for Disease Control and Prevention's (CDC's) four overarching Health Protection Goals is "Healthy People in Healthy Places." This goal is based on the idea that the places where people live, work, learn, and play will protect and promote health and safety, especially for those people at greater risk of health disparities. Here, social determinants of health are factors in the social environment that contribute to or detract from the health of individuals and communities. These factors include socioeconomic status, transportation, housing, access to services, discrimination by social grouping (e.g., race, gender, or class), and social or environmental stressors. Inequitable distribution of these conditions across various populations is a significant contributor to persistent and pervasive health disparities in the United States.

The CDC's 2008 report *Promoting Health Equity: A Resource to Help Communities Address Social Determinants of Health* is a workbook for community-based organizations seeking to affect the social determinants of health through community-based participatory approaches and nontraditional partnerships.[14] The social determinants of health are the circumstances in which individuals are born, grow up, live, work, play, learn, and age, and the systems that are created to deal with illness. These circumstances are in turn shaped by a wider set of societal forces such as economics, social policies, and politics as well as psychosocial factors such as opportunities for employment, access to health care, hopelessness, and freedom from racism, including institutional racism and discrimination.[15]

Race and place in America are interconnected.[16] Race continues to polarize and spatially divide cities.[17] Place affects access to jobs, education and public services, culture, shopping, level of personal security, and medical services.[18] Place even affects the air we breathe.[19] Race maps closely to economic geography. Race does not cause illness, racism does: More than 100 studies now link racism to worse health.[20] Some employers use place as a "signal" associated with perceptions about race, class, worker skills, and attitudes.[21] Using these signals, many employers often recruit suburban White workers while avoiding central-city Black workers.

All communities are not created equal. Some communities are more equal than others. If a community happens to be poor, working class, or a community of color, its residents generally have fewer choices and opportunities—in a range of residential amenities such as housing, schools, jobs, shopping, parks, green space, hospitals, and police and fire protection—than do affluent, middle-class, or White residents.[22] Where Whites choose to live, work, play, go to school, and worship is not accidental.[23] Many of their choices are shaped by race.[24] Much of the "edge" (the advantage which some people or groups actually benefit, deliberately or inadvertently, from racial bias) that accrues to middle-class Americans comes from White privilege.[25] Five decades after *Brown v. Board of Education*, White privilege is still the norm in the United States rather than the exception.[26]

Middle-class White families use their social and cultural advantage, which is unavailable to Black middle-class families, to choose homes in areas with the best schools. White advantage is institutionalized by lending practices and reproduced again and again by subsequent generations. Enforcing existing federal fair lending laws is one area where more work is needed.[27] The significance of race endures in the residential color line, racial exclusion, violence, and overt discrimination.[28]

In metropolitan Atlanta, for example, space "inside" and "outside" of I-285 (a perimeter highway that encircles the city of Atlanta) has become racialized.

Businesses and employers are keenly aware of and contribute to racialized space.[29] A business location advertised as "inner-city and inside the perimeter" is code for Black, whereas a location defined as "outside the perimeter" connotes suburban and White. Racialized place creates perpetual demarcations. Redlining practices used by insurance companies, banks, mortgage companies, grocery stores, sit-down restaurants, theaters, and even coffee shops are built largely around racialized zip codes.[30]

The Boston Public Health Commission (BPHC) took action to undo racism by focusing on lack of equal opportunity, discrimination, and race-related differences in exposure to health risks and instituting quality improvement initiatives within the health care system.[31] The core framework the BPHC adopted includes three main strategies: building and supporting community partnerships, promoting antiracist work environments, and realigning external activities to address racism.

Racialized place provides privilege and advantage for Whites while placing a "tax" on Blacks and other people of color. Even when income is equalized, Black homeowners receive 18% less value for their homes than do White homeowners. This differential amounts to an 18% "segregation tax" for people living in Black neighborhoods.[32] For every dollar of income, White homeowners owned $2.64 worth of house in 2001; by contrast, Black homeowners owned only $2.16 worth of house. The higher the segregation, the wider the Black/White gap. Fewer than 50% of Black families own their homes, compared with more than 70% of Whites. Home ownership is positively correlated with rising property values, educational attainment and achievement, decreased dropout rates, increased civil involvement, and residential stability.[33]

The color line is no imaginary line in the United States. Whether embedded in racial stigma[34] or in institutionalized discrimination, the color line is a stark reality for millions of poor and middle-class Blacks.[35] America has never been color-blind when it comes to people of color.[36] On average, communities of people of color have fewer parks, green space, and shopping, including full-service supermarkets, than White communities and more than their fair share of industrial polluting facilities and nonresidential land uses that bring down property values and diminish overall quality of life.[37]

People of color have fewer housing and residential choices than do Whites. Blacks and Latinos are denied mortgages and home improvement loans at twice the rate of Whites. Housing segregation and institutional racism in the real estate market render Black homes, on average, worth $42,800 less than White homes. Government housing policies have contributed to residential segregation and subsidized inequities between neighborhoods of people of color and White neighborhoods.[38]

The Legacy of Environmental Racism

The built environment, infrastructure, and environmental quality all have a direct impact on our health and well-being. Old, substandard housing affects health and proximity to polluting industries; waste, freeways, and other hazards affect the air we breathe, the water we drink, and the land on which we live. Neighborhood residents located close to major highways often suffer disproportionately from respiratory problems.[39] Noise pollution also negatively affects our anxiety and stress levels, which increase our risk for chronic illness.

This is not rocket science. Communities that ensure access to quality services, promote good physical and psychological well-being, and protect the natural and physical environment are essential for health equity.[40] A community environment with more protective factors is a healthier environment.[41] A community's physical environment influences the health of its residents in many ways. For example, clean water and air, the presence of sidewalks, walkable and bikable neighborhoods, access to full-service grocery stores and healthy foods, parks, safe streets, transit, and affordable, high-quality housing all contribute to a healthy community.

Middle-income homeowners in Black and Latino neighborhoods have fewer services, retail shopping, banking, good schools, and other residential amenities—amenities that are commonplace in most middle-class neighborhoods, which White homeowners take for granted.[42] Discrimination in real estate and mortgage markets and educational environments robs current and future generations of African Americans and other people of color of important wealth-creating opportunities. Racial and economic segregation exacerbate inner-city poverty and health disparities.[43]

Lower-income households tend to be exposed to more formidable and ongoing stressors, for example, job insecurity, unpaid bills, inadequate child care, underperforming schools, dangerous or toxic living conditions, crowded homes, and even noisy streets. They are also less likely to have access to the money, power, status, knowledge, social connections, and other economic resources they need to gain control over the many challenges that threaten to upset their lives.

Environmental racism creates unhealthy environments in which a disproportionately large share of poor people and people of color live. Environmental racism refers to any policy, practice, or directive that differentially affects or disadvantages (whether intended or unintended) individuals, groups, or communities based on race or color. It combines with public policies and industry practices to provide benefits for corporations while shifting costs to people of color.[44] Government, legal, economic, political, and military institutions reinforce environmental racism, and it influences local land use, enforcement of environmental regulations, industrial facility siting, and the locations where people of color live, work, and play.

The roots of environmental racism are deep and have been difficult to eliminate. Environmental decision-making often mirrors the power arrangements of the dominant society and its institutions. It disadvantages people of color while providing advantages or privileges for corporations and individuals in the upper echelons of society. The question of *who pays* and *who benefits* from environmental and industrial policies is central to this analysis of environmental racism.

The question of environmental justice is not anchored in a debate about whether or not decision-makers should tinker with risk management. The framework seeks to prevent environmental health threats before they occur. Environmental justice and health equity advocates have always emphasized prevention and precaution. This holistic framework targets the built environment and its impact on public health as well as government policies and private practices, with special emphasis on the health of vulnerable populations, including children, low-income families, and families of color. Much of the emphasis during the past three decades has concentrated on addressing social determinants of health as well as confronting institutionalized barriers, including various forms of racism and discrimination, including environmental racism.

Local and national groups have aligned themselves to challenge factors in the social environment that contribute to or detract from the health of individuals and community health. They are also working with planners and policymakers to reshape the built environment to improve individual and community health outcomes—with the ultimate goal of creating healthy places and healthy people.

References

1. Robert D. Bullard, *The Quest for Environmental Justice: Human Rights and the Politics of Pollution* (San Francisco: Sierra Club Books, 2005).

2. Ibid., xvi.

3. Carolyn Raffensperger and Joel Tickner, *Protecting Public Health and the Environment: Implementing the Precautionary Principle* (Washington, DC: Island Press, 1999).

4. Robert D. Bullard, "Solid Waste Sites and the Black Houston Community," *Sociological Inquiry* 53, no. 2–3 (Spring 1983): 273–288.

5. Robert D. Bullard, *Dumping in Dixie: Race, Class and Environmental Quality* (Boulder, CO: Westview Press, 2000).

6. Benjamin Goldman and Laura Fitton, *Toxic Wastes and Race Revisited* (Washington, DC: Center for Policy Alternatives, 1994).

7. Eileen McGurty, *Transforming Environmentalism: Warren County, PCBs, and the Origins of Environmental Justice* (New Brunswick, NJ: Rutgers University Press, 2007), p. 4.

8. Exchange Project, *Real People, Real Stories: Afton, NC (Warren County)* (Chapel Hill: Department of Health and Health Education, University of North Carolina at Chapel Hill, September 2006), http://www.learnnc.org/lp/media/uploads/2010/12/afton_long_story_07-0426_for_web.pdf (accessed January 30, 2008).

9. Wade Rawlins, "Dump's Days Fade," *The News & Observer*, November 11, 2003, p. 1.

10. Marianne Lavelle and Marcia Coyle, "Unequal Protection," *National Law Journal*, September 21, 1992, pp. S1–S2.

11. Ibid., S2.

12. Luke W. Cole and Sheila R. Foster, *From the Ground Up: Environmental Racism and the Rise of the Environmental Justice Movement* (New York: New York University Press, 2000).

13. Robert D. Bullard, "Race and Environmental Justice in the United States," Yale Journal of International Law 18 (Winter 1993): 319–335; and Robert D. Bullard, "The Threat of Environmental Racism," *Natural Resources & Environment 7* (Winter 1993): 23–26, 55–56.

14. Laura K. Brennan Ramirez, Elizabeth A. Baker, and Marilyn Metzler, *Promoting Health Equity: A Resource to Help Communities Address Social Determinants of Health* (Atlanta, GA: U.S. Department of Health and Human Services, Centers for Disease Control and Prevention, 2008).

15. Thomas A. LaVeist, *Race, Ethnicity, and Health: A Public Health Reader* (New York: Jossey-Bass, 2002).

16. John W. Frazier, Florence M. Margai, and Eugene Tettey-Fio, *Race and Place* (Boulder, CO: Westview Press, 2003).

17. Reynolds Farley, Sheldon Danziger, and Harry J. Holzer, *Detroit Divided* (New York: Russell Sage Foundation, 2002).

18. Peter Dreier, John Mollenkoph, and Todd Swanstromm, *Place Matters: Metropolitics for the Twenty-First Century* (Lawrence, KS: University Press of Kansas, 2001).

19. Robert D. Bullard, *Unequal Protection: Environmental Justice and Communities of Color* (San Francisco, CA: Sierra Club Books, 1996).

20. California Newsreel, *Unnatural Causes . . . Is Inequality Making Us Sick?* "Backgrounder from the Unnatural Causes Health Equity Database," 2008, http://www.unnaturalcauses.org/assets/uploads/file/primers.pdf (accessed November 28, 2009).

21. Chris Tilly, Philip Moss, Joleen Kirschenman, and Ivy Kennelly, "Space as a Signal: How Employers Perceive Neighborhoods in Four Metropolitan Labor Markets," in *Urban Inequality: Evidence From Four Cities*, ed. Alice O'Connor, Chris Tilly, and Lawrence D. Bobo, p. 306 (New York: Russell Sage Foundation, 2003).

22. Robert D. Bullard, Glenn S. Johnson, and Angel O. Torres, eds., *Sprawl City: Race, Politics, and Planning in Atlanta* (Washington, DC: Island Press, 2000).

23. Annette Lareau, Home Advantage: Social Class and *Parental Intervention in Elementary Education*, 2nd ed. (Lanham, MD: Rowman & Littlefield, 2000).

24. George Lipsitz, *The Possessive Investment in Whiteness* (Philadelphia, PA: Temple University Press, 1998).

25. Paula S. Rothenberg, *White Privilege: Essential Readings on the Other Side of Racism,* 2nd. ed. (New York: Worth, 2005).

26. Derek A. Bell, *Silent Covenants: Brown v. Board of Education and the Unfilled Hope of Racial Reform* (New York: Oxford University Press, 2004).

27. Stephen Ross and John Yinger, *The Color of Money: Mortgage Discrimination, Research Methodology and Fair-Lending Enforcement* (Cambridge, MA: MIT Press, 2002).

28. Alice O'Connor, Chris Tilly, and Lawrence D. Bobo, eds., *Urban Inequality: Evidence from Four Cities* (New York: Russell Sage Foundation, 2003), p. 5.

29. Ibid., p. 313.

30. Robert D. Bullard, *The Black Metropolis in the Twenty-First Century: Race and the Politics of Place.* (New York: Rowman & Littlefield, 2007).

31. Brennan Ramirez, Baker, and Metzler, *Promoting Health Equity*, p. 22.

32. David Rusk, *The Segregation Tax: The Cost of Racial Segregation on Black Homeowners* (Washington, DC: Brookings Institution Center on Urban and Metropolitan Policy, 2001).

33. Nancy A. Denton, "Housing as a Means of Asset Accumulation: A Good Strategy for the Poor?" in *Assets for the Poor: The Benefits of Spreading Asset Ownership*, ed. Thomas M. Shapiro and Edward N. Wolff (New York: Russell Sage, 2001), pp. 232–233.

34. Glenn C. Loury, The Anatomy of Racial Inequality (Cambridge, MA: Harvard University Press, 2003).

35. Mary Waters, *Black Identities* (Cambridge, MA: Harvard University Press, 1999).

36. Michael K. Brown, Martin Carnoy, Elliot Currie, Troy Duster, David B. Oppenheimer, Marjorie M. Schultz and David Wellman, *Whitewashing Racism: The Myth of a Color-Blind Society* (Berkeley: University of California Press, 2003).

37. Robert D. Bullard, *Growing Smarter: Achieving Livable Communities, Environmental Justice, and Regional Equity* (Cambridge, MA: MIT Press, 2007), pp. 2–8.

38. Douglas Massey and Nancy A. Denton, *American Apartheid* (Cambridge, MA: Harvard University Press, 1993).

39. Shobha Srinivasan, Liam R. O'Fallon, and Allen Dearry, "Creating Healthy Communities, Healthy Homes, Healthy People: Initiating a Research Agenda on the Built Environment and Public Health," *American Journal of Public Health* 93, no. 9 (2003): 1446–1450.

40. World Health Organization (WHO) Commission on the Social Determinants of Health, *Closing the Gap in a Generation: Health Equity Through Action on Social Determinants of Health.* (London, England: WHO, November 2008).

41. Judith Bell and Victor Rubin, *Why Place Matters: Building a Movement for Healthy Communities* (Oakland, CA: PolicyLink, 2007), p. 22.

42. Sheryll Cashin, *The Failures of Integration: How Race and Class Are Undermining the American Dream* (New York: Public Affairs, 2004).

43. Paul Jargowsky, *Poverty and Place* (New York: Russell Sage Foundation, 1997).

44. Bullard, *The Quest for Environmental Justice*, p. 32.

1

Environmental Health and Racial Equity in the Twenty-First Century

RACE AND ENVIRONMENTAL QUALITY have become hot topics of research, policy, conferences, and community organizing in recent years. Much of the impetus behind this surge emerged out of grassroots and community-based environmental struggles. The demand for equal protection later became the heart and soul of environmental justice—a framework built on the principle that all Americans have a right to equal protection of the nation's environmental, health, housing, transportation, employment, and civil rights laws and regulations.[1]

Mounting grassroots mobilization pressured the federal government to acknowledge and recognize environmental disparities, environmental inequality, and environmental justice. The U.S. Environmental Protection Agency (EPA) defines environmental justice as

> the fair treatment and meaningful involvement of all people regardless of race, color, national origin, or income with respect to the development, implementation, and enforcement of environmental laws, regulations and policies. Fair treatment means that no group of people, including racial, ethnic, or socioeconomic groups should bear a disproportionate share of the negative environmental consequences resulting from industrial, municipal, and commercial operations, or the execution of federal, state, local, and tribal programs and policies.[2]

Environmental degradation, poverty, and vulnerability are interrelated. Poverty impacts health because it determines how many resources poor people have and defines the amount of environmental risks they will be exposed to in their immediate environment.[3] Race and ethnicity map closely with the geography of environmental and health risks.[4] Residents in fenceline communities—those within one half mile of a polluting facility—comprise a special population that deserves special attention.[5] Many of these communities are disproportionately and adversely impacted by industrial pollution and unequal enforcement of environmental regulations. Environmental racism—any policy, practice, or directive that differentially (whether intended or unintended) affects or disadvantages individuals, groups, or communities based on race or color[6]—places millions of Americans' health at special risk.[7]

Movement Building

On October 23, 2002, after several false starts and two years of planning, the United Church of Christ (UCC) and environmental justice leaders convened the Second National People of Color Environmental Leadership Summit (Summit II) in Washington, DC. Summit II organizers planned the 4-day meeting for 500 participants. However, more than 1,400 delegates from grassroots and community-based organizations, faith-based groups, organized labor, civil rights, youth, and academic institutions made their way to the nation's capital to participate in the historic gathering, a clear indication that the movement was alive and well.

The Summit II planners made a special effort to raise funds and reach out to grassroots groups, community-based organizations, and youth and student groups. A special budget was carved out for Summit II youth and student programming. The vast majority, over 75%, of Summit II attendees were people of color from community-based organizations and networks. A diverse set of leaders from community-based organizations, environmental networks, faith-based groups, and university-based environmental justice centers committed to bringing young people to the Summit and growing a new generation of leaders to meet current and emerging challenges in communities of people of color and among marginalized populations in the United States and abroad.

Summit II brought three generations (elders, seasoned leaders, and youth activists) of the environmental justice movement together. The "new" faces—persons who were not present at the First National People of Color Environmental Leadership Summit held in 1991—outnumbered the veteran environmental justice leaders two to one. Summit II attendees were diverse in another respect, as they came from nearly every state, including Alaska and Hawaii, and from the Commonwealth of Puerto Rico. Today, the movement continues to expand and mature. The 1992 *People of Color Environmental Groups Directory* listed only 300 environmental justice groups in the United States. By 2000, the list had grown to over 1,000 groups in the United States, Canada, and Mexico.

Students and young people have fueled every successful social movement in the United States, from the civil rights movement to the environmental movement, the antiwar movement, and the women's movement. Four youth and student leaders served on the Summit II steering committee. Several hundred youths and students attended the conference and made their voices heard through a well-timed protest demonstration and long hours of hard work. The young people were able to incorporate many of their issues and priorities into the program. Nevertheless, during the second day of the Summit, more than 100 youths and students presented a set of demands to the gathering—calling for youths and students to be integrated into the leadership of the movement.

Summit II delegates reaffirmed the "Principles of Environmental Justice" and "A Call to Action," both adopted at the 1991 Summit. These principles are as true today as they were in 1991. Delegates adopted three new principles (Principles of Working Together, Youth Principles, and Principles Opposing the War Against Iraq) and presented 15 resolutions. The working groups put many hours into developing and completing these documents.

On October 26, 2002, the last day of the Summit, more than 150 youth attendees issued a statement, "An Overview of Youth Leadership in the Environmental Justice Movement," that outlined essential concepts of youth organizing and environmental justice. The statement reads:

> As youth we feel society has a negative perception of us. Society places stereotypes on us based on our race, class, gender, sexuality, and age. Our voices and concerns are often not heard by decision makers that affect our society. We believe that we have unique and diverse perspectives that can enhance the Environmental Justice Movement. We want to learn from our elders, their experiences, stories, and knowledge. We believe that through being mentored by our elders and by being involved in decision-making processes, we can build a powerful movement ensuring environmental justice for all.[8]

Summit II ended with the leaders reaffirming their commitment to return to their respective communities and work for environmental and economic justice. Growing new leaders has always been a top priority of the movement. This new leadership has emerged through mentoring, train-the-trainer, and college- and university-based programs. No social movement can sustain itself without bringing in new members—especially young people—and allowing them to assume leadership roles. Building a multiethnic, multiracial, multi-issue, antiracist, and intergenerational movement is not easy. Much work is still needed to build trust, mutual respect, and principled relationships across racial, ethnic, cultural, gender, and age lines.

Soon after the summit, the Ford Foundation, one of the funders of Summit II, showed interest in "second-generation" leaders. The Foundation approached the Oakland-based Movement Strategy Center to document youth involvement in the environmental justice movement. The research—interviews and site visits with 40 people at 27 organizations in 15 states along with ten individuals at private foundations—culminated in the 2005 *Regeneration: Youth Leadership in Environmental Justice* report.[9] The *Regeneration* report arrived at nine major findings:

- Youths organizing in the environmental justice movement are transforming strategies of organizing and leadership.
- Environmental justice organizations forge definitions of "youth" that reflect their communities and organizing strategies.
- Youth environmental justice work can take an intergenerational form and youth-led form, and both are important and complementary.
- Youth environmental justice work is deeply grounded in political education.
- Innovative cultural work is a strong feature of youth environmental justice organizing.
- Youth environmental justice organizations blend organizing with long-term youth development and support.
- Environmental justice organizations and networks are struggling to support generational transitions.
- Youth environmental justice organizations maintain a connection to movement building through networks and training institutes.
- Youth leadership development is evolving within a larger focus on movement sustainability.

Multigenerational environmental health and racial equity organizing offers many advantages for leadership development and movement building. It supports models of social change that promote diversity, cultural pluralism, antiracist public policies, and organizing of disenfranchised and marginalized low-income people and families and children of color. Multigenerational organizations have exploded on the scene all across the United States fighting to protect communities against the unequal distribution of environmental hazards undermining the health of families and children forced to live in neighborhoods with locally unwanted land uses (LULUs).

Community leaders have formed alliances with groups advocating for smart growth, healthy and sustainable communities, equitable development, and a "green economy," understanding that they must also continue to fight to secure safe and sanitary housing and toxin-free neighborhoods.[10] A growing network of groups have pushed for tougher enforcement of clean air regulations and campaigned to stop "dirty diesel" buses and bus depots from being sited in their neighborhoods. Others have focused their energies on transportation-oriented development, linking public transit systems with jobs and economic activity centers, representation on boards and commissions, receiving their fair share of public infrastructure investments, and ensuring workers are paid a livable wage so they can also have options, including home and car ownership.[11]

Land-Use Zoning and the Local Politics of Race

Land-use zoning has shaped much of the urban built environment. Zoning is probably the most widely applied mechanism to regulate urban land use in the United States. Zoning laws broadly define land for residential, commercial, or industrial uses, and may impose narrower land-use restrictions: for example, minimum and maximum lot size, number of dwellings per acre, and square footage and height of buildings.[12]

Zoning laws and regulations influence land use and in turn have important environmental justice implications.[13] Local land-use and zoning policies are the "root enabling cause of disproportionate burdens and environmental injustice" in the United States.[14] A 2003 National Academy of Public Administration (NAPA) report, *Addressing Community Concerns: How Environmental Justice Relates to Land Use Planning and Zoning*, found that most planning and zoning board members are men; more than nine out of ten members are White; most members are aged 40 years or older; and boards contain mostly professionals and few, if any, nonprofessional or community representatives.[15]

Zoning ordinances, deed restrictions, and other land-use mechanisms have been widely used as a NIMBY (not in my backyard) tool, operating through exclusionary practices. Exclusionary zoning (and rezoning) has been a subtle form of using government authority and power to foster and perpetuate discriminatory practices—including environmental planning. Exclusionary zoning has been used to zone against something rather than for something. On the other hand, "expulsive" zoning has pushed out residential uses and allowed "dirty" industries to invade communities.[16] Largely the poor, people of color, and renters inhabit the most vulnerable communities. Zoning laws are often legal weapons "deployed in the cause of racism" (as Rabin puts it) by allowing certain "undesirable" people (immigrants, people of color, and poor people) to be excluded from some areas and operations (polluting industries) to be excluded from other areas.

Land-use planning is a job primarily for local, regional, and state jurisdictions. Generally, residents look to their local government to address land-use problems. Nevertheless, some federal government decisions and guidance impact local and regional land use from zoning regulations to the construction of transportation systems (highways vs public transit and other alternatives to driving) that respond to a region's needs to comply with the federal Clean Air Act. For example, the January 2001 EPA report, *EPA Guidance: Improving Air Quality Through Land Use Activities*, supports this point. It reads:

> In recent years, many of EPA's stakeholders have explored using land use activities as strategies for improving air quality. These stakeholders, including state and local planning agencies, have suggested that EPA improve guidance on how to recognize land use strategies in the air quality planning process that result in improvements in local and regional air quality.[17]

The EPA issued the guidance "to inform state and local governments that land use activities which can be shown (through appropriate modeling and quantification) to have beneficial impacts on air quality, may help them meet their air quality goals."[18] Some regional authorities have used land-use zoning by deploying buffer zones to keep polluting facilities away from sensitive areas. For example, the South Coast Air Quality Management District in Los Angeles (SCAQMD), the air pollution control agency for all of Orange County and the urban portions of Los Angeles, Riverside, and San Bernardino counties, requires buffer zones for such sensitive areas as schools to protect against the risks posed by toxic emissions from high-impact sources.[19] The SCAQMD guidance also suggests policies that school districts can use to prevent or reduce potential air pollution impacts and protect the health of their students and staff.

The objective of SCAQMD's guidance is to facilitate stronger collaboration between school districts and SCAQMD to reduce exposure to source-specific air pollution impacts.[19] With or without zoning, deed restrictions, or other devices, various groups are unequally able to protect their environmental interests. More often than not, a disproportionate share of low-income and residential neighborhoods are "zoned for garbage" and deemed compatible with industrial use.[20] They also get shortchanged in the neighborhood protection game.[21] Zoning, whether local, regional, or federal, has been ineffective in protecting some communities and populations from environmental threats. No amount of zoning has insulated the most vulnerable communities from the negative health impacts of industrial pollution.[22]

Impact of the 1987 Toxic Wastes and Race Report

The UCC 1987 report, *Toxic Wastes and Race in the United States*, ushered in a new era of environmentalism, environmental research, policy analysis, and community activism.[23] Armed with the facts, the report's author, the UCC Commission for Racial Justice put government and industry on notice that low-income people and people of color would no longer sit back and allow their communities to become toxic waste dumping grounds. The UCC report propelled an entire generation of social science researchers investigating the interplay between race, class, the environment, and public health.

The landmark study also spawned a series of academic books, including *Dumping in Dixie: Race, Class, and Environmental Quality* in 1990, the first to chronicle the convergence of two movements—the social justice movement and environmental movement—into the environmental justice movement.[24] Out of the small and seemingly isolated environmental struggles emerged a potent grassroots community-driven movement. Many of the on-the-ground environmental struggles in the 1980s, 1990s, and through the early years of the new millennium have seen the quest for environmental and economic justice become a unifying theme across race, class, gender, age, and geographic lines.

The 1991 First National People of Color Environmental Leadership Summit broadened the framework beyond its early antitoxics focus to include issues of public health, worker safety, land use, transportation, housing, resource allocation, and community empowerment. The meeting also demonstrated that it is possible to build a multiracial grassroots movement around environmental and economic justice.[25] Held in Washington, DC, the 4-day summit was attended by more than 650 grassroots and national leaders from around the world. Delegates came from all 50 states, Puerto Rico, Chile, Mexico, and as far away as the Marshall Islands. People attended the Summit to share their action strategies, redefine the environmental movement, and develop common plans for addressing environmental problems affecting people of color in the United States and around the world.

On October 27, 1991, summit delegates adopted 17 "Principles of Environmental Justice." These principles were developed as a guide for organizing, networking, and relating to government and nongovernmental organizations (NGOs). By June 1992, Spanish and Portuguese translations of the principles were being used and circulated by NGOs and environmental justice groups at the Earth Summit in Rio de Janeiro, Brazil.

In July 1992, after much prodding from environmental and racial equity advocates, the EPA published *Environmental Equity: Reducing Risks for All Communities*, one of the first EPA reports to acknowledge environmental disparities by race and class.[26] Many of the beneficial policies, programs, and initiatives that were begun under the first Bush administration were continued and expanded under the Clinton administration. The urgency for addressing environmental health and racial disparities trickled up to the White House with the signing of Executive Order 12898 in 1994.

In 1997, as stated earlier, the EPA defined environmental justice as

fair treatment and meaningful involvement of all people regardless of race, color, national origin or income with respect to the development, implementation and enforcement of environmental laws, regulations and policies. Fair treatment means that no group of people, including racial, ethnic or socioeconomic groups, should bear a disproportionate share of the negative environmental consequences resulting from industrial, municipal and commercial operations or the execution of federal, state, local and tribal programs and policies.[27]

Toxic Wastes and Race 20 Years Later

In 2007, communities all across the nation celebrated the 20th anniversary of the *Toxic Wastes and Race* report. As part of the celebration, the UCC commissioned the *Toxic Wastes and Race at Twenty 1987–2007* report. The new report uses 2000 census data and applies distance-based methods to a current database of commercial hazardous waste facilities to assess the extent of racial and socioeconomic disparities for the nation as a whole. Disparities are also examined by region and state, and separate analyses are conducted for metropolitan areas, where most hazardous waste facilities are located.

People of color make up the majority (56%) of those living in neighborhoods within two miles of the nation's commercial hazardous waste facilities, nearly double the percentage in areas beyond two miles (30%).[28] People of color make up a much larger (over two thirds) majority (69%) in neighborhoods with clustered facilities. Siting disparities are widespread. Nine out of ten EPA regions have racial disparities in the location of hazardous waste sites. Forty of 44 states (90%) with hazardous waste facilities have disproportionately high percentages of people of color in host neighborhoods—on average about two times greater than the percentages in nonhost areas (44% vs 23%). Host neighborhoods in an overwhelming majority of the 44 states with hazardous waste sites have disproportionately high percentages of Hispanics (35 states), African Americans (38 states), and Asians/Pacific Islanders (27 states). Host neighborhoods of 105 of 149 metropolitan areas with hazardous waste sites (70%) have disproportionately high percentages of people of color, and 46 of these metro areas (31%) have a majority of people-of-color host neighborhoods.

Racial and socioeconomic disparities in the location of the nation's hazardous waste facilities are geographically widespread throughout the country. People of color are concentrated in neighborhoods and communities with the greatest number of facilities; and people of color were more concentrated in areas with commercial hazardous sites in 2007 than in 1987. Race continues to be a significant independent predictor of commercial hazardous waste facility locations when socioeconomic and other nonracial factors are taken into account.

One key question is, "Which came first, people or pollution?" Recent evidence shows that disproportionately high percentages of people of color and low-income populations were present at the time the 413 commercial hazardous waste facilities examined in the *Toxic Wastes and Race at Twenty* report were sited.[29] Nationally, commercial hazardous waste facilities sited since 1965 have been sited in neighborhoods that were disproportionately minority at the time of siting.

In 2008, using a national, census tract-level data set, two University of Colorado sociologists discovered that Black, White, and Hispanic households with similar incomes live in neighborhoods of dissimilar environmental quality, that the association between neighborhood and household income levels and neighborhood hazard levels varies according to neighborhood and household racial composition, and that increases in neighborhood and household income levels are more strongly associated with declining hazard levels in Black neighborhoods and households than in White neighborhoods and households.[30]

The authors found "blacks experience such high pollution burden that black households with incomes between $50,000 and $60,000 live in neighborhoods that are, on average, more polluted than the average neighborhood in which white households with incomes below $10,000 live."[31] These findings suggest that the "impact of higher incomes on black/white proximity to environmental hazards has less to do with the increases in white geographic mobility (relative to black geographic mobility) than with the ability of the higher income blacks to escape the highly polluted, disorganized, and deteriorated neighborhoods to which so many low-income blacks are confined."[32]

Environmental Health and Reproductive Justice

Women of color make up the backbone of the leadership among groups fighting for environmental and reproductive justice. They comprise nearly three fourths of the leaders profiled in the 2000 *People of Color Environmental Groups Directory*,[33] and have provided the essential leadership for framing the intersection of environmental health and racial justice. They make up the majority of the leaders in the U.S. grassroots environmental organizations that are working to make people, products, communities, and ecosystems healthier. These small and unfunded groups have helped seed the environmental health and racial equity movement. According to the 2008 Health and Environmental Funders

Network *Environmental Health and Justice Scoping Report,* the movement has a number of key strengths that include its interdisciplinary and multifaceted approach, work based in the community, multiracial and intergenerational base-building, public policy face, and innovativeness and creativity.[34]

The environmental health, racial equity, and reproductive justice movements differ dramatically from the mainstream conservation and environmental movements in that the leadership of the former is dominated by women. For example, the 2002 Summit II was kept on track by the brains and backbone of a few hardworking, fearless, and dedicated women of color.[35] Although a few men were actively involved and played an important role in planning the meeting, it was the women who kept the very complex event together. Women chaired the overall meeting and all but one of its key subcommittees, in which most of the real work occurred.

The impetus behind the grassroots organizing at the intersection of environmental justice and reproductive justice is also led largely by women of color. The 2009 Movement Strategy Center's *Fertile Ground: Gender, Organizing, and Movement Building at the Intersection of Environmental Justice and Reproductive Justice* states:

> Reproductive justice grew out of a rich legacy of grassroots organizing by women of color, building upon the environmental and reproductive rights movement. By centralizing the question of how control of bodies, gender, and sexuality impacts family, economic opportunity, health, safety, reproductive justice fundamentally links the well-being of individuals to that of communities and families.[36]

The *Fertile Ground* report explores the work of the Environmental Justice/Reproductive Justice (EJ/RJ) Collaborative, which 12 community leaders convened over the course of two years beginning in 2008. Clearly, work grounded in the EJ/RJ frame can generate stronger movements and social change outcomes. Combining forces generates a shared vision and framework that can lead to deeper change in policy, communications, messaging, and public thought; unifies and aligns segments of the social justice movement for greater impact; connects constituents across movements and builds a broader base; supports linkages across movements and builds leadership; creates campaigns and outcomes that better reflect communities' lived experiences; and paves the way for collaborative funding streams that are more agile and encourage the breakout of single-issue agendas.

With limited resources, EJ/RJ work is paying off in terms of changing the environmental policies and practices regarding chemicals and exposure. Groups are working to address the disproportionate impact of chemicals in consumer products and chemical production on communities of color. They are also organizing around the concept of workplace exposure to dangerous chemicals and challenging corporate, military, and government practices surrounding the use of toxins and their release into the environment—with special emphasis on water quality. EJ/RJ organizing is also timely as new findings link toxic products, chemicals, and pollutants to the health of children.

Government Response to Environmental Disparities

The mission of the EPA was never to address environmental policies and practices that result in unfair, unjust, and inequitable outcomes. The EPA is a regulatory agency. Nevertheless, many of the EPA's regulations, such as the Clean Air Act, are health-based. The EPA and other government officials are not likely to ask the questions that go to the heart of environmental injustice: What groups are most affected? Why are they affected? Who did it? What can be done to remedy the problem? How can communities be justly compensated and reparations paid to individuals harmed by industry and government actions? How can the problem be prevented?

The EPA has a spotty record protecting environmental civil rights under the statutory authority of Title VI of the Civil Rights Act, which prohibits discrimination on the basis of race, color, and national origin. In 1994, President Bill Clinton signed Executive Order 12898, *Federal Actions to Address Environmental Justice in Minority Populations and Low-Income Populations*, which seeks "to ensure that no segment of the population, regardless of race, color, national origin, income, or net worth bears disproportionately high and adverse human health and environmental impacts as a result of EPA's policies, programs and activities."[37]

In 1997, the President's Council on Environmental Quality issued environmental justice guidance.[38] In 1998, the EPA's Office of Civil Rights issued its *Interim Guidance for Investigating Title VI Administrative Complaints Challenging*

Permits, which provided a framework for processing environmental discrimination complaints.[39]

Efforts to eliminate environmental health disparities stalled and were met with intense resistance inside the EPA beginning in 2000 with the presidential election of George W. Bush.[40] In August 2000, 125 community groups, environmental justice organizations, coalitions, networks, individuals and Native American nation, in commenting on a revision to the guidance, provided a testament to how their administrative complaints had languished for years.[41] By 2001, more than 100 complaints had been filed, yet few had been resolved, often without adequate investigation, such as the *Select Steel* case in Michigan. Furthermore, none of the rulings were in favor of the complainant, in what amounts to a "conscious policy of non-enforcement."[42] Although the EPA issued its final guidance in March 2006, it did not develop legally binding standards for what constitutes an adverse disparate impact and continues to abrogate its enforcement responsibility to oversee discriminatory practices of state environmental agencies in a credible manner.

Disparate impact pursuant to Title VI of the Civil Rights Act of 1964 had shown promise as a private legal tool to obtain redress from the disparate siting of environmental harms in minority communities. However, on April 24, 2001, the U.S. Supreme Court in *Alexander v. Sandoval* eliminated a major judicial tool for pursuing litigation when it ruled that there is no private right of action to enforce disparate impact regulations promulgated under Title VI.[43]

In January and February 2003, the U.S. Commission on Civil Rights held hearings on environmental justice. Experts presented evidence of environmental inequities in communities of color, including disproportionate incidences of environmentally-related disease, lead paint in homes, hazardous waste sites, toxic playgrounds and schools located near Superfund sites and facilities that release toxic chemicals. In its 2003 report, *Not in My Backyard: Executive Order 12898 and Title VI as Tools for Achieving Environmental Justice*, the Commission concluded that "Minority and low-income communities are most often exposed to multiple pollutants and from multiple sources . . . There is no presumption of adverse health risk from multiple exposures, and no policy on cumulative risk assessment that considers the roles of social, economic and behavioral factors when assessing risk."[44] The report was distributed to members of Congress and to President Bush.

A March 2004 Office of Inspector General report, *EPA Needs to Consistently Implement the Intent of the Executive Order on Environmental Justice*, summed up the treatment of environmental justice under the Bush administration. After a decade, the EPA "has not developed a clear vision or a comprehensive strategic plan, and has not established values, goals, expectations and performance measurements" for integrating environmental justice into its day-to-day operations.[45]

A July 2005 U.S. Government Accountability Office (GAO) report, *Environmental Justice: EPA Should Devote More Attention to Environmental Justice When Developing Clean Air Rules*, also criticized the EPA for its handling of environmental justice issues when drafting clean air rules.[46] In July 2005, the EPA was met with a firestorm of public resistance when it proposed dropping race from its draft Environmental Justice Strategic Plan as a factor in identifying and prioritizing populations that may be disadvantaged by the agency's policies.[47]

A 2005 Associated Press (AP) study found African Americans are 79% more likely than are Whites to live in neighborhoods where industrial pollution is suspected of posing the greatest health danger.[48] Using the EPA's own data and scientists, the AP found that Blacks in 19 states and Latinos in 12 states were more than twice as likely as were Whites to live in neighborhoods where pollution poses the greatest health danger. The AP also found that residents of the at-risk neighborhoods were generally poorer and less educated and unemployment rates in those districts were nearly 20% higher than the national average.

Since 1987, the EPA has collected and stored Toxics Release Inventory (TRI) information in a central database that is accessible on the Internet. It has been used by thousands of neighbors, journalists, and local officials to evaluate the environmental performance of nearby facilities. The TRI program is widely credited with reducing releases of program chemicals by 65%. According to the EPA's Science Advisory Board (SAB), TRI data provide the only reliable source of longitudinal data to evaluate changes in facility and firm environmental performance, to conduct risk assessments of changes in toxic release levels, and to conduct spatial analysis of toxic hazards.[49] The SAB reports more than 120 scholarly articles have been published using TRI data to address a wide range of public health, economic, and social science issues.

Clearly, the TRI has become a useful resource for many different organizations including government, business, academic, and community groups. The

EPA's 2003 report, *How Are the Toxics Release Inventory Data Used? Government, Business, Academic, and Citizen Uses*, concludes:

> A variety of stakeholders work with TRI data on a regular basis. Some data uses, such as risk screening, were recognized when the TRI was first implemented; other uses have developed as the program has matured and expanded. TRI data have been a key tool in the Environmental Justice Movement and in the drive toward more environmentally responsible investment. The applications of TRI data will likely increase in number as environmental awareness grows and opportunities are identified for integrating TRI data with other types of information.[50]

In the fall of 2005, the EPA announced plans to change the TRI program. Many environmental justice leaders saw this as a personal attack on their movement. According to many environmental advocates, the new changes would severely weaken the program, deny the public information, and set back EPA efforts to confront the most serious public issues related to toxic chemicals.[51] In July 2006, the EPASAB Committee opposed these changes in a harsh letter to EPA administrator Stephen L. Johnson.

In December 2006, the EPA announced final rules that undermined this critical program by eliminating detailed reporting requirements for more than 5,000 facilities that release up to 2,000 pounds of chemicals every year and for nearly 2,000 facilities that manage up to 500 pounds of chemicals known to pose some of the worst threats to human health, including lead and mercury. Some of the critical changes included a reporting requirement of only every two years, raising the threshold amount required to report toxic releases, the elimination of the requirement of detailed reports, and the weakening of other important programs at the EPA because of the lack of relevant information previously generated with TRI data.[52]

On September 18, 2006, the EPA's Office of Inspector General issued another study, *Evaluation Report: EPA Needs to Conduct Environmental Reviews of Its Programs, Policies, and Activities*, chastising the agency for falling down on the job when it comes to implementing environmental justice.[53] The EPA continued to dismantle long-standing environmental justice initiatives around the country.[54] In October 2007, a GAO report indicated that the EPA's rules weakening TRI could reduce availability of toxic chemical information used to assess environmental justice and reduce the amount of information about toxic chemical releases without providing significant savings to facilities.[55] According to the GAO, the EPA's new rules would make significantly less information available to communities, but would save companies little—an average of less than $900 per facility per year.

Shortly after taking the helm at the EPA, administrator Lisa P. Jackson in April 2009 signed a final rule to reinstate the stricter TRI reporting requirements for industrial and federal facilities that release toxic substances that threaten human health and the environment.[56] The 2009 Omnibus Appropriations Act, signed by President Barack Obama on March 11, 2009, mandated that prior TRI reporting requirements be reestablished. These changes apply to all TRI reports due July 1, 2009.

In the waning days of the Bush administration in 2008, the EPA published a new rule, "Revisions to the Definition of Solid Waste," that deregulates millions of tons of hazardous wastes.[57] Under this new rule, hazardous wastes destined for recycling are no longer included within the definition of "solid waste" subject to Resource Conservation and Recovery Act (RCRA) regulation. Thus, facilities that claim to recycle hazardous wastes are no longer required to comply with RCRA's safe-handling and reporting requirements.

Given this waste industry's dismal environmental record, less EPA oversight is a prescription for more toxic pollution, increased threats to human health and the environment, and more expensive cleanups. The rule completely disregards the overwhelming evidence—at Superfund sites across this country—that "recycling" of hazardous waste is a very dangerous practice, which, if not stringently regulated, frequently results in the release of extremely toxic chemicals. In the new rule, the EPA removed critical safeguards at these high-risk facilities, and history has shown that this will lead to the generation of Superfund sites and the imminent and substantial endangerment of public health and the environment from toxic waste.

The EPA's new rule exempts 1.5 million tons of hazardous waste from RCRA's protective "cradle to grave" management system and excuses thousands of companies from complying with rules that protect human health and the environment. Under the rule, unlicensed and barely supervised companies will handle hazardous industrial wastes, some of which are highly flammable, explosive, and corrosive, that contain dangerous chemicals known to cause cancer, neurological damage, birth defects, lupus, and immune disorders.

In 2007, the EPA identified 218 cases of serious contamination of air, water, and soil from unsafe hazardous waste recycling.[58] Of the 218 cases, 209 (95.9%) occurred at facilities that were exempt from RCRA's strict oversight. In contrast, only 4% of these cases occurred at facilities controlled by RCRA permits that set stringent standards for storage, transport, treatment, and disposal.[59] Thus, it is clear that strict oversight of this high-risk activity is absolutely critical. Exempting millions more tons of hazardous waste will only increase the public's exposure to toxic chemicals and raise the need for taxpayer-funded cleanups.

Approximately 80,000 different chemicals are now in commercial use with nearly 6 trillion pounds produced annually in the United States. More than 80% of these chemicals have never been screened to learn whether they cause cancer, much less tested to see if they otherwise harm the nervous, immune, endocrine, or reproductive systems. The current U.S. approach regarding testing of chemicals is also not based on real-life exposures, since people and animals are not generally exposed to one chemical in isolation, but to an array of toxic chemicals.

Preliminary mapping conducted in July 2009 by Earthjustice discovered that waste recycling sites in several regions of the United States are located in predominantly low-income communities and communities of color.[60] Given what the research shows nationally about the location of treatment, storage, and disposal facilities, there is a high likelihood that the national pattern of damage cases will also follow the pattern showing a concentration in communities of color and low-income communities.

During the process that resulted in "Revisions to the Definition of Solid Waste," the EPA failed to evaluate how the new RCRA exemption conforms with the Environmental Justice Executive Order 12898. After a June 30, 2009, public hearing in Arlington, Virginia, and loud public outcry from the environmental justice and public health community, the EPA decided to examine the environmental justice and equity implications of the rule before making its decision. Three weeks after the public hearing, the EPA "vow[ed] to examine the impact of hazardous waste on poor communities."[61]

On December 2, 2009, the EPA announced plans to repeal a last-minute attempt by the Bush administration to allow polluters to burn dangerous hazardous waste without complying with important clean air laws.[62] The so-called Emissions Comparable Fuels rule, requested by the National Association of Manufacturers and the American Chemistry Council, would have allowed industries to burn hazardous waste by calling it "fuel." Environmental justice and public health leaders applauded this reversal as a major victory, since communities most impacted by this repeal are often already overburdened with toxic pollution.

The National-Scale Air Toxics Assessment analysis predicts the concentrations of 124 different hazardous air pollutants, which are known to cause cancer, respiratory problems, and other health effects by coupling estimates of emissions from a variety of sources with models that attempt to simulate how the pollution will disperse in the air. The EPA uses the results of these assessments to work with communities in designing their own local-scale assessments, set priorities for improving data in emissions inventories, and help direct priorities for expanding and improving the network of air toxics monitoring.

In June 2009, 6 months before the Emissions Comparable Fuels ruling, the EPA's National-Scale Air Toxics Assessment for 2002 reported that millions of Americans living in nearly 600 neighborhoods are breathing concentrations of toxic air pollutants that put them at a much greater risk of contracting cancer.[63] The levels of 80 cancer-causing substances released by automobiles, factories, and other sources in these areas result in a 100 in 1 million cancer risk. The average cancer risk across the country is 36 in 1 million.

When the First National People of Color Environmental Leadership Summit was held in 1991, no state in the country had passed a law or an executive order on environmental justice. Two years later, New Hampshire passed its pioneering environmental justice policy in 1993. In 2007, at least three dozen states and the District of Columbia had adopted formal environmental justice statutes, executive orders, or policies. In addition, "forty-one states demonstrate significant and increased attention to the issue of environmental justice at the level of state government."[64] By 2009, all 50 states and the District of Columbia had instituted some type of environmental justice law, executive order, or policy—indicating that the area of environmental justice continues to grow and mature.[65] Although permitting and facility siting still dominate state environmental justice programs, a growing number of states are beginning to use land-use planning techniques, such as buffer zones, to improve environmental conditions, reduce potential health threats, and prevent environmental degradation in at-risk communities. States are also incorporating environmental justice in their brownfields, Supplemental Environmental Projects, and climate policies. Some states rely on enforcement procedures in environmentally burdened communities, while other states use grants and community education.

Advancements Under the Obama Administration

The election of Senator Barack H. Obama as the 44th President of the United States in November 2008 ushered in a new era for addressing environmental and health disparities. Some of the president's early high-level appointments—individuals who in the past had been friendly to environmental justice—signaled a fundamental break with the previous administration. President Obama was praised for creating a "Green Team" of advisors that included Steven Chu, the Nobel Prize-winning physicist and head of the Lawrence Berkeley National Laboratory, as the new Secretary of Energy; Carol Browner, former EPA administrator under President Clinton, as Special Advisor to Climate and Energy to the White House; and Lisa P. Jackson, a respected state environmental official from New Jersey, as head of the EPA.[66] A native of New Orleans, Jackson is the first African American to head the EPA.[67]

Nancy Sutley was tapped to head the Council on Environmental Quality. Born in Argentina and raised in Queens, New York, Sutley amassed a robust record on environmental and energy policy in California and Washington, DC. She was a special assistant to then-EPA administrator Carol Browner during the Clinton administration. While serving as the deputy mayor of Los Angeles, she led Mayor Antonio Villaraigosa's environmental initiatives in an attempt to make Los Angeles one of the "greenest big cities in America." She also headed up initiatives to overhaul the truck fleet at the Los Angeles and Long Beach ports and move the California Water and Power Department to wind and solar energy.[68]

Congresswoman Hilda Solis (D-CA) was selected as the U.S. Department of Labor Secretary. While in Congress, Solis sponsored numerous environmental justice, health, and right-to-know legislation. She became the first Latina and the first person of Central American heritage to be appointed to a cabinet-level post.[69] A nationally recognized leader on the environment, Solis became the first woman to receive the John F. Kennedy Profile in Courage Award in 2000 for her pioneering work on environmental justice issues. The environmental justice legislation she authored and helped pass as a California state legislator in 1999 was the first of its kind in the nation to become law. A recognized leader on clean energy jobs, she authored the Green Jobs Act of 2007, which provided funding for "green collar" job training for veterans, displaced workers, at-risk youths, and low-income individuals.[70]

Not surprisingly, the EPA appears to be the biggest benefactor of the new push to address environmental disparities. Under Jackson, several environmental leaders were appointed to high-level positions, including Michelle DePass as Assistant Administrator of International Affairs.[71] Before joining the EPA, DePass directed the Ford Foundation's Environmental Justice and Healthy Communities Program. Mathy Stanislaus was selected as the EPA's Assistant Administrator for the Office of Solid Waste and Emergency Response (OSWER). Stanislaus is a one of the founders of the New York City Environmental Justice Alliance and the cofounder of the New Partners for Community Revitalization.[72]

In a November 2009 memorandum to EPA employees, "Next Steps—Environmental Justice and Civil Rights," EPA Administrator Jackson stated:

> Fifteen years ago, the first Executive Order on Environmental Justice was signed by President Clinton. Since that time, EPA and its partners have made progress on identifying and addressing the health and environmental burdens faced by communities disproportionately impacted by pollution. We should be proud of the work we've done to expand the reach of environmentalism and give those communities a voice in critical decisions that impact their lives. But a great deal of work remains ahead of us, and as EPA Administrator, I am more committed than ever to environmental justice.[73]

As part of her commitment to environmental justice, Jackson announced two further appointments. Lisa H. Garcia was appointed Senior Advisor for Environmental Justice.[74] Garcia is a former Chief Advocate for Environmental Justice and Equity at the New York State Department of Environmental Conservation. According to Jackson, Garcia will seek to "promote meaningful, working relationships with EJ communities, build strong partnerships to address some of our most persistent challenges, and ensure that EJ needs receive attention at the highest level of this Agency. She will also be working closely with [the] Office of Environmental Justice to strengthen all of EPA's EJ initiatives and promote agency-wide partnerships in our efforts."

Patrick Sungwook Chang was appointed Senior Counsel for External Civil Rights. He is the former Deputy Section Chief for the Coordination and Review Section in the Civil Rights Division of the U.S. Department of Justice, where he worked on implementation of Title VI of the Civil Rights Act of 1964 across the Federal Government. According to Jackson, Chang "will focus on resolving the Agency's backlog of pending Title VI complaints and will work closely with senior leaders in the Agency to evaluate and reform the Title VI program." He will also "evaluate potential long-term institutional changes to the Agency's Title VI complaint process to avoid future delays, with a particular focus on ensuring that all appropriate Agency components are used to create a timely and effective Title VI process."[75]

In addition to staff appointments, the Obama administration has reversed some of former President George W. Bush's environmental policies that proved troublesome—especially for people of color and low-income individuals who are burdened with more pollution in their homes and workplaces than the rest of the nation. Shortly after taking office in January 2009, President Obama directed federal regulators to act quickly on California and 13 other states' applications to set strict automobile emission and fuel efficiency standards. The president directed the Transportation Department to finalize interim nationwide regulations requiring the automobile industry to increase fuel efficiency standards to comply with a 2007 law, rules that the Bush administration decided at the last minute not to issue.[76] The administration proposed tougher standards that raise fuel efficiency targets to 35.5 miles per gallon (up from 27 miles per gallon) for new passenger vehicles and light trucks by 2016.[77]

In February 2009, the EPA asked the Supreme Court to drop the previous administration's appeal of a successful lawsuit by Earthjustice and other environmental groups seeking protective federal mercury emissions limits for the nation's power plants. More than 700,000 pounds of mercury pollution were allowed to be released during the previous administration. Coal-fired power plants generate more pollution than any other industry in the United States—spewing more than 96,000 pounds of mercury into the air each year.[78] In March 2009, the EPA and the Justice Department began a national initiative targeting electric utilities whose coal-fired power plants violated the law.[79]

In April 2009, the EPA announced that the agency would reconsider George W. Bush–era regulations on air pollution controls for facilities that emit fine particles ($PM_{2.5}$).[80] The agency also declared greenhouse gases a threat to public health and the environment and subject to regulation under the Clean Air Act, a move that could affect sources of greenhouse gas pollution ranging from vehicles to factories to power plants.[81] That same month, EPA Administrator

Jackson announced that she had signed a final rule to reinstate stricter reporting requirements for industrial and federal facilities that release toxic substances that threaten human health and the environment—reversing Bush-era rules that had been in place in 2006.[82]

In June 2009, the Obama administration "put the brakes on" mountaintop removal coal mining by announcing a plan for curbing the use of streamlined federal permitting and boosting efforts to protect rivers and streams from mining debris.[83] Mountaintop removal mining produces 126 million tons of coal a year and employs more than 14,000 workers in mostly rural West Virginia, Kentucky, and Tennessee, but has damaged more than 1,200 miles of streams in the Appalachian mountain region.

In July 2009, the EPA introduced the Environmental Justice Strategic Enforcement Assessment Tool (EJSEAT), a tool designed to help the agency identify areas with potentially disproportionately high and adverse environmental and public health burdens. It will allow the federal government to target billions of economic recovery dollars in communities seeking environmental justice. In the EJSEAT, "census tracts in each state are assigned an EJSEAT score. The scores combine data such as cancer rates, poverty levels, child mortality, toxic emissions, education and racial characteristics and density of industrial facilities."[84] The tool is currently a draft in development and is expected to take a year for the EPA to complete.[85]

In November 2009, the EPA announced a national initiative to address environmental justice in ten "Showcase Communities," or one community per EPA region. According to EPA Administrator Jackson:

> These 10 communities will serve as models for the EPA's committed environmental justice efforts, and help highlight the disproportionate environmental burdens placed on low-income and minority communities all across the nation. By expanding the conversation on environmentalism, we can give a voice to vulnerable groups that haven't always had a voice on these issues. Our 10 Showcase Communities will provide lessons for how we make every community a better place for people to live, for business to invest and bring jobs, and for opportunities to grow.[86]

The ten "Showcase Communities" are Bridgeport, Connecticut; Staten Island, New York; Washington, DC; Jacksonville, Florida; Milwaukee, Wisconsin; Port Arthur, Texas; Kansas City, Missouri, and Kansas City, Kansas; Salt Lake City,

Utah; Los Angeles, California; and Yakima, Washington. The EPA has committed $1 million to this effort over the next 2 years—$100,000 per project to "help address concerns in communities disproportionately exposed to environmental risks. These demonstration projects will test and share information on different approaches to increase EPA's ability to achieve environmental results in communities."[87]

In December 2009, the EPA announced a plan to overturn the "Revisions to the Definitions of Solid Waste" rule, which allowed unregulated burning of hazardous waste as fuel that would otherwise be regulated as hazardous waste.[88] It also announced plans to strengthen its assessment of pesticide health risks, particularly in regards to workers, including farmworkers and farm children, as well as risks posed by pesticides that are not used on food.[89] Mathy Stanislaus, assistant administrator for OSWER, unveiled the agency's action plan for its Community Engagement Initiative, which is designed to assist local stakeholder and community participation in government decisions on land cleanup, emergency response, and the management of hazardous materials and waste.[90]

On December 7, 2009, the EPA issued a final ruling that greenhouse gases pose a danger to human health and the environment. The announcement came as the United Nations Climate Change Conference began in Copenhagen, Denmark. Administrator Jackson signed two distinct findings regarding greenhouse gases under section 202(a) of the Clean Air Act[91]:

Endangerment Finding: The Administrator finds that the current and projected concentrations of the six key well-mixed greenhouse gases—carbon dioxide (CO_2), methane (CH_4), nitrous oxide (N_2O), hydrofluorocarbons (HFCs), perfluorocarbons (PFCs), and sulfur hexafluoride (SF_6)—in the atmosphere threaten the public health and welfare of current and future generations.

Cause or Contribute Finding: The Administrator finds that the combined emissions of these well-mixed greenhouse gases from new motor vehicles and new motor vehicle engines contribute to greenhouse gas pollution which threatens public health and welfare.[92]

On January 4, 2010, the EPA released its "National Priorities for Enforcement and Compliance Assurance for Fiscal Years 2010–2013."[93] The agency sets these priorities every 3 years to focus resources toward the most significant environmental problems and human health challenges identified by EPA staff, states, tribes, and the public. This year, the priority candidates include:

- Air toxics
- Concentrated animal feeding operations
- Environmental justice—community-based approach
- Indian Country drinking water
- Marine debris
- Mineral processing
- Municipal infrastructure
- New source review/prevention of significant deterioration (NSR/PSD)
- RCRA enforcement
- RCRA financial assurance
- Resource extraction
- Pesticides at day care facilities
- Surface impoundments
- Wetlands
- Worker protection standards

An EPA background paper explained the significance of making environmental justice a priority candidate for targeted enforcement from the Office of Enforcement and Compliance Assurance (OECA). It states:

> This priority candidate would further support the Agency's commitment to protect vulnerable communities. It would empower communities, giving them a role in the process of ensuring compliance at facilities, which directly affects their lives. Making EJ a separate enforcement priority should not diminish the importance of, or take the place of, incorporating EJ concerns in all of the national enforcement priorities. Rather, it would signify OECA's commitment to apply enforcement tools as an important means of protecting at-risk communities.[94]

The paper went on to explain that the approach to the environmental justice enforcement priority would be geographically based rather than sector based. Each region would identify a "disadvantaged community" in a geographic area in which the EPA would perform targeted enforcement (including targeting of facilities within national priority sectors). This might be problematic for some EPA regions in which states have a long history of environmental racism, environmental injustice, unequal protection, and dumping pollution on low-income people and people of color—especially African Americans of various income and class levels.[95]

On January 6, 2010, the EPA proposed more stringent ground-level ozone standards to comply with recommendations made by the agency's science advisers—who during the previous administration proposed setting the standards within the range of 60 to 70 parts per billion (ppb) averaged over 8 hours.[96] Ozone is the main ingredient in smog. In March 2008, the Bush administration tightened the ozone limit from 84 pbb to 75 pbb—even though the EPA's independent science advisory panel unanimously had said the standard should be no higher than 70 ppb to be protective.[97] The Obama administration is also proposing a separate "secondary" standard to protect vegetation and ecosystems, including parks, wildlife refuges, and wilderness areas.

A January 12, 2010, memorandum from EPA Administrator Jackson listed the top priorities and seven key themes on which the agency will focus its work.[98] They include:

- Taking action on climate change
- Improving air quality
- Assuring the safety of chemicals
- Cleaning up our communities
- Protecting America's waters
- Expanding the conversation on environmentalism and working for environmental justice
- Building strong state and tribal partnerships

These seven priorities guided the EPA's work in 2010 and will continue to guide the agency in future years. It is important to note that again, achieving environmental justice has been deemed one of the top priorities. We should also note that the other six themes all have environmental justice and racial equity implications.

On January 15, 2010, the EPA announced a draft plan for assessing the potential impacts of its hazardous waste recycling rule on low-income, minority, and tribal populations.[99] The agency is reaching out to various stakeholder groups, including the environmental justice community, requesting public comment before the analysis begins. The EPA will use lessons learned from the analysis of the DSW (definition of solid waste) rule to inform its ongoing effort to strengthen the consideration of environmental justice in rule-making.

In September 2010, EPA Administrator Jackson and White House Council on Environmental Quality Chair Sutley reconvened the Interagency Working Group on Environmental Justice (EJ IWG) in a historic meeting, the first such gathering in more than a decade, held at the White House.[100] The meeting, attended by five cabinet members, highlight the federal government's dedication to ensuring all Americans have strong federal protection from environmental and health hazards. The EJ IWG agreed to the following next steps:

- Hold monthly EJ IWG meetings, including assigning senior officials from each cabinet agency to coordinate EJ activities
- Organize regional listening sessions in early 2011
- Hold follow-up EJ IWG principals' meetings in April and September 2011
- Each agency will be tasked to develop or update its EJ strategy by September 2011
- Plan a White House forum for EJ leaders and stakeholders on environmental justice

Conclusion

Much progress has been made in mainstreaming environmental protection as a civil rights and social justice issue. The key is getting the government to enforce environmental and health laws and regulations equally across the board—without regard to race, color, or national origin. Twenty-seven years after the release of *Toxic Wastes and Race,* significant racial and socioeconomic disparities persist in the distribution of the nation's commercial hazardous waste facilities.

People of color in 2007 were more concentrated in areas with commercial hazardous sites than they were in 1987. This discovery raises serious questions about the ability of current policies and institutions to adequately protect vulnerable populations from toxic threats, as people of color and low-income households are still disproportionately impacted by environmental threats inside and outside their homes.

Despite four decades of environmental laws and regulations, ushered in largely by environmentalists beginning in the 1970s, neighborhoods of color are still the dumping grounds for LULUs and polluting facilities that others do not want. Individuals that have organizations and resources to hire lawyers, experts, and scientists are often more successful in defending their physical space and protecting their health by blocking polluting facilities from entering their communities. On the other hand, polluting industries often take the path of least resistance, which too often has meant low-income communities and communities of color receiving more than their fair share of health threats from polluting plants.

More than a dozen environmental justice networks exist today that were not around in 1987. The last decade in particular has seen some positive change in the way these groups relate to one other. We now see an increasing number of community-based groups, networks, environmental and conservation groups, legal groups, faith-based groups, labor, academic institutions, and youth organizations teaming up on environmental and health issues that differentially impact low-income individuals and people of color. Environmental racism and environmental justice panels have become "hot" topics at national conferences and forums sponsored by law schools, bar associations, public health groups, scientific societies, professional meetings, and university lecture series.

In just a short time, environmental health and racial equity advocates have had a profound impact on public policy, industry practices, national conferences, private foundation funding, research, and curriculum development. A growing number of courses and curricula on the subject can be found at nearly every university in the country. Groups have been successful in blocking numerous permits for new polluting facilities, and have forced government and private industry buyout and relocation of several communities impacted by Superfund sites and industrial pollution. There has also been a resurgence of environmental justice, civil rights, and health protection under the Obama administration. In just 2 years, environmental justice has been elevated and has seen heightened visibility in staffing, policies, and programs at the EPA. The next step is to ensure these changes translate into real health and environmental improvements throughout the nation.

References

1. Robert D. Bullard, *The Quest for Environmental Justice: Human Rights and the Politics of Pollution* (San Francisco, CA: Sierra Club Books, 2005).

2. U.S. Environmental Protection Agency (EPA), *Guidance for Incorporating Environmental Justice in EPA's NEPA Compliance Analysis* (Washington, DC: U.S. EPA, 1998); and Robert Bullard and Glenn Johnson, "Environmental and Economic Justice: Implications for Public Policy," *Journal of Public Management & Social Policy* 4, no. 4 (1998): 137–148.

3. Kenneth Olden, "The Complex Interaction of Poverty, Pollution, Health Status," *Scientist* 12, no. 2 (February 1998): 7; and National Institute of Environmental Health Sciences (NIEHS)-National Institutes of Health, Division of Extramural Research and Training: Health Disparities Research, http://www.niehs.nih.gov/dert/programs/translat/hd/ko-art.htm (accessed August 17, 2010).

4. Robert D. Bullard, *Dumping in Dixie: Race, Class, and Environmental Quality* (Boulder: Westview Press, 1990; 2000).

5. Bullard, *The Quest for Environmental Justice.*

6. Robert D. Bullard, *Confronting Environmental Racism: Voices From the Grassroots* (Boston, MA: South End Press, 1993).

7. Luke W. Cole and Sheila R. Foster, *From the Ground Up: Environmental Racism and the Rise of the Environmental Justice Movement* (New York: New York University Press, 2000); and Laura Westra, Bill E. Lawson, and Peter S. Wenz, *Faces of Environmental Racism: Confronting Issues of Global Justice*, 2nd ed. (Lanham, MD: Rowan & Littlefield, 2001).

8. Robert D. Bullard, Second National People of Color Environmental Leadership Summit, October 26, 2002, http://www.ejrc.cau.edu/SummitPolicyExSumm.html (accessed November 26, 2010); and Robert D. Bullard, "Environmental Justice for People of Color Draws 1,200 Delegates to Washington," *Black Commentator*, Issue No. 16, November 14, 2002, http://www.blackcommentator.com/16_re_print.html (accessed November 26, 2010).

9. Julia Quiroz-Martinez, Diana Pei Wu, and Kristin Zimmerman, *Regeneration: Youth Leadership in Environmental Justice* (Oakland, CA: Movement Strategy Center, December 2005).

10. Robert Pollin, Heidi Garrett-Peltier, James Heintz, and Helen Scharber, *Green Recovery: A Program to Create Good Jobs and Start Building a Low-Carbon*

Economy (Amherst: Political Economy Research Institute, University of Massachusetts–Amherst, September 2008); and Van Jones, *The Green Collar Economy: How One Solution Can Fix Our Two Biggest Problems* (New York: Harper One, 2008).

11. Robert D. Bullard, *Growing Smarter: Achieving Livable Communities, Environmental Justice, and Regional Equity* (Cambridge, MA: MIT Press, 2007).

12. Charles M. Haar and Jerold S. Kayden, eds., *Zoning and the American Dream: Promises Still to Keep* (Chicago, IL: American Planning Association, 1999).

13. Bullard, *Growing Smarter*.

14. Juliana Maantay, "Zoning, Law, Health, and Environmental Justice: What's the Connection?" *Journal of Law, Medicine & Ethics* 30, no. 4 (Winter 2002): 572.

15. National Academy of Public Administration (NAPA), *Addressing Community Concerns: How Environmental Justice Relates to Land Use Planning and Zoning* (Washington, DC: NAPA, July 2003), 50.

16. Yale Rabin, "Expulsive Zoning: The Inequitable Legacy of Euclid," in *Zoning and the American Dream: Promises Still to Keep*, ed. Charles M. Haar and Jerold S. Kayden, pp. 106–108 (Chicago, IL: American Planning Association, 1999).

17. U.S. Environmental Protection Agency (EPA), *EPA Guidance: Improving Air Quality Through Land Use Activities* (Washington, DC: EPA Transportation and Regional Programs Division, January 2001), 1.

18. Ibid., 2.

19. ICF Consulting, *Air Quality Issues in School Site Selection: Guidance Document* (Diamond Bar, CA: South Coast Air Quality Management District, June 2005; rev. 2007), http://www.aqmd.gov/prdas/aqguide/doc/School_Guidance.pdf (accessed December 21, 2009).

20. Bullard, *The Quest for Environmental Justice*, pp. 43–61.

21. Manuel Pastor, James Sadd, and John Hipp, "Which Came First? Toxic Facilities, Minority Move-In, and Environmental Justice," *Journal of Urban Affairs* 23, no. 1 (2001): 3; and Daniel R. Faber and Eric J. Krieg, *Unequal Exposure to Ecological Hazards: Environmental Injustices in the Commonwealth of Massachusetts* (Boston, MA: Northeastern University, 2001).

22. Bullard, *The Quest for Environmental Justice*.

23. United Church of Christ (UCC) Commission for Racial Justice, *Toxic Wastes and Race in the United States* (New York: UCC, 1987).

24. Bullard, *Dumping in Dixie.*

25. Dana Alston, "Transforming a Movement: People of Color Unite at Summit Against Environmental Racism," *Sojourner* 21 (1992): 30–31.

26. U.S. Environmental Protection Agency (EPA), *Environmental Equity: Reducing Risks for All Communities* (Washington, DC: EPA, 1992).

27. U.S. Environmental Protection Agency, *Guidance for Incorporating Environmental Justice.*

28. Robert D. Bullard, Paul Mohai, Robin Saha, and Beverly Wright, *Toxic Wastes and Race at Twenty: 1987–2007* (Cleveland, OH: United Church of Christ Witness & Justice Ministries, March 2007), http://www.ejrc.cau.edu/TWART-light.pdf (accessed December 15, 2009).

29. Paul Mohai and Robin Saha, "Reassessing Racial and Socioeconomic Disparities in Environmental Justice Research," *Demography* 43, no. 2 (2007): 383–399; and Paul Mohai and Robin Saha, "Racial Inequality in the Distribution of Hazardous Waste: A National-Level Reassessment," *Social Problems* 54, no. 3 (2007): 343–370.

30. Liam Downey and Brian Hawkins, "Race, Income, and Environmental Inequality in the United States," Sociological Perspective 51, no. 4 (October 2008): 759–781.

31. Ibid., 778.

32. Ibid., 759.

33. Robert D. Bullard, *People of Color Environmental Groups Directory* (Battle Creek, MI: Charles Stewart Mott Foundation, 2000).

34. Tina Eshaghpour, *Environmental Health and Justice Scoping Report: Assessing the State of the Field and Opportunities for Philanthropic Investment in Environmental Health Through a Racial Justice Lens*, December 2008, p. 11, http://www.hefn.org/resources/files/Scoping%20Projects%202008%20EHEJ%20Final%20Version.pdf (accessed December 11, 2009).

35. Robert D. Bullard, "Crowning Women of Color: The Real Story Behind the EJ Summit II," Environmental Justice Resource Center Web site, http://www.ejrc.cau.edu (accessed December 21, 2009).

36. Movement Strategy Center, *Fertile Ground: Gender, Organizing, and Movement Building at the Intersection of Environmental Justice and Reproductive Justice* (Oakland, CA: Movement Strategy Center 2009).

37. President William J. Clinton, *Federal Actions to Address Environmental Justice in Minority Populations and Low-Income Populations*, 59 Fed. Reg. 7629 (February 16, 1994).

38. President's Council on Environmental Quality, *Environmental Justice Guidance Under the National Environmental Policy Act*, December 10, 1997.

39. U.S. Environmental Protection Agency (EPA), *Process for Revising EPA's Interim Guidance for Investigating Title VI Administrative Complaints Challenging Permits* (Washington, DC: EPA, June 2000), http://www.epa.gov/ocr/reviguid2.htm (accessed November 1, 2009).

40. Bullard, Mohai, Saha, and Wright, *Toxic Wastes and Race at Twenty*.

41. Center on Race, Poverty and the Environment et al., "Comments on *Draft Revised Guidance for Investigating Title VI Administrative Complaints Challenging Permits and Draft Title IV Guidance for EPA Assistance Recipients Administering Environmental Permitting Programs*" (San Francisco, CA: Center on Race, Poverty and the Environment, August 26, 2000).

42. Margaret Kriz, "EPA Stuck with Backlog of Environmental Justice Decisions," *National Journal*, July 30, 2001, http://www.govexec.com/daily/fed/0701/073001nj2.htm (accessed October 1, 2009); John Callewaert, "The Importance of Local History for Understanding and Addressing Environmental Injustice," *Local Environment* 7, no. 3 (2002): 257–267; and Julie H. Hurwitz and E. Quita Sullivan, "Using Civil Rights Laws to Challenge Environmental Racism: From Bean to Guardians to Chester to Sandoval," *Journal of Law in Society* 2 (Winter 2001): 5–70.

43. "The Supreme Court—Leading Case, 115," *Harvard. Law Review* 306 (2001): 497–498.

44. U.S. Commission on Civil Rights, *Not in My Backyard: Executive Order 12898 and Title VI as Tools for Achieving Environmental Justice* (Washington, DC: U.S. Commission on Civil Rights, 2003), 27.

45. Office of the Inspector General, *EPA Needs to Consistently Implement the Intent of the Executive Order on Environmental Justice*, Report No. 2004-P-00007 (Washington, DC: U.S. Environmental Protection Agency, 2004), i.

46. U.S. Government Accountability Office, *Environmental Justice: EPA Should Devote More Attention to Environmental Justice When Developing Clean Air Rules* (Washington, DC: U.S. Environmental Protection Agency, 2005), 3–6.

47. Manu Raju, "EPA's Draft Equity Plan Drops Race as a Factor in Decision," *Inside EPA*, July 1, 2005, http://www.precaution.org/lib/06/prn_epa_drops_race_from_ej_guide.050701.htm (accessed December 15, 2009).

48. David Pace, "AP: More Blacks Live With Pollution," *Associated Press*, December 14, 2005.

49. Letter from EPA Science Advisory Board to EPA Administrator Stephen L. Johnson, "Toxics Release Inventory Data," July 12, 2006, http://www.epa.gov/science1/pdf/sab-com-06-001.pdf (accessed November 15, 2009).

50. U.S. Environmental Protection Agency, *How Are the Toxics Release Inventory Data Used? Government, Business, Academic, and Citizen Uses* (Washington, DC: Office of Environmental Information, March 2003), 17.

51. OMB Watch, "Congress White House Going in Opposite Directions on TRI," February 21, 2007, http://www.ombwatch.org/node/3184 (accessed September 1, 2010); and http://www.ombwatch.org/tricenter/TRIpress.html (accessed December 27, 2006).

52. Ibid.

53. Office of the Inspector General, *Evaluation Report: EPA Needs to Conduct Environmental Justice Reviews of Its Programs, Policies, and Activities*, Report No. 2006-P-00034 (Washington, DC: U.S. Environmental Protection Agency, September 18, 2006), 7.

54. James Hagengruber, "EPA Cutbacks Greeted With Criticism: Groups Say Office of Civil Rights and Environmental Justice Gutted," October 31, 2006, http://www.spokesman review.com/Idaho/story.asp?ID=157291&mail=yes (accessed November 15, 2009).

55. U.S. Government Accountability Office (GAO), *Environmental Right-to-Know: EPA's Recent Rule Could Reduce Availability of Toxic Chemical Information Used to Assess Environmental Justice* (Washington, DC: GAO, October 4, 2007), 5.

56. U.S. Environmental Protection Agency (EPA), "EPA Administrator Reinstates Full TRI Reporting Requirements," Press Release, April 21, 2009, http://yosemite.epa.gov/OPA/ADMPRESS.NSF/d0cf6618525a9efb85257359003fb69d/1693fb3535db2495852 5759f0053b22b!OpenDocument (accessed November 15, 2009).

57. U.S. Environmental Protection Agency, *Final Rule*, 73 Fed. Reg. 64668 (October 30, 2008).

58. U.S. Environmental Protection Agency (EPA), *An Assessment of Environmental Problems Associated With Recycling of Hazardous Secondary Materials* (EPA-HQ-RCRA-2002-0031-0355), 2007, http://www.epa.gov/waste/hazard/dsw/rulemaking.htm (accessed November 15, 2009).

59. Ibid., 12.

60. Earthjustice, "Protect Your Community From Toxic Waste: Help Undo Bush-Era Polluter Loophole," July 2009, http://www.earthjustice.org/features/protect-your-community-from-toxic-waste-help-undo-bush-era-polluter-loophole (accessed August 31, 2010).

61. Amy Littlefield, "EPA Vows to Assess Impact of Hazardous Waste on Poor Communities," *Los Angeles Times*, July 22, 2009.

62. Earthjustice, "EPA Dumps Misguided Rule Allowing Unregulated Hazardous Waste Burning," Press Release, December 2, 2009, http://www.earthjustice.org/news/press/2009/epa-dumps-misguided-rule-allowing-unregulated-hazardous-waste-burning.html (accessed December 5, 2009).

63. U.S. Environmental Protection Agency (EPA), *National-Scale Air Toxics Assessment for 2002* (Washington, DC: EPA, Technology Transfer Network, June 24, 2009), http://www.epa.gov/nata2002 (accessed December 8, 2009).

64. Public Law Institute, *Environmental Justice for All: A Fifty State Survey of Legislation, Policies and Cases*, 3rd ed. (San Francisco: University of California Hastings College of Law, 2007), p. 3.

65. Ibid., iv.

66. Bryan Walsh, "High Hopes for Obama's Green Dream Team," *Time*, December 16, 2009, http://www.time.com/time/health/article/0,8599,1866682,00.html (accessed December 21, 2009).

67. Jonathan Tilove, "Obama Taps New Orleans Native Lisa Jackson to Lead Environmental Protection Agency," *Times-Picayune*, December 15, 2008.

68. "Nancy Sutley: Why She Matters," Who RunsGov.com, *Washington Post*, October 7, 2009, http://www.whorunsgov.com/Profiles/Nancy_Sutley (accessed December 21, 2009).

69. "Hilda Solis Confirmed as Labor Secretary–Finally," *San Francisco Chronicle*, February 24, 2009, http://www.sfgate.com/cgi-bin/blogs/nov05election/detail?blogid=14&entry_id=36224 (accessed December 21, 2009).

70. Janet Wilson, "Obama's Labor Pick Expected to Champion Green Jobs," *Grist*, January 8, 2009, http://www.grist.org/article/Laboring-for-change (accessed December 21, 2009).

71. Dan Farber, "Two New EPA Nominees," *Legal Planet*, March 19, 2009, http://legalplanet.wordpress.com/2009/03/19/two-new-epa-nominees (accessed December 20, 2009).

72. Aaron Short, "Greenpointer Appointed to the EPA," *Greenpoint Gazette*, April 16, 2009, http://www.greenpointnews.com/news/greenpointer-appointed-to-the-epa (accessed December 20, 2009).

73. U.S. Environmental Protection Agency, Lisa P. Jackson, "Memo to Employees: Next Steps-Environmental Justice and Civil Rights," November 12, 2009, http://blog.epa.gov/administrator/2009/11/12/memo-to-employees-next-steps-environmental-justice-and-civil-rights (accessed December 1, 2009).

74. Ibid.

75. Ibid.

76. John M. Broder, "Obama's Order Is Likely to Tighten Auto Standards," *New York Times*, January 26, 2009.

77. Steven Mufson, "Vehicle Emission Rules to Tighten: U.S. Would Also Raise Fuel Mileage Standards by 2016," *Washington Post*, May 19, 2009.

78. Earthjustice, "New Administration Reverses Course on Power Plant Mercury Regulations," Press Release, February 4, 2009, http://www.earthjustice.org/news/press/2009/new-administration-reverses-course-on-power-plant-mercury-regulations.html (accessed December 20, 2009).

79. Joe Koncelik, "In a Major Reversal, Obama Administration Restarts NSR Enforcement Initiative," Ohio Environmental Law Blog, March 6, 2009, http://www.ohioenvironmentallawblog.com/2009/03/articles/air/in-a-major-reversal-obama-administration-restarts-nsr-enforcement-initiative (accessed December 21, 2009).

80. Earthjustice, "EPA to Review Bush-Era Air Pollution Rules: Environmental Groups Who Sued Over New Source Review Rules, Cautiously Optimistic," Press Release, April 27, 2009, http://www.commondreams.org/newswire/2009/04/27-10 (accessed December 21, 2009).

81. John M. Broder, "E.P.A. Clears Way for Greenhouse Gas Rule," *New York Times*, April 18, 2009.

82. "EPA Reverses Bush-Era Toxics Release Inventory Blackout," *Society of Environmental Journalists*, http://www.sej.org/publications/watchdog-tipsheet/epa-reverses-bush-era-toxics-release-inventory-blackout (accessed December 21, 2009).

83. Eric Bontrager, "Obama Puts Brakes on Mountaintop Removal; Goal Is to Prevent Coal-Mining From Smothering Rivers and Streams," *Scientific American*, June 11, 2009, http://www.scientificamerican.com/article.cfm?id=obama-restricts-mountain-top-removal (accessed January 4, 2010).

84. CBS News, "Environmental Justice Tool in the Works: Lauded as Stimulus Achievement, Pollution Scores for Poor and Minority Neighborhoods Still on Drawing Board," July 24, 2009, http://www.cbsnews.com/stories/2009/07/24/tech/main5186668.shtml (accessed December 20, 2009).

85. Ibid.

86. U.S. Environmental Protection Agency (EPA), "EPA Announces Environmental Justice Showcase Communities," November 17, 2009, http://yosemite.epa.gov/OPA/ADMPRESS.NSF/d0cf6618525a9efb85257359003fb69d/b3d235503bc70b3a852576710060f044!OpenDocument (accessed December 20, 2009).

87. Ibid.

88. Jennifer Berry, "Rule Allowing Burning of Hazardous Waste May Be Overturned," Earth911.com, December 8, 2009, http://earth911.com/blog/2009/12/08/rule-allowing-burning-of-hazardous-waste-may-be-overturned (accessed December 21, 2009).

89. U.S. Environmental Protection Agency (EPA), "EPA to Strengthen Oversight of Pesticide's Impact on Children and Farmworkers," December 8, 2009, http://yosemite.epa.gov/opa/admpress.nsf/0/ba658fe761020fa2852576860059025a (accessed December 21, 2009).

90. U.S. Environmental Protection Agency, "Community Engagement Initiative," http://www.epa.gov/oswer/engagementinitiative.htm (accessed December 21, 2009).

91. U.S. Environmental Protection Agency, "Endangerment and Cause or Contribute Findings for Greenhouse Gases Under the Clean Air Act," Press Release, December 7, 2009, http://www.epa.gov/climatechange/endangerment.html (accessed December 21, 2009).

92. Ibid.

93. U.S. Environmental Protection Agency, "National Priorities for Enforcement and Compliance Assurance," January 4, 2010, http://www.epa.gov/oecaerth/data/planning/priorities/index.html (accessed January 7, 2010).

94. U.S. Environmental Protection Agency, "Background Paper for Candidate National Enforcement Priority: Environmental Justice (EJ), January 2010," January 2010, http://www.epa.gov/oecaerth/resources/publications/data/planning/priorities/fy2011candidates/fy2011candidate-ej.pdf (accessed January 7, 2010).

95. Bullard, *Dumping in Dixie*; Bullard, "Need for EPA Inspector General Investigation of Region 4 Treatment of African Americans," *Dissident Voice*, September 14, 2009, http://dissidentvoice.org/2009/09/need-for-epa-inspector-general-investigation-of-region-4-treatment-of-black-communities (accessed December 21, 2009); and Bullard, "Poisoned Communities Put Spotlight on EPA Region 4," *OpEd News*, October 24, 2009, http://www.opednews.com/articles/Poisoned-Communities-Put-S-by-Robert-Bullard-091021-905.html (accessed December 21, 2009).

96. U.S. Environmental Protection Agency, "Ozone Standards: Proposed Revisions to National Standards for Ground-Level Ozone," January 6, 2010, http://www.epa.gov/groundlevelozone/actions.html (accessed January 7, 2010).

97. Traci Watson and Wendy Koch, "EPA Sets Tougher Air-Quality Standards," *USA Today*, March 12, 2008.

98. U.S. Environmental Protection Agency, Lisa P. Jackson, "Memorandum: Seven Priorities for EPA's Future," January 12, 2010, http://blog.epa.gov/administrator/2010/01/12/seven-priorities-for-epas-future (accessed November 26, 2010).

99. U.S. Environmental Protection Agency (EPA), "In Renewed Effort on Environmental Justice, EPA to Assess Impact of Waste Rule on Disadvantaged Communities: Agency's Draft Plan on Hazardous Waste Recycling Rule Open for Public Comment," Press Release, January 15, 2010, http://yosemite.epa.gov/opa/admpress.nsf/d0cf6618525a9efb85257359003fb69d/8f5211bd9333b721852576ac005ac062!OpenDocument (accessed January 15, 2010).

100. U.S. Environmental Protection Agency (EPA), "EPA Hosts Historic Meeting on Environmental Justice/Obama Administration Cabinet Members Show Commitment to Healthy Environment and Strong Economy for All Americans," news release from headquarters, September 22, 2010, http://yosemite.epa.gov/opa/admpress.nsf/bd4379a92ceceeac8525735900400c27/d651c10d4a830640852577a600583d81!OpenDocument (accessed October 1, 2010).

2

What We Know After Three Decades of Research

MORE THAN THREE DECADES of research have laid the foundation for environmental health research. New subfields burst on to the scene in the early 1980s, giving rise to and supporting a national movement around racial equity and environmental justice. Building on decades of research findings on social inequality, researchers began to study environmental health through a racial equity lens. The research began to untangle the web of factors that contribute to some populations being at greater risk from exposure to environmental hazards from lead poisoning to pollution from refineries, chemical plants, power plants, incinerators, landfills, hazardous waste facilities, and cars, trucks, and buses.

Environmental justice has always been about the link between the environment and public health. From the beginning of the environmental justice movement, advocates, activists, and academics targeted the fundamental system and institutions, including business and governmental entities, that create, maintain, and support environmental, health, economic, and racial inequities, including institutionalized racism.[1] It was not difficult for people of color to view environmental and health issues through a racial equity lens, since many of their communities were systematically targeted for some of the nation's worst polluting facilities. Environmental inequality was seen as socially produced and an extension of White racism.[2]

Vulnerable communities, populations, and individuals often fall between the regulatory cracks. They are in many ways "invisible" communities.[3] The environmental justice movement serves to make these marginalized communities visible, vocal, and empowered. At the outset of the movement, many White allies in the mainstream environmental movement were reluctant to use the term "environmental racism." Some of the groups were even hostile to the idea. However, the vast majority of people of color environmental justice leaders not only embraced the environmental racism concept, but set their core organizing around dismantling environmental racism.

After three decades, environmental racism has become a household word. Out of the small and seemingly isolated environmental struggles emerged a potent grassroots community-driven movement. Many of the on-the-ground environmental struggles in the 1980s, 1990s, and through the early years of the new millennium have seen the quest for environmental and economic justice become a unifying theme across race, class, gender, age, and geographic lines.

The "chicken or egg" waste facility siting debate has nearly been put to rest, since recent evidence shows that disproportionately high percentages of minorities and low-income populations were present at the time that the commercial hazardous waste facilities were sited. Hundreds of empirical studies have found race and class disparities in the location of polluting facilities. In a 2001 study published in the *Journal of Urban Affairs,* researchers Manuel Pastor, Jim Sadd, and John Hipp confirmed that during a 30-year period, polluting facilities were deliberately sited in existing minority communities in the Los Angeles Basin.[4] Likewise in a 2005 study published in the journal *Social Problems,* researchers Robin Saha and Paul Mohai report that in Michigan, during the last 30 years, commercial hazardous waste facilities were sited in neighborhoods that were disproportionately poor and disproportionately non-White at the time of siting.[5]

In 2007, Paul Mohai and Robin Saha provided compelling evidence of the demographic composition at or near the time of siting for the neighborhoods of the 413 facilities examined in the *Toxic Wastes and Race at Twenty* report.[6] Again, their research found that nationally commercial hazardous waste facilities sited since 1965 have been sited in neighborhoods that were disproportionately minority at the time of siting.

In a 2009 study, using data from the Americans' Changing Lives Study, Paul Mohai and his colleagues found significant disparities in exposure to environmental hazards among racial groups. African Americans and persons at lower educational levels were more likely to live within a mile of a polluting facility. Racial disparities were especially pronounced in metropolitan areas in the Midwest and West and in suburban areas of the South. The researchers also provide a paradigm for studying changes over time in the links to health.[7]

This chapter brings together a wide range of seemingly disparate environmental challenges facing vulnerable populations and vulnerable communities under the racial equity framework. We trace the national research priority from emphasizing the elimination of childhood lead poisoning to the expanded goal of healthy homes. Research on air pollution provides clear cut evidence that dirty air is not a randomly distributed and unequal health burden borne by those populations most susceptible to the threat—whether in metropolitan areas and cities, neighborhoods, near schools, as well as indoor pollution inside schools and homes.

Our analysis also chronicles research that tracks pollution from companies to communities, toxic threats near schools, and health threats from "dirty power," coal-fired power plants. We also explore research that documents the convergence of the green building and healthy homes movement and the contribution of buildings, automobile-dependent transportation systems, and electric power generation to climate change—and the health and equity implications.

Reports From the National Academy of Sciences

After mounting pressure and hundreds of reports and studies on environmental justice, the National Academy of Sciences produced five environmental justice reports between 1999 and 2009. In 1999, the National Academy of Sciences Institute of Medicine (IOM) released *Toward Environmental Justice: Research, Education, and Health Policy Needs,* concluding that "low-income and people of color communities are exposed to higher levels of pollution than the rest of the nation and that these same populations experience certain diseases in greater number than more affluent White communities."[8]

The IOM study also offers detailed examinations to assist in identifying environmental hazards and assessing risk for populations of varying ethnic, social, and economic backgrounds, and the need for methodologies that uniquely suit the populations at risk; identifying basic, clinical, and occupational research needs and meeting challenges to research on minorities; expanding environmental education from an ecological focus to a public health focus for all levels of health professionals; and legal and ethical aspects of environmental health issues.

In 2001, the National Academy of Public Administration (NAPA) released the first of three studies. The first study, *Environmental Justice in EPA Permitting: Reducing Pollution in High-Risk Communities Is Integral to the Agency's Mission*, concluded that the Environmental Protection Agency (EPA) must work more proactively to integrate environmental justice into its core mission.[9] The NAPA study is designed to help low-income individuals and people of color gain a better understanding of how they can more effectively bring environmental justice concerns to the attention of the EPA's permitting programs.

In 2002, NAPA released *Models for Change: Efforts by Four States to Address Environmental Justice*, its second report on environmental justice.[10] The report provides information on the legislation, policy, procedures, and tools that four states (Indiana, Florida, New Jersey, and California) have used to address the widely recognized fact that some low-income communities and communities of color are exposed to significantly greater environmental and public health hazards than other communities. The report foreword states, "Fairness, justice, and equity are critical to good public administration."[11]

In 2003, NAPA released *Addressing Community Concerns: How Environmental Justice Relates to Land Use Planning and Zoning*, its third environmental justice report.[12] This report is designed to help local, state, and federal officials better understand how local land-use planning and zoning laws can be used to resolve current environmental justice concerns now and prevent them in the future. It recommends that local governments make full use of their land-use planning and zoning authorities to solve environmental problems. It urges local, state, and federal environmental, planning, and zoning agencies to launch meaningful environmental justice initiatives and integrate those efforts into the implementation of their core program.

And in May 2009, NAPA released *Putting Community First: A Promising Approach to Federal Collaboration for Environmental Improvement: An Evaluation of the Community Action for a Renewed Environment (CARE) Demonstration Program*.[13] CARE is a competitive grants program that builds broad-based local partnerships to reduce toxics and pollutants in communities at high risk for a range of environmental hazards. The NAPA panel also provided some useful insights and broader lessons learned over 3 years engaged with the CARE program:

- CARE provides necessary and appropriate support to communities.
- CARE provides a national platform for sharing lessons about how to improve environmental protection.
- Communities' diverse challenges and solutions are valuable for the EPA.
- Working with communities can make national regulatory programs more effective.
- Working with communities can build ties with other federal agencies.
- Working with communities can mobilize new energy within the EPA.
- Working with communities can help the EPA find new ways to deploy its resources effectively.

The report offers the EPA's leadership practical recommendations for building on the strong foundation of the CARE demonstration to create a model for working with communities and other federal programs that promotes the principles of transparency, participation, and collaboration, and ultimately, helps the EPA effectively achieve its mission. The NAPA panel concludes with sobering words about engaging the Obama administration on environmental justice and health issues in overburdened communities:

> At a time when the new administration is seeking ways to promote civic and community engagement, and partnership and collaboration, the Environmental Protection Agency is in a good position to benefit from this tested model for working with communities that has gained the support of agency managers and program staff. The CARE program is an approach to community-based environmental protection— built on the shoulders of the Environmental Justice program and others before it— that complements and strengthens the EPA's regulatory and national-program-office efforts to protect human health and the environment. This appears to be especially true for environmentally-burdened communities that have multi-layered, multi-media (air, water, waste) local environmental concerns from various sources.[14]

The CARE program is built on the EPA's environmental justice work. The program's strengths rest with the interagency and intra-agency approach and the focus on environmental protection at the local level, and emphasis on building partnerships between federal, state, tribal, regional, county, local, and neighborhood organizations.

From Childhood Lead Poisoning Prevention to Healthy Homes

The Center for Disease Control and Prevention's 2009 *Fourth National Report on Human Exposure to Environmental Chemicals* cites the reduction in childhood lead poisoning as a major public health success story.[15] Children's blood lead levels continue to decline in the United States, even in historically high-risk groups for lead poisoning. The lead threat has been especially problematic for poor children, children of color, and children living in inner cities, especially in the Northeast. Children with elevated blood lead levels, ≥10 μg/dL, decreased from 8.6% in 1988–1991 to 1.4% in 1999–2004, an 84% decline.[16] Still, some children continue to be at a greater risk for exposures to lead than others. From 1988 to 1991 and 1999 to 2004, children's geometric mean blood lead levels declined in non-Hispanic Black (5.2–2.8 μg/dL), Mexican American (3.9–1.9 μg/dL), and non-Hispanic White children (3.1–1.7 μg/dL). Still, the greatest risk factors for high lead levels were older housing, poverty, age, and being non-Hispanic Black.

Lead concentrations increased in many children living in Washington, DC, after the local water authority altered the treatment used to disinfect drinking water.[17] In 2001, the District of Columbia's water authority switched from chlorination to an alternative water-disinfection technology known as chloramination. The goal was to reduce the potentially carcinogenic by-products of chlorinated drinking water. However, an unintended consequence of this technique was the sudden release of lead into the drinking water that serves the nation's capital—resulting in a "lead crisis" that persisted for several years, until water engineers found a way to fix the chloramination process. Children in the nation's capital were dosed with potentially dangerous amounts of lead, which could have an impact of somewhere between 4 and 7 IQ points. Failure to protect young children from exposure to lead-tainted drinking water is a crime against children.

Recent studies suggest that a young person's lead burden is linked to lower IQ, lower high school graduation rates, and increased delinquency.[18] Lead poisoning causes about 2 to 3 points of IQ lost for each 10-μg/dL lead level.[19] The Centers for Disease Control and Prevention (CDC) considers 10 ug/dL to be the "level of concern," even though recent studies have shown that there is evidence of adverse health effects in children with blood lead levels below 10 μg/dL. Environmental and medical interventions are recommended at ≥20 μg/dL.[20] No threshold for these effects has been found. Thus, childhood lead poisoning is not only a health, environmental, and housing problem; it is also an education problem.

A U.S. House of Representatives subcommittee investigating the CDC's performance uncovered that more than twice as many Washington, DC, children as previously reported by federal and local health officials had high levels of lead in their blood amid the city's drinking water crisis. Children who lived in neighborhoods with the highest concentrations of lead in the water—Capitol Hill, Columbia Heights, and northern sections of Ward 4—were much more likely to have elevated lead in their bloodstream.[21]

Other recent studies are finding renovations, repairs, and painting to be major sources of new lead poisoning cases. A study of New York State children (excluding New York City), found that such activities were important sources of lead exposure among children with blood lead levels ≥20 µg/dL, more than 14% of all new cases.[22] Another study of new cases in New York City found that despite notable progress, children of color still suffer disproportionately from lead poisoning, with 85% of children identified with lead poisoning being Black, Hispanic, or Asian, and most new cases being Hispanic and Black children.[23]

According to the CDC, by the end of fiscal year 2010, blood lead levels of 10 µg/dL or higher in the United States are expected to be eliminated as a public health problem. Because of this dramatic reduction in childhood lead poisoning and because many factors influence health and safety in homes, the CDC launched a broad "Healthy Homes" initiative to address and improve health conditions inside U.S. homes, especially those of low-income families, since homes are the source of a number of health-related conditions, including childhood lead poisoning, respiratory disease, unintentional injuries, and radon-related illnesses that can be mitigated, eliminated, or reduced by appropriate intervention.[24] The surgeon general's 2009 *Call to Action to Promote Healthy Homes* outlines "a society-wide comprehensive and coordinated approach to healthy homes that will result in the greatest possible public health impact and reduce disparities in the availability of healthy, safe, affordable, accessible, and environmentally-friendly homes."[25]

Research shows that lead poisoning is just one of many adverse health conditions that are related to housing deficiencies. In addition to lead, many low-income families and children are exposed to multiple indoor hazards such as mold, vermin, pesticides, and a lack of safety devices such as smoke alarms. For example, according to the Natural Resources Defense Council (NRDC), children's "exposure to neurotoxin compounds at levels believed to be safe for adults could result in permanent loss of brain function if it occurred during the prenatal and early childhood period of brain development."[26] A 2009 Environmental Working Group report, *Pollution in People: Cord Blood Contaminants in Minority Newborns*, found up to 232 toxic chemicals in the umbilical cord blood of ten babies from racial and ethnic minority groups.[27] The findings represent evidence that each child was exposed to a host of dangerous chemicals while still in the mother's womb. The ten babies in the study were born in Michigan, Florida, Massachusetts, California, and Wisconsin.

Clearly, housing conditions can significantly affect public health.[28] By moving from a single focus on lead poisoning to eliminating multiple housing-related hazards, the CDC embarked on an initiative to promote housing factors that enhance well-being through research, surveillance, and translation of science into public health practice. The benefits of a comprehensive "Healthy Homes" initiative are many.[29] They include reduction in the annual occurrence of 18,000 deaths from unintentional injury, 12 million nonfatal injuries, nearly 3,000 deaths in house fires, 14,000 burn injuries, 590 unintentional firearm deaths, 322 deaths from carbon monoxide exposure, 240,000 cases of childhood lead poisoning, 2 million emergency department visits and 500,000 hospitalizations for asthma, and the annual 168,000 viral and 34,000 bacterial illnesses caused by contaminated water and food.[30]

A September 2009 *New York Times* study, "Toxic Waters: Clean Water Laws Are Neglected, at a Cost in Suffering," is clear evidence that the health of millions of Americans is at risk from lax enforcement of existing laws.[31] Nationally, polluters in the last 5 years have violated federal clean water laws more than 500,000 times, with many violators escaping fines and punishment. About 60% of the polluters were deemed in "significant noncompliance," which translates into the most serious violations such as dumping cancer-causing chemicals. The *New York Times* research shows 10% of Americans have been exposed to drinking water that contains dangerous chemicals or fails to meet a federal health benchmark, and 40% of the nation's public water systems violated the Safe Drinking Water Act (originally passed in 1974) at least once.

Addressing Unequal Air Pollution Burden

According to Argonne National Laboratory researchers, 57% of Whites, 65% of African Americans, and 80% of Hispanics live in 437 counties with substandard air quality.[32] More than 61.3% of African American children, 69.2% of Hispanic children, and 67.7% of Asian American children live in areas that exceed the 0.08 parts per million (ppm) ozone standard, while 50.8% of White children live in such areas. Half the pediatric asthma population, 2 million children, live in these areas. Air pollution claims 70,000 lives a year, nearly twice the number killed in traffic accidents.[33] Diesel engine emissions in particular contribute to serious public health problems, including premature mortality, aggravation of existing asthma, acute respiratory symptoms, chronic bronchitis, and decreased lung function. Long-term exposure to high levels of diesel exhaust (generally at the level of occupational exposure) increase risk of developing lung cancer.[34] Diesel engine emissions have also been linked to increased incidences of various other cancers in more than 30 health studies.[35] Diesel particulate matter alone contributes to 125,000 incidences of cancer in the United States each year.[36]

Air pollution exacerbates asthma and other respiratory illnesses. Reduction in motor vehicle emissions can result in marked health improvements. The CDC reports that "when the Atlanta Olympic Games in 1996 brought about a reduction in auto use by 22.5%, asthma admissions to emergency rooms (ERs) and hospitals also decreased by 41.6 percent."[37]

Long-term exposure to air pollution shortens lives and contributes to cardiovascular and lung disease. A January 22, 2009 study published in the *New England Journal of Medicine* shows Americans are living longer because the air they breathe is becoming cleaner.[38] The average drop in air pollution seen across 51 metropolitan areas between 1980 and 2000 appears to have added nearly 5 more months to the lives of residents. Life expectancy for the corresponding time periods rose from 74 to 77 years. Researchers calculated that reductions in air pollution accounted for as much as 15% of the increase in life expectancy. Residents of cities that were the most effective at cleaning up air pollution showed the largest increases in life expectancy.

Asthma and other respiratory diseases are exacerbated by polluted air. Asthma is one of the nation's most common and costly diseases, with an estimated 20 million Americans (1 in 15) suffering from the disease, at a cost of nearly $18 billion each year. Asthma is the leading cause of school absenteeism among children, accounting for more than 15 million missed days of school.[39] Students with asthma may also be at higher risk for poor performance. Asthma prevalence has been increasing since the early 1980s across all age, sex, and racial groups. The lifetime asthma prevalence rate in African Americans is 19.4% higher than the rate in Whites. In 2007, the age-specific asthma prevalence rate was 39% higher in Blacks than in Whites (103.2 per 1,000 persons vs 74.5 per 1,000 persons, respectively).[40] African Americans are also three times more likely to be hospitalized from and die from asthma.[41] African American women have the highest asthma mortality rate of all groups, more than 2.5 times higher than the rate in White women.

Studies show that Puerto Ricans have higher age-adjusted asthma death rates (40.9 per million) than all other Hispanic subgroups and non-Hispanic Whites (14.7 per million) and African Americans (38.1 per million).[42] Racial and ethnic differences in asthma prevalence, morbidity, and mortality are highly correlated with poverty, urban air quality, indoor allergens, and lack of patient education and inadequate medical care.[43]

While asthma rates have been rising, government has not done all it can to address health threats from air pollution. In November 2009, however, the EPA proposed stronger air quality standards for sulfur dioxide (SO_2) to protect millions of the nation's most vulnerable citizens.[44] This was is the first time in nearly 40 years the EPA has proposed strengthening the nation's SO_2 air quality standard. This was a step in the right direction to protect the public's health, as exposure to SO_2 can aggravate asthma, cause respiratory difficulties, and result in ER visits and hospitalization.

The EPA's proposed new SO_2 standard of between 50 and 100 parts per billion (ppb) is designed to protect against short-term exposures ranging from 5 minutes to 24 hours. Because these revised standards would be more protective, the EPA is proposing to revoke the current 24-hour and annual SO_2 health standards. The agency is also proposing changes to monitoring and reporting requirements for SO_2. Monitors would be placed in areas with high SO_2 emission levels as well as in urban areas. The EPA's new proposal would change the Air Quality Index to reflect the revised SO_2 standards. It would also improve states' ability to alert the public when short-term SO_2 levels may affect their health.

The EPA will address the secondary standard—designed to protect the public welfare, including the environment—as part of a separate proposal in 2011. The agency held a public hearing on January 5, 2010, in Atlanta. In June 2010, the first time since setting a 24-hour primary standard for SO_2 at 140 ppb and an annual average standard at 30 ppb to protect health, both in 1971, the EPA revised the health standard, resetting the 1-hour standard to 75 ppb to protect against short-term exposure and revoking the 24-hour and annual standards.

Tracking Toxic Pollution From Companies to Communities

In April 2009, a team of environmental justice scholars released a ground-breaking study that tracked pollution from individual companies to specific communities. The study, *Justice in the Air: Tracking Toxic Pollution From America's Industries and Companies to Our States, Cities, and Neighborhoods*, was the first empirical study to use this innovative approach.[45] The researchers used the EPA's Risk-Screening Environmental Indicators (RSEI) project, a screening system developed in the 1990s to assess the human health risks resulting from toxic chemical emissions at industrial sites. The RSEI combines three variables to assess the human health risks posed by toxic releases: fate and transport, or how the chemical spreads from the point of release to the surrounding area; toxicity, or how dangerous the chemical is on a per-pound basis; and population, or how many people live in the affected areas. The EPA's own RSEI analysis confirmed that the most polluted places nationwide tend to have significantly higher-than-average percentages of African Americans, Latinos, and Asians.[46]

Using the RSEI, the researchers introduced the new concept of a "corporate environmental justice" performance scorecard—a measure based on the human health impacts from toxic air pollution released by a company and whether people of color and low-income persons bear a larger share in particular states, metropolitan areas, cities, and neighborhoods.[47] The scorecard is a new tool that can be used to promote informal regulations and corporate responsibility.

Not surprisingly, the 2009 RSEI study found racial disparities in total human health risks from industrial air toxics in the nation's 100 largest metropolitan areas. Birmingham, Alabama, topped the list of ten metropolitan areas with the largest discrepancies between the share of people of color in their health risk from industrial air toxics and their share in the population—where 65% of the health risks were borne by people of color despite only comprising 34% of the population. Cities rounding out the top 10 high-risk metropolitan areas are Baton Rouge, Louisiana; Memphis, Tennessee; Chicago, Illinois; Harrisburg, Pennsylvania; Louisville, Kentucky; Gary, Indiana; San Diego, California; Milwaukee, Wisconsin; and Tacoma, Washington.

The Delaware-based DuPont Company topped all companies on the "toxic score," a rating that conveys the firm's relative share of industrial toxic air pollution in the country—with the single largest item in its score coming from chloroprene releases at a DuPont-owned plant in Louisville, Kentucky. The other industries that round out the top 10 on the "Toxic 100" list are Dow Chemical, Bayer Group, Eastman Kodak, General Electric, Arcelor Mittal, U.S. Steel, ExxonMobil, and AK Steel Holding. The top ten companies alone account for 11% of the total human health risks from industrial air toxics in the country.

The researchers found that ten industrial sectors accounted for more than half (57%) of the total human health risks from industrial pollution nationwide.[48] Among the top ten companies on the "Toxic 100' list that have the highest share of people of color in their toxic score, people of color bear more than half of the human health impacts from the companies' toxic air releases. An example of this disparity is ExxonMobil, as people of color account for 69.1% of the impact from facilities owned by the company, but comprise 31.8% of the population nationwide.

Toxic Health Threats to School Children

Over 870,000 of the 1.9 million (46%) housing units for poor families and children, inhabited largely by people of color, sit within about a mile of factories that reported toxic emissions to the EPA.[49] The 2001 *Poisoned Schools: Invisible Threats, Visible Actions* report found more than 600,000 students in Massachusetts, New York, New Jersey, Michigan, and California were attending nearly 1,200 public schools that were located within a half mile of federal Superfund or state-identified contaminated sites.[50] No state except California has a law requiring school officials to investigate potentially contaminated property and no federal or state agency keeps records of public or private schools that operate on or near toxic waste or industrial sites.

A December 2008 *USA Today* study showed that the air at 435 schools in 34 states appears worse than at a Cincinnati, Ohio-area elementary school shut down in 2005 because of carcinogenic chemicals on the premises. Only 3% of the 127,800 public, private, and parochial schools ranked were within a mile of a long-term monitor set up to detect hazardous air pollutants.[51] On March 2, 2009, the EPA's administrator Lisa Jackson announced plans to determine whether industrial pollution taints the air outside schools across the nation. On March 31, 2009, the EPA announced it would test pollution around 63 schools in 22 states.[52]

In early October 2009, the EPA announced the first results from its air toxics monitoring near 63 schools. According to the EPA, "early sampling at all the schools show that levels of air toxics are below levels of short-term concern." However, EPA scientists caution the public about drawing conclusions at this point, since the project is designed to show whether long-term, not short-term, exposure poses health risks to school children and staff. Once monitoring is complete and the full set of results are in from all of the schools, the EPA will then evaluate the potential health concerns from long-term exposure to these pollutants.[53]

Convergence of Green Buildings and Healthy Schools

Over the last decade, we have seen the convergence of the green building movement—which typically focuses on energy efficiency and resource conservation—and the healthy schools movement. The green building movement seeks high-performance school design and construction consistent with children's needs for healthy environments; the healthy schools movement promotes a healthy environment for existing schools and environmental public health for children who are disproportionately affected by environmental exposures in "sick schools." The National Research Council's 2006 *Green School: Attributes for Health and Learning* report describes how the indoor environment affects children's health and their academic performance.[54] There are no federal laws that set standards for indoor air quality or ventilation standards, or guidelines for pesticides in and outside of classrooms.

Gregory Kats' 2006 *Greening America's Schools: Costs and Benefits* report details how the location and design of healthy school buildings enhances student learning, reduces health and operating costs, and ultimately, increases school quality and competitiveness.[55] Kats found that "green schools" cost on average about 2%, or $3, more per square foot to build than do conventional schools. However, the financial and health benefits of greening schools—which included energy and water cost savings, greater teacher retention, and reduction in colds, flu, and asthma—are about $70 per square foot, more than 20 times the cost of going green.

Much of the environmental justice movement's energy over the years has been spent fighting for toxin-free neighborhoods. Some of the most intense struggles have involved pollution threats to school children or schools constructed on or near toxic waste sites, abandoned landfills, and polluting facilities. Yet, no federal law or standards exist today for locating new schools near industrial facilities that emit toxins.

The pollution threat in neighborhoods extends into school classrooms. Not surprisingly, poor children in poor schools in poor environments face the highest health risk from "sick schools."[56] Quite often, resources play a major role in determining the health of schools, thereby exacerbating social, economic, environmental, and academic disparities.[57] Typically, low-income students of color attend schools in older, poorly maintained buildings that have multiple indoor environmental quality problems, including indoor air pollution, toxic chemical and pesticide use, mold infestation, asbestos and radon, lead in paint and drinking water, and other heavy metals.

People of color comprise about one third of the nation's population. However, students of color make up about 45% of the children attending "sick schools." Students of color are concentrated at even higher numbers in states such as Mississippi (53.5%) and Louisiana (50%). These two states alternate each year as the "poorest" and "most polluted" states in the country.[58] No federal guidelines or legislation exist today to fully support the healthy schools movement.

In too many cases, the indoor environment is making school children sick. One in eight U.S. school-aged children has asthma, resulting in an estimated 15 million missed school days.[59] An estimated 32 million students (60% of all students) are at risk daily solely as a result of school conditions. Over half (57%) of schools have at least one unsatisfactory environmental factor and more than two thirds (68%) have at least one inadequate building feature. Few states regulate air quality in schools or provide minimum ventilation standards. The *Sick Schools 2009* study found that 38 states offer grants for green school construction, 28 states have actually conducted some kind of infrastructure assessment, 21 states have adopted high-performance green school design, 15 states require integrated pest management, and only eight states have green cleaning laws.[60]

More than 55 million children and 7 million adults (20% of the total U.S. population and 98% of all children) spend their days in public and private K–12 schools in which poor air quality, hazardous chemicals, and other unhealthy conditions make students sick and handicap their ability to learn.[61] A large portion of the nation's 125,000 schools are housed in "unhealthy" buildings that can harm and hinder learning. These building pose a special health risk to children who are growing and developing.[62] Up to one half of the nation's schools have problems with indoor environmental air quality.

Poor air quality inside schools has been linked to higher absenteeism and increased respiratory ailments, lower teacher and staff productivity, lower student motivation, slower learning, lower test scores, increased medical costs, and lowered lifelong achievement and earnings. According to the EPA, the concentration of air pollutants indoors is typically higher than it is outdoors, in some instances as high as 10 or even 100 times.[63]

A number of federal initiatives have been undertaken to promote high-performance healthy schools, including the No Child Left Behind Act of 2001 (no funds were appropriated to help school districts implement them).[64] The Energy Independence and Security Act of 2007 (EISA) authorized an appropriation for the EPA of $10 million over 5 years for work on school environments. EISA Subtitle E, Healthy High Performance Schools, directs the EPA to promote healthy school environments by working with state agencies, by creating federal guidelines for siting schools, and by developing model guidelines for children's environmental health in schools. The American Recovery and Reinvestment Act of 2009 allocates funds for school renovations and directs grant funds that Title I schools can allocate to public school renovations; and the American Recovery and Reinvestment Tax Act of 2009 provides greatly expanded federal bond financing for "the construction, rehabilitation, or repair of a public school facility, or for the acquisition of land on which such a facility is to be constructed."[65]

Impact of "Dirty Power" on Public Health

Environmental health scientists have documented the ill health effects of our addiction to fossil fuel. Fine particles, polycyclic aromatic hydrocarbons (PAHs), sulfur and nitrogen oxides, benzene and mercury emitted from dirty coal-fired power plants, and diesel- and gasoline-powered vehicles all have been linked to infant mortality, lower birthweight, respiratory symptoms, childhood asthma, developmental disorders, and cancer.[66] Children are hit especially hard by "dirty power." Fine particles, ozone, diesel, and PAHs are known or suspected contributors to childhood asthma.[67] Such health effects represent a major societal and public health challenge.[68]

More than 68% of African Americans live within 30 miles of a coal-fired power plant—the distance within which the maximum effects of the smokestack plume are expected to occur. By comparison, 56% of Whites and 39% of Latinos live in such proximity to a coal-fired power plant.[69] Over 35 million American children live within 30 miles of a power plant, of which an estimated 2 million are asthmatic. Coal-burning power plants are the major source of mercury pollution, a neurotoxin especially harmful to children and developing fetuses. About 8% of U.S. women of childbearing age are at risk from mercury pollution. Much of this mercury stays airborne for 2 years and spreads around the globe.

Power plants are responsible for about 40% of all human-induced carbon dioxide (CO_2) emissions, the most significant greenhouse gas, emitted from burning fossil fuels in the United States—placing power plants at the center of the debate on climate change and climate justice. SO_2 emissions from power plants significantly harm the cardiovascular and respiratory health of people who live near the plants. More than 23,600 U.S. deaths occur each year as a result of emissions from power plants.

Because much of the mercury emitted from power plants falls within 100 miles of its source, utilities that buy credits instead of installing controls could worsen local mercury "hot spots" found around the country.[70] In 2005, over the objections of environmentalists, the EPA introduced a weak "cap-and-trade" rule that allowed power plants to either reduce their own mercury pollution or buy pollution credits from other plants. In February 2008, a federal appeals court ruled that the EPA's approach to power plant mercury emissions violates the Clean Air Act, and vacated the regulation.

The 12 states, or "dirty dozen," with the heaviest concentrations of the dirtiest power plants or in terms of total tons of CO_2 emitted are Texas (five of the ten dirtiest plants), Pennsylvania (four), Indiana (four, including two of the top ten dirtiest plants), Alabama (three), Georgia (three, including two of the top three dirtiest plants), North Carolina (three), Ohio (three), West Virginia (three), Wyoming (two), Florida (two), Kentucky (two), and New Mexico (two).[71]

Nationwide, Native American lands are grossly underserved by electricity services. According to a recent Energy Information Administration report, an average of 14.2% of tribal households in the country are without electricity.[72] This is ten times the average for the rest of America. Ironically, 20% of the energy resources in the United States are located in Indian country, which combined occupies land areas equal to the size of Texas.

Even with talk about the nation going green, dirty energy still follows the path of least resistance, allowing low-income, people of color, and indigenous people's communities to become environmental "sacrifice zones" and the dumping grounds for all kinds of health-threatening operations, including landfills, incinerators, dirty coal-fired power plants, oil refineries, petrochemical plants, and mountaintop removal mining of coal—often called "strip mining on steroids." Mountaintop mining in the southern Appalachians has damaged more than 1,200 miles of streams and turned more than 400,000 acres of forested mountains into lunar landscapes.[73]

Climate Change and Vulnerable Populations

Climate change looms as one of the major environmental and public health issues of the twenty-first century. The most vulnerable populations will suffer the earliest and most damaging setbacks because of where they live, their limited income and economic means, and their lack of access to health care. Yet, low-income people and people of color contribute least to global warming. For example, the average African American household emits 20% fewer greenhouse gases than does its White counterpart.[74] African Americans are also at greater risks from energy price shocks, spending 30% more of their income on energy than do Whites.

Global warming is a major public health threat, as future climate change could detrimentally affect air quality and thereby harm human health.[75] Global warming is expected to double the number of cities that exceed air quality standards. It will also increase temperatures on hot summer days, potentially leading to more unhealthy "red alert" air pollution days.[76] A 2007 NRDC report, *Heat Advisory: How Global Warming Causes More Bad Air Days*, says global warming will increase the number of "bad air days" by as much as 155% in some cities.[77] Researchers project that by mid-century, people living in 50 cities in the eastern United States will see a 68% (5.5 days) increase in the average number of days exceeding the health-based 8-hour ozone standard set by the EPA. On average, Americans will have 15% fewer healthy air days.

Global warming will also likely increase heat-related deaths. There is a positive relationship between the proportion of people of color living in an area and the proportion of concrete, heat-trapping surfaces in the same area, and a negative relationship between proportion of people of color and amount of tree cover.[78] Racial segregation plays an important role in this equation in the inner city.[79] A 2008 Environmental Justice Climate Change (EJCC) Initiative report, *A Climate of Change: African Americans, Global Warming, and a Just Climate Policy in the United States*, found that more than 43% of African Americans live in these urban "heat islands," compared to only 20% of Whites.

African Americans consistently experience higher rates of heat-related mortality during heat waves.[80] During the 1995 Chicago heat wave, excess mortality rates were 50% higher for non-Hispanic African Americans than for non-Hispanic Whites.[81] African Americans in Los Angeles are twice as likely to die from heat wave-related illnesses than other city residents. Similarly, Latinos have the highest rates of heat wave-related ER visits and hospitalizations in California. Low-income households face greater challenges in adapting to elevated temperatures. Nationally, African Americans have a 5.3% higher prevalence of heat-related mortality than Whites, and 64% of this disparity is traced to disparities in prevalence of home air conditioning.[82]

The 2009 *Climate Gap: Inequalities in How Climate Change Hurts Americans and How to Close the Gap* report examined the "sometimes hidden and unequal impact" of climate change on communities of color and the poor in California— vulnerable groups that will be hit especially hard.[83] The researchers found that climate change will increase pollution, harm public health, raise the costs of food, energy and water, and result in job losses, with the greatest burden falling on communities of color and the poor.

Low-income households face greater challenges in adapting to climate change. The working poor spend a much higher portion of their income on housing and transportation. For working-poor homeowners, nearly 25% of their household income is consumed by housing and commuting expenses compared with just 15.3% for other households. Working-poor renters on average spend nearly a third (32.4%) of their income on housing and transportation compared to other renter households (19.7%).[84] Nationally, American families spend about 4% of their take-home income on gasoline. By contrast, in some rural counties in the mostly Black and poor Mississippi Delta, that figure has surpassed 13%. Gasoline expenses rival what many households spend on food and housing.[85]

Conclusion

Grassroots environmental groups have always centered their focus on public health—especially the health of vulnerable populations such as low-income families and children and people of color. However, many of the environmental health challenges facing these populations have slipped between the cracks of various local, state, regional, and federal agencies, including the EPA.[86]

Despite significant improvements in environmental protection over the past several decades, millions of Americans continue to live, work, play, and go to school in unsafe and unhealthy physical environments.[87] Over the past three decades, the federal EPA has not always recognized that many of our government and industry practices (whether intended or unintended) have adverse impacts on poor people, people of color, and children. Racial discrimination is a fact of life in America, despite its being unjust, unfair, and illegal. Nevertheless, discrimination continues to deny millions of Americans their basic civil and human rights, particularly in regards to their right to live in a safe environment.

Eliminating environmental and health disparities will make us a much stronger nation as a whole. We are becoming a more diverse nation each day. As the United States moves toward becoming a majority people of color nation, eliminating environmental and health inequality is not something that should be ignored or given mere lip service. To ignore or marginalize these historic trends and their potential impact is not in the best interest of keeping the United States competitive in the world. The question is, will adequate resources be committed to erasing the glaring environmental and health disparities that currently exist in the nation? Government and private foundations have established expanded research and intervention programs to address a range of health issues, including healthy homes. Still, much work is needed to eliminate environmental health and racial disparities in the United States.

References

1. Robert D. Bullard, *Confronting Environmental Racism: Voices From the Grassroots* (Boston, MA: South End Press, 1993); Luke W. Cole and Sheila R. Foster, *From the Ground Up: Environmental Racism and the Rise of the Environmental Justice Movement* (New York, NY: New York University Press, 2000); and Robert J. Brulle and David N. Pellow, "Environmental Justice: Human Health and Environmental Inequalities," *Annual Review of Public Health* 27 (2006): 3.1–3.22.

2. Joe R. Feagin, Hernan Vera, and Pinar Batur, *White Racism: The Basics* (Cambridge, UK: Routledge, 2001).

3. Robert D. Bullard, *Invisible Houston: The Black Experience in Boom and Bust* (College Station: Texas A&M University Press, 1987).

4. Manuel Pastor, Jim Sadd, and John Hipp, "Which Came First? Toxic Facilities, Minority Move-In, and Environmental Justice," *Journal of Urban Affairs* 23, no. 1 (2001): 1–21.

5. Robin Saha and Paul Mohai, "Historical Context and Hazardous Waste Facility Siting: Understand Temporal Trends in Michigan," *Social Problems* 52, no. 4 (2005): 618–648.

6. Paul Mohai and Robin Saha, "Which Came First, People or Pollution? How Race and Socioeconomic Status Affect Environmental Justice." Paper presented at the Annual Meeting of the American Association for the Advancement of Science, San Francisco, February 17, 2007.

7. Paul Mohai, Paula M. Lantz, Jeffrey Morenoff, et al., "Racial and Socioeconomic Disparities in Residential Proximity to Polluting Industrial Facilities: Evidence From the Americans' Changing Lives Study," *American Journal of Public Health* 3, no. 99 (2009): 649–656.

8. Institute of Medicine, *Toward Environmental Justice: Research, Education, and Health Policy Needs* (Washington, DC: National Academy of Sciences, 1999), chap. 1.

9. National Academy of Public Administration (NAPA), *Environmental Justice in EPA Permitting: Reducing Pollution in High-Risk Communities Is Integral to the Agency's Mission* (Washington, DC: NAPA, December 2001).

10. National Academy of Public Administration (NAPA), *Models for Change: Efforts by Four States to Address Environmental Justice* (Washington, DC: NAPA, June 2002).

11. Ibid., vii.

12. National Academy of Public Administration (NAPA), *Addressing Community Concerns: How Environmental Justice Relates to Land Use Planning and Zoning* (Washington, DC: NAPA, June 2003).

13. National Academy of Public Administration (NAPA), *Putting Community First: A Promising Approach to Federal Collaboration for Environmental Improvement: An Evaluation of the Community Action for a Renewed Environment (CARE) Demonstration Program* (Washington, DC: NAPA, May 2009), http://www.napawash. org/pc_management_studies/CARE/5-13-09_Final_Evaluation_Report.pdf (accessed December 21, 2009).

14. Ibid., xviii.

15. Centers for Disease Control and Prevention (CDC), *Fourth National Report on Human Exposure to Environmental Chemicals* (Atlanta, GA: CDC, National Center for Environmental Health, 2009), http://www.cdc.gov/exposurereport/pdf/ FourthReport.pdf (accessed December 21, 2009).

16. Robert L. Jones, David M. Homa, Pamela A. Meyer, et al., Caldwell, "Trends in Blood Lead Levels and Blood Lead Testing Among US Children Aged 1 to 5 Years, 1988–2004," *Pediatrics* 123, no. 3 (2009): e376–e385.

17. Janet Raloff, "Water Clean-Up Experiment Caused Lead Poisoning," *Science News*, January 21, 2009, http://www.sciencenews.org/view/generic/id/40275/title/ Science_%2B_the_Public__Water-cleanup_experiment_caused_lead_poisoning (accessed December 21, 2009).

18. Centers for Disease Control and Prevention, "Recommendations for Blood Lead Screening of Young Children Enrolled in Medicaid: Targeting a Group at High Risk," *Morbidity and Mortality Weekly Report* 49, no. RR-14 (December 8, 2000): 1–13; and National Institutes of Health (NIH), National Institute of Environmental Health Sciences (NIEHS), Health Disparities Research, http://www.niehs.nih.gov/oc/ factsheets/disparity/home.htm (accessed December 15, 2006).

19. Peter Montague, "Pediatricians Urge a Precautionary Approach to Toxic Lead," *Rachel's Democracy and Health News* 827 (September 29, 2005), http://www.omega. twoday.net/stories/1068040 (accessed October 1, 2010).

20. Centers for Disease Control and Prevention (CDC), *Preventing Lead Poisoning in Young Children* (Atlanta, GA: CDC; 2005), http://www.cdc.gov/nceh/lead/ publications/prevleadpoisoning.pdf (accessed December 1, 2009).

21. Carol D. Leonnig, "More D.C. Kids Had Elevated Lead Than Stated," *Washington Post*, August 4, 2009.

22. Centers for Disease Control and Prevention, "Children With Elevated Blood Lead Levels Related to Home Renovation, Repair, and Painting Activities–New York State, 2006–2007," *Morbidity and Mortality Weekly Report* 58, no. 3 (January 30, 2009): 55–58.

23. New York City Department of Health and Mental Hygiene, *Report to the New York City Council on Progress in Preventing Childhood Lead Poisoning in New York City, 2008*, submitted September 30, 2009, http://www.nyc.gov/html/doh/downloads/pdf/lead/lead-city%20council-lpp-report_2008.pdf (accessed December 1, 2009).

24. U.S. Department of Health and Human Services (HHS), *The Surgeon General's Call to Action to Promote Healthy Homes* (Washington, DC: HHS, 2009).

25. Ibid., v.

26. Natural Resources Defense Council, *Our Children at Risk: The 5 Worst Environmental Threats to Their Health*, chap. 5, "Pesticides," November 1997, http://www.nrdc.org/health/kids/ocar/ocarinx.asp (accessed October 1, 2010).

27. Environmental Working Group, in partnership with Rachel's Network, *Pollution in People: Cord Blood Contaminants in Minority Newborns* (Washington, DC: Environmental Working Group, 2009), http://www.ewg.org/files/2009-Minority-Cord-Blood-Report.pdf (accessed December 21, 2009).

28. Mary Jean Brown, "Cost and Benefits of Enforcing Housing Policies to Prevent Childhood Lead Poisoning," *Medical Decision Making* (November/December 2002): 482–492.

29. U.S. Department of Health and Human Services, *The Surgeon General's Call to Action to Promote Healthy Homes*, pp. 19–28.

30. U.S. Environmental Protection Agency (EPA), *Onsite Wastewater Treatment Systems Manual*, Report No. EPA 625/R-00/008 (Washington, DC: EPA, 2002).

31. Charles Duhigg, "Toxic Waters—Clean Water Laws Are Neglected, at a Cost of Suffering," *New York Times*, September 13, 2009.

32. Dee R. Wernette and Leslie A. Nieves, "Breathing Polluted Air: Minorities Are Disproportionately Exposed," *EPA Journal* 18, no. 1 (March/April 1992): 16–17.

33. Earth Policy Institute, "Air Pollution Fatalities Now Exceed Traffic Deaths by 3 to 1," September 17, 2002, http://www.earth-policy.org/Updates/Update17.htm (accessed December 21, 2009).

34. U.S. Environmental Protection Agency (EPA), National Center for Environmental Assessment, *Health Assessment Document for Diesel Exhaust*, EPA/600/8-90/057E (Washington, DC: EPA, September 2002); and Health Effects Institute (HEI), *Diesel Exhaust: A Critical Analysis of Emissions, Exposure, and Health Effects* (Cambridge MA: HEI, 1995).

35. Nsedu Obot Witherspoon, "Policy Directives Toward the Protection of Children's Health in School Environments," Draft Policy Paper submitted to the Environmental Justice Resource Center at Clark Atlanta University for the Second People of Color Environmental Leadership Summit, Washington, DC, October 23–27, 2002.

36. State and Territorial Air Pollution Program Administrators (STAPPA) and the Association of Local Air Pollution Control Officials (ALAPCO), *Cancer Risk From Diesel Particulate: National and Metropolitan Area Estimates for the United States* (Washington, DC: STAPPA and ALAPCO, March 15, 2000); and Swati R. Prakash, "Breathe at Your Own Risk: Dirty Diesels, Environmental Health and Justice," Draft Policy Paper submitted to the Environmental Justice Resource Center at Clark Atlanta University for the Second People of Color Environmental Leadership Summit, Washington, DC, October 23–27, 2002.

37. Richard J. Jackson and Chris Kochtitzky, *Creating a Healthy Environment: The Impact of the Built Environment on Public Health* (Washington, DC: Sprawl Watch Clearinghouse Monograph Series, November 2001), p. 3.

38. C. Arden Pope, Majid Ezzati, and Douglas W. Dockery, "Fine-Particulate Air Pollution and Life Expectancy in the United States," *New England Journal of Medicine* 360, no. 3 (January 22, 2009): 376–386.

39. National Center for Environmental Health, Centers for Disease Control and Prevention (CDC), *Asthma's Impact on Children and Adolescents* (Atlanta, GA: National Center for Environmental Health, CDC, June 8, 2005).

40. American Lung Association (ALA), *Trends in Asthma Morbidity and Mortality* (Washington, DC: ALA Epidemiology and Statistics Unit, January 2009), http://www.lungusa.org/assets/documents/ASTHMA-JAN-2009.pdf (accessed December 21, 2009).

41. National Institute of Allergy and Infectious Diseases (NIAID), "Asthma: A Concern for Minority Populations" NIAID Fact Sheet (Washington, DC: National Institutes of Health, 2001).

42. David M. Homa, David M. Mannino, and Marielena Lara, "Asthma Mortality in U.S. Hispanics of Mexican, Puerto Rican, and Cuban Heritage, 1990–1995," *American Journal of Respiratory and Critical Care Medicine* 161 (February 2000): 504–509.

43. Asthma and Allergy Foundation of America, "Asthma Facts and Figures," http://www. aafa.org/display.cfm?id=8&sub=42 (accessed December 22, 2009).

44. U.S. Environmental Protection Agency (EPA), "EPA Proposes Stronger Air Quality Standards for Sulfur Dioxide: New Standard to Protect Millions of the Nation's Most Vulnerable Citizens," Press Release, November 17, 2009, http://www.epa.gov/aging/press/epanews/2009/2009_1117_2.htm (accessed December 24, 2009).

45. Michael Ash, James K. Boyce, Grace Chang, et al., *Justice in the Air: Tracking Toxic Pollution From America's Industries and Companies to Our States, Cities, and Neighborhoods* (Amherst: Political Economy Research institute, University of Massachusetts-Amherst, April 2009), http://www.peri.umass.edu/fileadmin/pdf/dpe/ctip/justice_in_the_air.pdf (accessed December 21, 2009).

46. Nicolaas Bouwes, Steven Hassur, and Marc Shapiro, "Information for Empowerment: The EPA's Risk-Screening Environmental Indicators Project," in *Natural Assets: Democratizing Environmental Ownership*, ed. James K. Boyce and Barry G. Shelley, pp. 117–134 (Washington, DC: Island Press, 2003).

47. Ibid., 19.

48. Ibid., 10.

49. "Study: Public Housing Is Too Often Located Near Toxic Sites," *Dallas Morning News*, October 3, 2000.

50. Child Proofing Our Communities Campaign, *Poisoned Schools: Invisible Threats, Visible Actions*. (Falls Church, VA: Center for Health, Environment and Justice, March 2001).

51. Blake Morrison and Brad Heath, "Schools Near Industry Face Chemical Dangers," *USA Today*, December 10, 2008.

52. Blake Morrison and Brad Heath, "EPA to Monitor 62 Schools' Air," *USA Today*, March 31, 2009.

53. U.S. Environmental Protection Agency (EPA), "EPA Posts New Schools Air Toxics Monitoring Initiative Data" Press Release, October 29, 2009, http://www.yosemite. epa.gov/opa/admpress.nsf/eeffe922a687433c85257359003f5340/c50f116862dc425885 25765e0050836e!OpenDocument (accessed December 7, 2009).

54. National Research Council, National Academy of Sciences, *Green Schools: Attributes for Health and Learning* (Washington, DC: National Academies Press, 2006).

55. Gregory Kats, *Greening America's Schools: Costs and Benefits*, A Capital E Report, October 2006, http://www.cape.com/ewebeditpro/items/O59F9819.pdf (accessed December 21, 2009).

56. Brent Ibata, *Public Health Law and the Built Environment in American Public Schools: Detailed History With Policy Analysis* (Saarbrücken, Germany: VDM Verlag Dr. Müller, 2009).

57. Tobi Bernstein, *School Indoor Air Quality: State Policy Strategies for Maintaining Healthy Learning Environments* (Washington, DC: Environmental Law Institute, August 2009), http://www.elistore.org/Data/products/d19_06.pdf (accessed December 21, 2009).

58. U.S. Census Bureau, *State Rankings–Statistical Abstract of the United States, Persons Below Poverty Level 2003*, FactFinder, http://www.factfinder.census. gov (accessed December 21, 2009); and David Sutton, "America's Healthiest and Unhealthiest States," *Forbes*, December 5, 2008, http://www.forbes. com/2008/12/04/healthy-unhealthy-obesity-forbeslife-cx_ds_1205health.html (accessed December 21, 2009).

59. Healthy Schools Network, *Sick Schools 2009: America's Continuing Environmental Health Crisis for Children*, p. 8 (Washington, DC: Coalition for Healthier Schools, 2009), http://www.healthyschools.org/SICK_SCHOOLS_2009.pdf (accessed December 21, 2009).

60. Ibid., 8.

61. Kats, *Greening America's Schools*.

62. Mark J. Mendell and Garvin A. Heath, "Do Indoor Pollutants and Thermal Conditions in Schools Influence Student Performance? A Critical Review of the Literature," *Indoor Air* 15 (2004): 27.

63. U.S. Environmental Protection Agency, *Indoor Air Quality*, January 6, 2003, http:// www.epa.gov/iaq (accessed December 21, 2009).

64. Tina Adler, "Learning Curve: Putting Healthy School Principles Into Practice," *Environmental Health Perspectives* 117, no. 10 (October 2009): A453.

65. U.S. Department of Education Legislation, *School Modernization: American Recovery and Reinvestment Act of 2009*, p. 166, Sec. 14002(b), http://www.ed.gov/policy/gen/leg/recovery/modernization/leg-arra.html (accessed December 21, 2009).

66. Philippe Grandjean and Philip J. Landrigan, "Developmental Neurotoxicity of Industrial Chemicals," *Lancet* 368 (2006): 2167–2178.

67. Ruth A. Etzel, "How Environmental Exposures Influence the Development and Exacerbation of Asthma," *Pediatrics* 112 (2003): 233–239; and David P. Strachan, "The Role of Environmental Factors in Asthma," *British Medical Bulletin* 56 (2000): 865–882.

68. Frederica P. Perea "Children Are Likely to Suffer Most From Our Fossil Fuel Addiction," *Environmental Health Perspectives* 116, no. 8 (August 2008): 987–990.

69. Clear the Air, et al., *Air of Injustice: African Americans & Power Plant Pollution* (Atlanta, GA: Clear the Air, October 2002).

70. Samantha Levine, "Who'll Stop the Mercury Rain?" *U.S. News & World Report*, March 29, 2004.

71. Environment News Service, "Mercury Emissions Up at Coal-Burning Power Plants," November 21, 2008, http://www.ens-newswire.com/ens/nov2008/2008-11-21-092.asp (accessed December 21, 2009).

72. U.S. Energy Information Administration (EIA), *Energy Consumption and Renewable Energy Development Potential on Indian Lands* (Washington, DC: EIA, April 2001).

73. John Feffer, "The Art of Extraction," *Common Dreams*, December 23, 2009, http://www.commondreams.org/view/2009/12/23-11 (accessed December 28, 2009).

74. Congressional Black Caucus Foundation (CBCF), *African Americans and Climate Change: An Unequal Burden* (Washington, DC: CBCF, 2004).

75. Michelle L. Bell, Richard Goldberg, Christian Hogrefe, et al., "Climate Change, Ambient Ozone, and Health in 50 U.S. Cities," *Climate Change* 82 (2007): 61–76.

76. Jonathan A. Patz, Patrick L. Kinney, Michelle L. Bell, et al., *Heat Advisory: How Global Warming Causes More Bad Air Days* (New York, NY: Natural Resources Defense Council, July 2004).

77. Daniel A. Lashof, *Heat Advisory: How Global Warming Causes More Bad Air Days.* (New York, NY: Natural Resources Defense Council, September 2007), http://www.nrdc.org/globalwarming/heatadvisory/heatadvisory07.pdf (accessed December 21, 2009).

78. Rachel Morello Frosch, Manuel Pastor, Jim Sadd, and Seth Shonkoff, *The Climate Gap: Inequalities in How Climate Change Hurts Americans & How to Close the Gap* (Los Angeles: University of Southern California, Program for Environmental and Regional Equity, May 2009).

79. Amy J. Schulz, David R. Williams, Barbara A. Israel, and Lora Bex B. Lempert, "Racial and Spatial Relations as Fundamental Determinants of Health in Detroit," *Milbank Quarterly* 80, no. 4 (2002): 677–707.

80. J. Andrew Hoerner and Nia Robinson, *A Climate of Change: African Americans, Global Warming, and a Just Climate Policy in the United States* (Oakland, CA: Environmental Justice Climate Change Initiative, June 2008).

81. Marie O'Neill, Antonella Zanobetti, and Joel Schwartz, "Disparities by Race in Heat-Related Mortality in Four U.S. Cities: The Role of Air Conditioning Prevalence," *Journal of Urban Health* 82, no. 2 (2005): 191–197.

82. Ibid.

83. Frosch, Pastor, Sadd, and Shonkoff, *The Climate Gap.*

84. Elizabeth Roberto, *Commuting to Opportunity: The Working Poor and Commuting in the United States* (Washington, DC: Brookings Metropolitan Policy Program, February 2008).

85. Clifford Krauss, "Rural U.S. Takes Worst Hit As Gas Tops $4 Average," *New York Times,* June 9, 2008.

86. Charles Duhigg, "Nation's Clean Water Laws Often Ignored," *New York Times,* September 13, 2009, A1.

87. Paul Mohai and Bunyan Bryant, "Race, Poverty, and the Environment," *EPA Journal* 18 (March/April 1992): 1–8; Robert D. Bullard, "In Our Backyards," *EPA Journal* 18 (March/April 1992): 11–12; Wernette and Nieves, "Breathing Polluted Air"; and Patrick C. West, "Health Concerns for Fish-Eating Tribes?" *EPA Journal* 18 (March/April 1992): 15–16.

3

Impetus for Change: Milestones and Timeline—1968–2010

IT HAS NOW BEEN more than four decades since Dr. Martin Luther King, Jr., went to Memphis, Tennessee, on an environmental, economic, health, and human rights mission on behalf of striking garbage workers. At the same time, Cesar Chavez and Dolores Huerta, cofounders of the National Farm Workers Association (which later became the United Farm Workers [UFW]) were leading the national struggle for farmworkers' rights, health, and safety—rights most U.S. workers take for granted. The environmental, health, and economic justice work of these national leaders and the sacrifices made by thousands of other brave individuals predate the nation's first Earth Day in 1970. The major milestones of the 1968–2010 era are highlighted in this chapter.

Now, nearly three decades after protesters in Warren County, North Carolina, put environmental racism on the map, a growing segment of our society continues its quest for equal protection and equal access to clean, healthy, and sustainable environments where they live, work, learn, and play, providing a voice for individuals, groups, and communities that have historically been left out of decision-making, especially decisions that impact low-income populations and people of color.[1]

The last four decades have seen some positive changes in the way groups in the United States relate to each other regarding health, environment, economic, and racial justice. We now see an increasing number of community-based groups, environmental health and racial equity networks, environmental and conservation groups, legal groups, faith-based groups, labor organizations, academic institutions, and youth organizations teaming up on environmental and health issues that differentially impact poor people and people of color. Many of these groups have adopted a racial equity lens to analyze and frame the issues, mobilize constituents, shape public policy, and craft legislation and legal strategies to dismantle institutionalized barriers to opportunity—including environmental racism.

Environmental health, environmental justice, and racial equity panels have become "hot" topics at national conferences and forums sponsored by law schools, bar associations, public health groups, scientific societies, professional meetings, and university lecture series. In just a short time, local and national advocates have had a profound impact on public policy, industry practices, national conferences, private foundation funding, and community-based participatory research, where community and "expert" are equal partners.

Environmental health and racial equity research, writing, and publications have flourished since the early 1990s. Today, there is a rich body of work that supports an array of disciplines from the social and behavioral sciences to physical sciences to law and legal studies. Courses and curricula on the environment, health, and racial equity can be found at nearly every college and university across the country. It is now possible for students to receive a baccalaureate and advanced degree in environmental health and racial equity. Similarly, college and university professors can select it as a major research concentration and receive tenure and promotion.

Grassroots community groups have been successful in blocking numerous permits for new polluting facilities and forced government and private industry buyout and relocation of several communities impacted by Superfund sites and industrial pollution. Environmental health and racial equity concepts and principles are making their way into initiatives that are moving the nation toward a "green economy," green buildings and healthy schools, clean and renewable energy, smart growth, and just climate policies.

When the First National People of Color Environmental Leadership Summit was held in 1991, no state in the country had passed a law or an executive order on environmental justice. Two years later, New Hampshire passed its pioneering environmental justice policy. In 2007, at least three dozen states and the District of Columbia had adopted formal environmental justice statutes, executive orders, or policies. In addition, "forty-one states demonstrate[d] significant and increased attention to the issue of environmental justice at the level of state government."[2] By 2009, all 50 states and the District of Columbia had instituted some type of environmental justice law, executive order, or policy—indicating that the area of environmental justice continues to grow and mature.[3] Although permitting and facility siting still dominate state environmental justice programs, a growing number of states are beginning to use land-use planning techniques, such as buffer zones, to improve environmental conditions, reduce potential health threats, and prevent environmental degradation in at-risk communities. States are also incorporating environmental justice in their brownfields, supplemental environmental projects, and climate policies. Some states rely on enforcement procedures in environmentally burdened communities, while other states use grants and community education.

On November 4, 2008, Senator Barack Obama (D-IL)—a former community organizer who worked for 3 years on environmental justice issues in Altgeld Gardens, a low-income public housing development located on Chicago's Southside and home to People Community Recovery, founded by Hazel Johnson in 1982—was elected president of the United States.[4] On January 20, 2009, he was sworn in as the 44th President, the first African American to hold this office.

The milestones detailed in this report attempt to capture some of the important environmental justice achievements and their impact during the past four decades. The timeline was derived primarily from two important documents— EJ Summit II Environmental Justice Timeline/Milestones (2002) and the 2007 United Church of Christ *Toxic Wastes and Race at Twenty* report, Chapter 2, "Environmental Justice Timeline—Milestones 1987–2007."[5]

Many of the entries were derived from a national call to grassroots groups, community-based organizations, networks, academic centers, legal clinics, practitioners, analysts, foundations, organized labor, faith-based groups, government officials, and others who have been involved in the movement to address environmental health and racial disparities over the years. The response was tremendous. No doubt some events and activities may have been inadvertently left out. Nevertheless, this list of milestones is intended to provide the reader with a better understanding and appreciation of the important contributions made by thousands of unsung heroes who have made sacrifices to advance environmental health and racial justice in the United States.

1968

Dr. Martin Luther King, Jr. leads a march in Memphis, Tennessee, on behalf of striking sanitation workers. He is assassinated in Memphis in April of that same year.

1969

Cesar Chavez and the United Farm Workers (UFW) declare National Grape Boycott Day.

Ralph Abascal of the California Rural Legal Assistance files suit on behalf of six migrant farmworkers that ultimately results in a ban of the pesticide DDT.

Congress passes the National Environmental Policy Act (NEPA).

1970

This year the U.S. Public Health Service acknowledges that lead poisoning was disproportionately impacting African Americans and Hispanic children.

1971

Presidents' Council on Environmental Quality (CEQ) annual report acknowledges racial discrimination adversely affects the urban poor and the quality of their environment.

1978

Northeast Community Action Group and Houston, Texas, Northwood Manor subdivision residents protest the Whispering Pines sanitary landfill.

1979

Linda McKeever Bullard files *Bean v. Southwestern Waste Management Corp.* lawsuit on behalf of Houston's Northeast Community Action Group, the first lawsuit challenging the siting of a waste facility using civil rights laws.

Robert D. Bullard completes the *Houston Waste and Black Community Study* for the *Bean v. Southwestern Waste Management Corp.* lawsuit.

1980

Environmental Health Coalition is founded in San Diego, California.

1981

Environmental Health Coalition sponsors the first Toxic Substances Conference, featuring Dr. Sam Epstein, author of *The Politics of Cancer*.

1982

Warren County residents protest the siting of a polychlorinated biphenyl (PCB) landfill in Warren County, North Carolina. It is in Warren County that Dr. Benjamin Chavis coined the term "environmental racism."

Hazel Johnson founds People for Community Recovery in Altgeld Gardens, a public housing development located on Chicago, Illinois's Southside—making People for Community Recovery one of the first environmental justice organizations in the country.

1983

"Solid Waste Sites and the Houston Black Community" article is published in *Sociological Inquiry*, a quarterly journal of the International Sociology Honor Society.

U.S. Government Accountability Office (GAO) publishes *Siting of Hazardous Landfills and Their Correlation With Racial and Economic Status of Surrounding Communities*. The GAO report found that three out of four of the off-site commercial hazardous waste facilities in U.S. Environmental Protection Agency (EPA) Region IV were located in African American communities, despite African Americans making up just one fifth of the region's population.

Urban Environment Conference's *Taking Back Our Health* conference is held in New Orleans, Louisiana.

The EPA, U.S. Department of Justice, U.S. Department of Defense, and Olin Chemical Company settle $25 million lawsuit with Black residents in Triana,

Alabama. The tiny all-Black community was contaminated with DDT from Redstone Arsenal U.S. Army base and was dubbed the "unhealthiest town in America."

Environmental Health Coalition successfully advocates for the passage of the first Community Right to Know Ordinance in California.

1984
Cesar Chavez and UFW announce a new grape boycott focusing on pesticides.

1985
The *Bean v. Southwestern Waste Management Corp.* case is removed from Judge Gabrielle McDonald, the only African American federal judge in Texas, and assigned to Senior Federal District Judge John Singleton. The *Bean* case finally goes to trial and Judge Singleton rules in favor of the defendants.

1986
West Harlem Environmental Action's (WE ACT's) community organizing begins in 1986 to combat the harmful impacts of the North River Sewage Treatment Plant on the people of the West Harlem, New York, community.

Environmental Health Coalition expands to address toxic pollution from maquiladora industries by cosponsoring the first International Environmental Conference in Tijuana, Mexico.

1987
United Church of Christ Commission for Racial Justice issues the famous *Toxic Wastes and Race in the United States* report, the first national study to correlate waste facility siting and race.

Texas Southern University sociologist Robert D. Bullard publishes *Invisible Houston: The Black Experience in Boom and Bust* (Texas A&M University Press, 1987) that chronicles the social, economic, political, educational, land use, and environmental quality of Black Houston neighborhoods as the "dumping grounds."

Environmental Health Coalition and Southeast San Diego neighborhood residents fight for emergency Superfund removal of cyanide waste.

1988

Revielletown, Louisiana, buyout and relocation by Georgia Pacific (now Georgia Gulf).

Britain's Black Environment Network is formed.

The Alston/Bannerman Fellowship Program begins to advance progressive social change by helping to sustain longtime activists of color.

Latino grassroots group Mothers of East L.A. defeats the construction of a huge toxic waste incinerator in their community.

In Dilkon, Arizona, a small group of Navajo community activists spearhead a successful effort to block siting of a $40 million toxic waste incinerator. The Great Louisiana Toxics March is led by the Gulf Coast Tenants and communities in "Cancer Alley" (the 85-mile corridor between Baton Rouge and New Orleans). The march brought public attention to the toxic living conditions in the region.

1989

Morrisonville, Louisiana, relocation (Dow Chemical Company buyout).

Paul Mohai and Bunyan Bryant are appointed Faculty Investigators of the University of Michigan's *1990 Detroit Area Study* and begin the first comprehensive examination of environmental inequality in the Detroit metropolitan area.

Indigenous communities, organizations, traditional societies, and tribal nations begin meeting together on environmental and natural resource extraction issues. This leads to national meetings in 1990 on the Diné (Navajo) territory and in 1991, near the sacred Bear Butte in South Dakota. The 1989 meeting ultimately led to the formation of the Indigenous Environmental Network (IEN) in 1990.

Presidential Commission on the Outdoors holds a conference focusing on *People of Color and the Environment*. The conference, organized by the Conservation Leadership Project, is held in Seattle, Washington, in August.

Luke Cole and Ralph Abascal establish the Center on Race, Poverty and the Environment (CRPE) in San Francisco, California.

1990
The Clean Air Act is passed by the U.S. Congress.

Under the leadership of Bunyan Bryant and Paul Mohai, the *Michigan Conference on Race and the Incidence of Environmental Hazards* convenes at the University of Michigan's School of Natural Resources and Environment in January, bringing together academics and activists to discuss the evidence and policy solutions bearing on disproportionate environmental burdens.

The "Michigan Coalition" (an ad hoc group formed during the conference) writes letters and meets with William Reilly (EPA) and Michael Deland (CEQ) in September.

Bush EPA administrator William Reilly establishes the Environmental Equity Work Group, the first federal government agency to recognize environmental justice as a need.

First of four meetings on environmental justice are held between environmental justice leaders, also known as the "Michigan Coalition," and EPA Administrator William Reilly.

Robert D. Bullard publishes *Dumping in Dixie: Race, Class, and Environmental Quality* (Westview Press, 1990), the first textbook on environmental justice.

The Southwest Network for Environmental and Economic Justice (SNEEJ) is established.

The *Proceedings of the Michigan Conference on Race and the Incidence of Environmental Hazards* is published in September, and delivered to the EPA.

In January, nine activists of color write a letter to the "Big 10" national environmental organizations, calling on them to dialogue with activists of color on the environmental crisis impacting communities of color and to hire people of color on their staffs and boards of directors.

In early April, the Southwest Organizing Project convenes more than 80 representatives from 32 organizations working on environmental and economic justice issues in the Southwestern United States.

A second letter is sent to the Big 10, this time signed by 103 activists of color representing grassroots, labor, youth, church, civil rights, and social justice advocates and coalitions in the Southwest. The letter reinforces the first letter challenging mainstream environmentalists on issues of environmental racism and lack of accountability toward third world communities in the Southwest.

Paul Mohai publishes "Black Environmentalism" in the journal *Social Science Quarterly*, the first national-level study to dispel the myth that African Americans are less concerned about the environment than are White Americans.

Environmental Health Coalition releases first comprehensive toxics report, *Communities At Risk: Your Right to Know About Toxics in San Diego*. Report ranks communities by toxic hazards and gives total amount of waste generated by local industries. San Diego environmental justice communities are identified.

1991
On December 30, *El Pueblo para el Aire y Agua Limpio v. County of Kings*, judge rules that permit process for toxic waste incinerator was flawed because failure to translate documents into Spanish meant the affected public was not "meaningfully involved" in the environmental review, in a case brought by CRPE. This was the second environmental justice lawsuit filed after the 1979 *Bean* case.

The Agency for Toxic Substances and Disease Registry convenes the National *Minority Environmental Health Conference* in Atlanta, Georgia.

In May, People Organized in Defense of Earth and her Resources (PODER) is formed and to date has sustained itself for 18 years without any city, county, or government funding. It is the only organization that addresses environmental justice issues in Austin, Texas.

In October, the First National People of Color Environmental Leadership Summit is held in Washington, DC, attracting more than 1,000 participants. The Seventeen Principles of Environmental Justice were developed at the 4-day summit.

In October, PODER actively participates in the first People of Color Summit which adopted the Principles of Environmental Justice in Washington, DC. This Summit led to President William Clinton's signing of Executive Order 12898, "Federal Actions to Address Environmental Justice in Minority Populations and Low-Income Populations" on February 11, 1994.

The EPA Accountability Campaign is initiated by SNEEJ, their grassroots members, and joined by other networks and their grassroots affiliates to ensure equitable treatment of communities of color by the EPA.

The Southern Organizing Committee (SOC) for Economic and Social Justice holds its 1992 postsummit in New Orleans.

Dumping in Dixie book receives National Wildlife Federation Conservation Achievement Award for Science.

Environmental Health Coalition proposes Toxic-Free Neighborhoods "buffer zone" ordinance to the San Diego City Council.

1992
First edition of the *People of Color Environmental Groups Directory* is published by the Charles Stewart Mott Foundation.

The "Environmental Justice Act of 1992" is introduced into Congress by Congressman John Lewis (D-GA) and Senator Albert Gore (D-TN).

First Title VI administrative complaint filed with the EPA by St Francis Prayer Center in Flint, Michigan, against Genesee Power. This complaint is lost by the EPA and not found and accepted for investigation until 1994. (EPA later dismissed the complaint on the grounds that the plaintiff could not show disparate impacts; since the company vowed to meet all the requisite air emissions standards, there could be no adverse health effects, and thus no disparate impact.)

The Deep South Center for Environmental Justice (DSCEJ) is founded at Xavier University of Louisiana (later moved to Dillard University in 2005) in New Orleans.

Bunyan Bryant and Paul Mohai publish the book *Race and the Incidence of Environmental Hazards: A Time for Discourse* (Westview Press, 1992), which contains the papers presented at the 1990 Michigan Conference and the first systematic review of the empirical evidence pertaining to racial disparities in the distribution of environmental hazards. It is the second environmental justice book of its kind.

Governmental Accountability Campaign persuades the EPA and the Agency for Toxic Substances and Disease Registry (ATSDR) to clean up waste sites and support sustainable economic development efforts and enforce laws and regulations in communities.

An environmental justice delegation participates in the United Nations Conference on Environment and Development, or Earth Summit, in Rio de Janeiro, Brazil.

The *National Law Journal* publishes a special issue on *Unequal Environmental Protection* that chronicles the double standards and differential treatment of people of color and Whites.

After mounting scientific evidence and much prodding from environmental justice advocates, the EPA releases its own study, *Environmental Equity: Reducing Risks for All Communities*, finally acknowledging the fact that some populations shoulder greater environmental health risks than others. This is one of the first comprehensive government reports to examine environmental justice.

Discussions begin regarding establishing a Northeast Environmental Justice Network.

The Environmental Justice and Labor Conference, a follow-up to the First National People of Color Environmental Leadership Summit and spearheaded by SOC, is held at Xavier University in New Orleans—attracting more than 2,000 attendees.

The EPA, ATSDR, and National Institute of Environmental Health Sciences (NIEHS) jointly sponsor the "Equity in Environmental Health: Research Issues and Needs" workshop in Research Triangle Park, North Carolina; papers from the workshop were later published in a 1993 special issue of *Toxicology and Industrial Health* journal.

The *EPA Journal* devotes its entire Volume 18, No. 1 (March/April 1992) issue to environmental justice.

WE ACT, with the assistance of the Natural Resources and Defense Council (NRDC) and the law firm of Paul, Weiss, Rifkind, Wharton & Garrison, sues the city of New York for operating the North River plant as a public nuisance to the people of the West Harlem Community. WE ACT settled its lawsuit with the city and was awarded a $1 million settlement. The city also agreed to set aside $55 million in capital funds to repair the air pollution and engineering design problems at the North River Wastewater Treatment facility.

Two environmental justice leaders, Dr. Benjamin Chavis and Dr. Robert D. Bullard, are appointed to the Clinton-Gore Presidential Transition Team in the Natural Resources Cluster (EPA, Departments of Energy, Agriculture, and Interior).

Deeohn Ferris coordinates national campaign for drafting of the "Environmental Justice Position Paper" for submission to the Clinton-Gore Transition Team.

Rigoberta Menchú Tum wins the Nobel Peace Prize. Tum is a (Quiche) Mayan Indian from Guatemala who fought for indigenous and women's rights, ethno-cultural reconciliation, and land reform in her country.

The EPA publishes *Tribes at Risk: The Wisconsin Comparative Risk Project*, which documents that the Ojibwe and other Native American nations in north-ern Wisconsin suffer a disproportionate environmental risk of illness and other health problems from eating fish, deer, and other wildlife contaminated with in-dustrial pollutants like airborne PCBs, mercury, and other toxins deposited on land and water.

The World Uranium Hearing is convened in Salzburg, Austria. The proceedings are published as *Poison Fire, Sacred Earth*.

The Office of Environmental Equity is established in November. The name was changed to the Office of Environmental Justice in 1994.

Environmental Health Coalition and community residents win revocation of permit to operate Chem Waste's toxic waste incinerator in Tijuana.

1993
The Environmental Justice Act is redrafted and reintroduced by Congressman John Lewis (D-GA) and Senator Max Baucus (D-MT).

The Texas Commission on Environmental Quality creates an Environmental Equity Program.

Virginia begins addressing environmental justice through the Joint Legislative Audit Review Commission.

Arkansas passes the Environmental Equity Act, which addresses environmental justice issues in the siting of solid waste disposal facilities.

The Connecticut Department of Environmental Protection develops an Environmental Equity Policy.

SOC works with the organization Communities at Risk and coordinates participation of Region IV task force members on a Superfund Reauthorization Roundtable.

The EPA establishes the 25-member National Environmental Justice Advisory Council (NEJAC).

Local community leaders and their allies defeat the Formosa Plastics Plant from locating in Wallace, Louisiana.

The first two EPA Title VI (Civil Rights Act) administrative complaints are filed against the Mississippi Department of Environmental Quality and Louisiana Department of Environmental Quality. Other network members follow and file administrative Title VI complaints against state agencies and the EPA.

The *Second Race and the Incidence of Environmental Hazards Conference* is held at the School of Natural Resources, University of Michigan.

Asian Pacific Environmental Network (APEN) forms in 1993 to inject an Asian/Pacific Islander perspective into the Environmental Justice Movement and to build an environmental justice framework and principles to work in Asian/Pacific Islander communities.

WE ACT leads fight over the North River Sewage Treatment Plant drawing in activists across 12 northeastern states. This initial gathering catalyzes the formation of a multistate regional network, the Northeast Environmental Justice Network.

The Farmworker Network for Economic and Environmental Justice is formed to support the struggle of more than 50,000 workers in nine independent farmworker organizations.

First wave of Title VI administrative complaints are filed with the EPA by Tulane Environmental Law Clinic and Sierra Club Legal Defense Fund (now known as Earthjustice) in New Orleans on behalf of groups in Louisiana and Mississippi.

Ken Sexton and Yolanda Banks Anderson serve as guest editors of *Toxicology and Industrial Health* special issue on "Equity in Environmental Health: Research Issues and Needs," Volume 9, No. 5 (September/October 1993).

The *Toxic Racism* documentary produced for WGBH Boston airs on PBS.

Predominantly Latino residents of Kettleman City, California, succeed in preventing siting of a toxic waste facility in their community.

Environmental justice courses are approved at the University of Michigan School of Natural Resources and Environment—setting the stage for the school's Environmental Justice Program—the nation's first and only academic program to offer bachelor's, master's, and doctoral degrees in environmental justice.

Stella M. Capek publishes "The Environmental Justice Frame: A Conceptual Discussion and an Application," *Social Problems*, Volume 40, No. 1, pp. 5–24.

In February, the Toxic "Tank Farm" (fuel storage facilities) was closed as a result of health risk to area residents. For more than 35 years, residents living near the tank farm had been exposed to many toxic chemicals and were physically ill. PODER and East Austin Strategy Team (EAST) began holding community meetings and informing residents about the release of chemicals in the air, water, and soil. PODER and EAST challenged Mobil's oil permit, which led to the relocation of six of the largest multinational multibillion-dollar corporations (Exxon, Citgo, Chevron, Mobil, Texaco, and Gulf Coastal States) from the East Austin community.

1994
The Environmental Justice Resource Center at Clark Atlanta University is formed in Atlanta, Georgia.

The Environmental Justice Resource Center publishes the second edition of the *People of Color Environmental Groups Directory* that lists more than 600 groups in the United States, Puerto Rico, Canada, and Mexico.

The Environmental Law and Justice Center is formed at Texas Southern University Thurgood Marshall School of Law in Houston, Texas.

The Washington Office on Environmental Justice opens in Washington, DC.

Environmental justice delegates participate in the International Conference on Population and Development in Cairo, Egypt. Environmental justice leaders meet with Dr. Kenneth Olden, director of NIEHS, to begin dialogue.

In February, NIEHS, along with six other federal agencies, host the "Symposium on Health and Health Research Needs to Ensure Environmental Justice" in Washington, DC.

On February 11, environmental justice reaches the White House when President William J. Clinton signs Executive Order 12898, Federal Actions to Address Environmental Justice in Minority Populations and Low-Income Populations. The order mandates federal agencies to incorporate environmental justice into all their work.

The New Hampshire Department of Environmental Services incorporates an environmental equity policy and implementation strategy into its agenda.

The EPA's Interagency Working Group on Environmental Justice is established.

Center for Policy Alternatives issues *Toxic Waste and Race Revisited*. The updated report strengthens the association between race and siting of waste facilities.

Women of Color Environmental Justice Conference takes place at the University of Michigan in March.

The University of Massachusetts issues a study, funded by Waste Management Inc., that challenges siting demographics. This study marks the start of the first wave of attacks on environmental justice.

The Title IV lawsuit *Labor/Community Strategy Center, Bus Riders Union, et al. v. Los Angeles County Metropolitan Transportation Authority* is filed. The lawsuit charges that the Los Angeles Metropolitan Transportation Authority operated separate and unequal bus and rail systems that discriminated against poor minority bus riders in Los Angeles, California.

The Playas de Tijuana community, after a great deal of organizing, are able to defeat the Chemical Waste Management incinerator with help from the organizations *El Pueblo y Agua Limpia* (from Kettleman City, California), Environmental Health Coalition, and SNEEJ.

The Mole Lake Sokaogon Chippewa becomes the first Wisconsin tribe granted independent authority under the federal Clean Water Act by the EPA to regulate water quality on their reservation. Tribal regulatory authority would affect all upstream industrial and municipal facilities, including Exxon's proposed Crandon mine. The state of Wisconsin immediately files suit against the EPA in federal court, demanding that the Federal Government reverse its decision to let Indian tribes establish their own water quality standards.

The GAO publishes report to Congressional Requesters, *Superfund Status, Cost, and Timeliness of Hazardous Waste Site Cleanups.*

The Environmental Health Coalition, SNEEJ, and Comité Ciudadano Pro Restauración del Canon del Padre file a petition to the EPA to clean up the New River; the EPA issues subpoenas to U.S.-owned maquiladoras, twin plants that operate on the U.S.-Mexico border.

1995
In January, the First Interagency Public Hearing on Environmental Justice Executive Order 12898 is held at Clark Atlanta University in Atlanta.

The Environmental Justice Resource Center holds the Environmental Justice and Transportation: Building Model Partnerships Conference at Clark Atlanta University in Atlanta. This national conference helps strengthen the links between groups working on environmental justice, transportation equity, and civil rights.

Diné Community Action for a Renewed Environment (CARE) is the first Native American community group to get the Department of Interior Bureau of Indian Affairs to produce an environmental impact statement (EIS) and a 10-year Forest Management Plan for a federally recognized tribe (Navajo Nation). Before this, EISs were produced by Peabody Coal Company and other corporations rubberstamping EISs on Indian lands.

Environmental justice delegates participate in the Fourth World Conference on Women, in Beijing, China.

Laotian Organizing Project (LOP) started as APEN's first organizing project in Richmond, California, to organize the Laotian refugee community as a new voice in the environmental justice movement. LOP also forms Asian Youth Advocates (AYA) as a youth leadership development and organizing arm for high-school aged Laotian young women. AYA's formation marks APEN's push to include a gender, race, and class framework into the environmental justice movement while committing to the development of a generation of new leaders.

The Environmental Justice Fund was founded by six networks to promote the creation of alternative funding strategies to support grassroots environmental justice organizing. The six networks are Asian Pacific Environmental Network, Southwest Network for Environmental and Economic Justice, Indigenous Environmental Network, Farmworker Network for Economic and Environmental Justice, Southern Organizing Committee for Economic and Social Justice, and the Northeast Environmental Justice Network.

Region IV Environmental Justice Task Force supports Communities at Risk Platform for Superfund Reauthorization.

The NIEHS establishes the Minority Worker Training Program in September 1995 to provide a series of national pilot programs to test a range of strategies for the recruitment and training of young persons who live near hazardous waste sites or in communities that are at risk of exposure to contaminated properties, with the specific focus to obtain work in the environmental field.

The Georgia House of Representatives 1995/1996 session enacts the HB-204 Environmental Justice Act of 1995.

The GAO publishes *Hazardous and Non-Hazardous Waste: Demographics of People Living Near Waste Facilities* (1995).

As part of the Good Neighbor Campaign, PODER works to persuade Congress to earmark 10% of SEMATECH's $100 million taxpayer subsidized budget for a environmentally sustainable manufacturing process. SEMATECH is a nonprofit research consortium funded by the federal government and several of the largest U.S.-owned semiconductor manufacturers in Montopolis, Texas, a community of people of color.

In June, PODER initiates Summer Youth Leadership Development Program and its Young Scholars for Justice. This project is dedicated to the development of youth and young adults of color to address education, environmental, economic, and social justice issues affecting them and ensure gender, racial, and resource equity.

San Diego–based Environmental Health Coalition wins first cleanup standards protective of human health and the environment for contamination in San Diego Bay.

1996
Washington Office on Environmental Justice facilitates environmental justice leaders' participation in the United Nations Conference on Human Settlements, Habitat II, in Istanbul, Turkey.

The Environmental Justice Resource Center and CAU-TV coproduce the *Just Transportation* documentary.

The Indigenous Anti-Nuclear Summit 1996 takes place in Albuquerque, New Mexico. Under sponsorship of the Seventh Generation Fund, with the IEN and affiliate support, the summit brings together a network of indigenous peoples from North America and the Pacific region negatively affected by the nuclear chain. A declaration is developed that establishes a mandate of work on nuclear issues.

In July, a ten-person environmental delegation visits South Africa and meets with diverse community, labor, health, youth, and other leaders who were struggling to throw off the shackles of apartheid.

Jean Sindab, an environmental justice trailblazer with the National Council of Churches, dies.

EPA Superfund Relocation Roundtable Meeting is held in Pensacola, Florida. As a result of the hard work of Margaret Williams and local grassroots leaders, the EPA decides to relocate the entire community of 358 African Americans and low-income households living next to the Escambia Wood Treatment Plant in Pensacola.

The People of Color Disenfranchised Communities Environmental Health Network is established. The Network addresses pollution-related issues in Department of Energy and Department of Defense federal facilities. As a result of the Network's work, the EPA forms the Federal Facilities Work Group in December.

ATSDR conducts the Community Tribal Forum.

Environmental Justice Enforcement and Compliance Assurance Roundtable is held in Texas and sponsored by the NEJAC Enforcement Committee and Region IX.

The African American Environmental Justice Action Network is established.

Institute of Medicine (IOM) sponsors a Toxic Tour of "Cancer Alley" as part of its fact-finding mission and preparation for its report on health and environmental justice.

PODER forces the city of Austin to relocate a Browning-Ferris Industries (BFI) recycling plant located in the Latino community. The community was impacted daily with industrial traffic, noise, rodents, and trash. BFI, a multinational waste management company, was contracted by the city of Austin to collect recyclables such as plastics, glass, cans, and newspapers of more than 350,000 households. The site was located in East Austin and became a "mini" landfill causing an infestation of rats, raising residents' public health concerns. The neighborhood received high levels of industrial traffic. The neighborhood called for a relocation plan and convinced the city of Austin to purchase the property in 1996 and its relocation. The community was successful in rezoning the BFI property to a neighborhood office.

1997
Earth Summit II is held in New York.

Ingram barge spill of toluene and benzene at Southern University site in Baton Rouge.

Environmental justice provisions are added to Louisiana's statutes.

The Just Transition Alliance is founded in 1997 as a coalition of environmental justice and labor organizations.

The Environmental Justice Center's Healthy Resource and Sustainable Communities Conference brings several hundred environmental justice leaders from across the country together to explore environmental justice and sustainable development strategies.

The Community Tribal Advisory Board for the ATSDR Board of Scientific Counselors is established and network members are appointed to the Board.

African American farmers bring a lawsuit against the U.S. Department of Agriculture (USDA) charging it with discrimination in denying them access to loans and subsidies.

President Clinton issues Executive Order 13045 protecting children from environmental health and safety risks.

Citizens Against Nuclear Trash (CANT) and residents in Homer, Louisiana, win a major victory over Louisiana Energy Services on Earth Day.

The Waste Management Division of Region IV EPA and SOC convene Environmental Justice Summit.

The Second Environmental Justice Enforcement Roundtable is sponsored by the NEJAC Enforcement Committee and Region IV Environmental Accountability Office.

The Environmental Justice Action Group organizes a regional environmental justice conference in Portland, Oregon, in October. The conference, attended by about 150 people, explored the formation of a Pacific Northwest environmental justice alliance.

The Tennessee legislature passes a resolution for Superfund sites, as a result of the work of the Defense Depot Memphis TN Concerned Citizens Committee. The resolution requires posting of warning signs at all Superfund sites.

The EPA establishes the *National Advisory Council on Policy Technology*, Title VI Implementation, to examine facility permitting.

The community of El Florido in Baja California, Mexico, wins a victory with the cleanup of the 60,000 metric tons of lead waste from the Alco Pacifico Lead Smelter Site. The company had abandoned a major Superfund site complex in West Dallas, Texas. Organizations from West Dallas also played a crucial role, along with the Environmental Health Coalition and SNEEJ.

Maryland enacts House Bill 1350, establishing the Maryland Advisory Council on Environmental Justice (MACEJ).

In August, Oregon Governor John Kitzhaber issues Executive Order 97-16 creating the Governor's Environmental Justice Advisory Board.

CEQ publishes *Environmental Justice Guidance Under the National Environmental Policy Act* (December 1997).

In July, PODER convinces the City Council to approve the East Austin Overlay Ordinance, which tightens restrictions on the types of industries allowed to move or expand into East Austin area neighborhoods and requires notification of all proposed projects.

1998

The EPA issues *Interim Guidance for Investigating Title VI Administrative Complaints Challenging Permits.*

The United Church of Christ Commission on Racial Justice convenes an array of grassroots environmental justice, civil rights, faith-based, legal, and academic centers' leaders at the Shintech plant planned for Convent, Louisiana, and publishes *From Plantations to Plant: Report of the Emergency National Commission on Environmental and Economic Justice in St. James Parish, Louisiana* (September 15, 1998).

After fierce public opposition and mounting political pressure, Japanese-owned Shintech suspends its effort to build a PVC plant in Convent, Louisiana.

CANT and residents in Homer win a major victory over Louisiana Energy Services on Earth Day.

The Conference of Black Trade Unionists, the nation's oldest and largest independent Black labor organization, initiated its Community Action and Response Against Toxics Team Program in an effort to address the fact that low-income and minority communities are more likely than are other communities to suffer from exposure to poor quality air, polluted water sources, and toxic hazards.

The First International Agricultural Worker Forum is held in 1998. The purpose of the Forum is to create a space for workers to present their problems and encourage leadership development through future training programs. More than 60 delegates attend.

IEN facilitates for the participation of Native American grassroots, tribal traditional leadership, and elders in the Native Peoples/Native Homelands Climate Change Workshop that is held in Albuquerque, New Mexico. This leads to the development of the "Albuquerque Declaration," which is sent to the United Nations (UN) Fourth Conference of the Parties of the UN Framework Convention on Climate Change. From this point on, IEN has participated in climate change meetings at the local, regional, national, and international levels.

The EPA denies the Title VI Select Steel complaint, its first administrative decision under Title VI.

The "Justice for All: Racial Equity and Environmental Well-Being" conference is attended by several hundred participants held at the University of Colorado–Boulder in September. The conference focuses on diversity at environmental institutions as well as access to open space for people of color and the poor.

The North Carolina Environmental Justice Network grows out of the First Annual North Carolina Environmental Justice Summit held at the Historical Franklinton Center at Bricks.

The Florida legislature passes the Environmental Equity and Justice Act.

The Center for Environmental Equity and Justice is created at Florida A&M University in Tallahassee, Florida.

The U.S. Supreme Court dismisses as moot *Seif v. Chester Residents Concerned for Quality Living*, 1998 WL 477242, as requested by the plaintiff, because the Pennsylvania Department of Environmental Protection (PADEP) revoked the permit at issue. The issue before the court was whether the plaintiffs had the right to bring their lawsuit under Title VI without alleging intentional discrimination.

More than a dozen bishops and national church leaders in the Council of Black Churches participate in "Toxic Tour of Cancer Alley." Church leaders on the tour represent more than 17 million African Americans.

The Wisconsin Mining Moratorium Law is passed by the legislature after a major grassroots lobbying campaign by Indian tribes and environmental and sport-fishing groups. The law prohibits the state from issuing a permit for metallic sulfide mining unless an applicant can provide at least one example from the United States or Canada in which a metallic sulfide mine has operated for 10 years without pollution and been closed for 10 years without pollution.

Louisiana Governor M. J. "Mike" Foster, Jr, issues an executive order to address environmental justice in the parishes bordering "Cancer Alley."

The Connecticut Coalition for Environmental Justice is founded in 1998 by a former director of the Hartford Health Department, Mark A. Mitchell, MD, MPH, as a results of his concerns about the need for community action to fight the increase in environmentally related diseases in communities of color. It established chapters in Hartford, New Haven, and Bridgeport, Connecticut.

As a member of Surface Transportation Policy Project for more than 10 years, PODER worked with other groups which were instrumental in having President Clinton sign TEA-21 (Transportation Equity Act for the 21st Century). TEA-21 was adopted to ensure an appropriate balance between highway and transit spending and to provide more choices such as bike lanes, wide curb lanes, sidewalks, and so on.

1999
The UN Intergovernmental Forum on Forests experts meeting takes place in Costa Rica.

A National Emergency Meeting of Blacks in the United States is held in New Orleans, Louisiana. Groups come from 37 states. This and subsequent meetings lay the foundation for the creation of the National Black Environmental Justice Network (NBEJN).

IEN establishes a Native Persistent Organic Pollutants campaign office in Alaska in partnership with Alaska Community Action on Toxics (ACAT).

The Black farmers' racial discrimination case against the USDA settles for a reported $995 million as of early 2010.

AYA wins a campaign victory at Richmond High School in Richmond, California, that increases advisory and guidance services to students. AYA broadens the notion of environmental justice to recognize school environments as a key arena for youths.

The Third Ministerial Conference of the World Trade Organization is held in Seattle, Washington (participants included SNEEJ, Southwest Workers Union, IEN, and International Indian Treaty Council).

Congressional Black Caucus (CBC) Chair James Clyburn (D-SC) convenes "Environmental Justice: Strengthening the Bridge Between Economic Development and Sustainable Communities" in Hilton Head, South Carolina.

IOM publishes *Toward Environmental Justice: Research, Education, and Health Policy Needs* (National Academies Press).

Dana Alston, a heroine of the environmental justice movement best known for her famous speech at the 1991 First People of Color Environmental Leadership Summit and *We Speak for Ourselves* booklet, dies.

California passes its first environmental justice law, SB 115 (Solis), designating the governor's Office of Planning and Research (OPR) as the lead agency for environmental justice programs and several of the state's environmental and state planning programs.

Pennsylvania establishes the Environmental Justice Working Group to review DEP programs. An environmental justice advisory board is created based on work group report.

"America's Parks, America's People: A Mosaic in Motion" conference is held in San Francisco in January. Hundreds of activists and government representatives attend this conference (Mosaic I), which focuses on diversity and access to open space for people of color and the poor.

The Michigan Department of Environmental Quality sponsors an Environmental Justice Working Group, which issues a report setting out four recommendations. Among these recommendations, the working group advises that the Michigan Department of Environmental Quality and the permit applicant consider a 1-mile radius around proposed sites to determine whether additional community outreach efforts would be prudent so as to address potential environmental justice issues.

The Florida state legislature creates the Community Environmental Health Program. The primary purpose of the program is to ensure the availability of public health services to members of low-income communities who may be adversely affected by contaminated sites located in or near the community.

The Minnesota Pollution Control Agency adopts environmental justice policy.

In July, the Little Village Environmental Justice Organization (LVEJO) hosts a community Bucket Brigade Training.

ACAT creates a documentary film, *I Will Fight Until I Melt*, that portrays the last words of Yupik elder Annie Alowa urging the military to clean up toxic waste left behind on St. Lawrence Island, Alaska. The video helped prompt long-term community-based research and actions that led state and federal agencies to prioritize cleanup of the military sites.

2000
Dursban—the most dangerous and widely used insecticide in the country—is taken off the market for indoor use thanks to a concerted national advocacy campaign focused on protecting children's health.

The Environmental Justice Resource Center publishes the third edition of the *People of Color Environmental Groups Directory*, which lists more than 1,000 environmental justice groups in the United States, Puerto Rico, Canada, and Mexico.

A special issue of *American Behavioral Scientist* titled "Advances in Environmental Justice: Research, Theory and Methodology," Volume 43 (January 4) is published. The issue is edited by Dorceta E. Taylor.

Diné CARE spearheads a national organizing effort with a multiracial and multistate coalition to amend the Radiation Exposure Compensation Act.

IEN develops a training partnership with Project Underground to hire and train a Native American mining campaigner to address mining issues, launching the Indigenous Mining Campaign Project as a response to address unsustainable mining and oil development on Native American lands.

On April 26, Executive Order No. 26, the Alabama Commission on Environmental Initiatives is created.

The Tennessee Department of Environment and Conservation completes a draft of an environmental justice plan.

Hundreds of environmental justice leaders participate in the Climate Justice Summit held during the COP6 meetings in The Hague, Netherlands.

In December, the a CBC Environmental Justice Braintrust forms the National Environmental Policy Commission.

The North Carolina General Assembly releases $7 million in appropriations to begin the detoxification of the Warren County PCB landfill.

Macon County Citizens for a Clean Environment block the siting of a mega-landfill near the historic Tuskegee University campus in Tuskegee, Alabama.

NBEJN holds a national press conference on "End Toxic Terror in Black Communities" in Washington, DC.

NBEJN a coordinates CBC hearing on environmental justice in Washington, DC.

The Fort Ord Environmental Justice Network hosts the first environmental justice forum in Monterey County, California, at California State University Monterey Bay.

The Florida Brownfield Redevelopment Act addresses environmental justice concerns. The statute states that minority and low-income communities are disproportionately impacted by environmental hazardous sites, and the existence of brownfields in a community may contribute to community decline.

Maryland HB 1350 and the House Joint Resolution 6 address environmental justice concerns in Anne Arundel County. The resolution requires the Department of Environment and MACEJ to develop a plan to promote environmental justice in the county because of its high cancer mortality rate.

The Missouri Department of Natural Resources includes environmental justice in its integrated strategic plan.

The North Carolina Department of Natural Resources issues its Environmental Equity Initiative.

California SB 89, authored by Senate Member Martha Escutia (D-Montebello), requires the Secretary for Environmental Protection to convene a working group on environmental justice.

WE ACT files Title 6 civil rights complaint at the U.S. Department of Transportation (DOT).

The Committee on Health Effects of Waste Incineration, Board on Environmental Studies and Toxicology, and National Research Council release *Waste Incineration and Public Health* (Washington, DC: National Academies Press).

ACAT prompts the Anchorage School Board to adopt nationally precedent-setting least-toxic pest management policy to prevent the use of harmful pesticides in schools.

2001
Jesus People Against Pollution founder Charlotte Keys wins the Robert Wood Johnson Health Leadership Award for her work in Columbia, Mississippi.

Trade Secrets documentary on the history of the chemical revolution and the companies behind it (including environmental justice cases) airs on PBS.

The "Celebrity Tour of Cancer Alley Louisiana" is held. This event sparked some celebrities, including writer Alice Walker and Congresswoman Maxine Waters (D-CA), to revisit and work with some of the impacted communities located along the Mississippi River chemical corridor.

EPA cleanup at Agriculture Street landfill neighborhood begins.

Judge Orlofsky rules in *South Camden Citizens in Action v. NJ Dept of Environmental Protection* that compliance with environmental laws does not equal compliance with civil rights laws, and determines that New Jersey has violated Title VI of the Civil Rights Act of 1964, the first environmental justice case to prevail under this theory. The decision was later overturned by Third Circuit Court on grounds that plaintiffs do not have the right to enforce the EPA's disparate impact regulations.

On April 25, residents of Anniston, Alabama, and the Sweet Valley/Cobb Town Environmental Task Force win a $42.8 million settlement against Monsanto Chemical Company. The community has to be relocated because of PCB contamination.

Environmental justice leaders participate in World Conference Against Racism held in Durban, South Africa.

The Warren County, North Carolina, PCB landfill community secures state and federal resources to detoxify the PCB landfill and build strategy for community-driven economic development.

An environmental justice delegation from the Environmental Justice Resource Center and the DSCEJ visits and meets with faculty and administrators at the University of Puerto Rico, community leaders in Vieques, and several dozen groups in the San Juan area.

Native American activists and their allies succeed in preventing siting of a nuclear waste dump in Ward Valley, California, after 10 years of struggle.

In April, UN Commission on Human Rights lists living free of pollution as a basic human right.

California AB 1390 is enacted in the 2001–2002 state budget and directs air districts to target at least 50% of the $48 million general fund appropriated for three diesel emission reduction programs to environmental justice communities.

Governor Parris Glendening creates Maryland's Commission on Environmental Justice and Sustainable Communities by executive order.

The Indiana Department of Environmental Management develops "Environmental Justice Strategic Plan."

California SB 32 authorizes local governments to investigate and clean up small parcels of property contaminated with hazardous waste.

California SB 828 adds deadlines for developing an interagency environmental justice strategy affecting boards, departments, and offices within the Cal/EPA.

Daniel Faber and Deborah McCarthy publish *Green of Another Color* study that highlights underfunding of environmental justice within environmental philanthropy.

The Central California Environmental Justice Network holds its first environmental justice conference in Fresno in California's Central Valley in November; more than 120 people attend. This is the first environmental justice conference ever held in the Central Valley.

Environmental justice lawyers Luke W. Cole and Sheila R. Foster publish *From the Ground Up: Environmental Racism and the Rise of the Environmental Justice Movement* (New York University Press, 2000). The authors analyze how grassroots activism from communities of color is transforming environmental politics.

WE ACT's Peggy Shepard is appointed to the National Advisory Environmental Health Sciences Council of National Institutes of Health.

National Academy of Public Administration (NAPA) produces *Environmental Justice in EPA Permitting: Reducing Pollution in High-Risk Communities Is Integral to the Agency's Mission.*

Manuel Pastor, Jr., publishes *Racial/Ethnic Inequality in Environmental-Hazard Exposure in Metropolitan Los Angeles* (University of California Policy Research Center).

Kathi Hanna and Christine Coussens publish a workshop summary for the Roundtable on Environmental Health Sciences, Research, and Medicine, Division of Health Sciences Policy titled *Rebuilding the Unity of Health and the Environment: A New Vision of Environmental Health for the 21st Century* (Washington, DC: National Academies Press).

An international coalition of more than 300 environmental justice and health groups from Asia, Africa, Europe, North America, Central America, South America, and the Pacific Islands (the International POP Elimination Network) prompt the governments of the world to sign the Stockholm Convention on persistent organic pollutants (POPs), a global legally binding treaty that bans 12 of the most toxic chemicals with precautionary provisions that allow for the inclusion of new POP chemicals under phaseout provisions of the treaty. Groups including IEN and ACAT ensured that language in the preamble of the convention reflected the particular vulnerability of Arctic indigenous peoples to the high levels of chemical contamination in the north and health effects resulting from contamination of their traditional foods.

In April, Connecticut College presents a conference "A Quest for Environmental Justice: Healthy High Quality Environments for all Communities," featuring Bunyan Bryant, Mark Mitchell, Manuel Lizarralde, and John A. Stewart. This resulted in the book, *Our Backyard: A Quest for Environmental Justice*, which focused on national and state environmental justice issues.

2002

California voters pass Proposition 40, the largest resource bond in U.S. history, which provides $2.6 billion for parks, clean water, and clean air, with an unprecedented level of support among communities of color and low income.

The NBEJN forms a partnership with the South African Environmental Justice Networking Forum to host a weeklong pre-World Summit on Sustainable Development side event, workshops, and site tours.

Environmental justice delegates participate in the Sustainable Development Rio +10 Earth Summit, in Johannesburg, South Africa.

The Diamond community in Norco, Louisiana, secures full relocation and buyout by the Shell Chemical Refinery.

The *Fenceline: A Company Town Divided*, a documentary film by Slawomir Grünberg with Jane Greenberg, airs July 23 on PBS television.

The Massachusetts Executive Office of Environmental Affairs adopts environmental justice policies.

The First North American Indigenous Mining Summit is held that forms working groups to develop action plans to address coal, uranium, and metallic mining activities on Native American lands. In 2002, a Native American oil campaigner is hired.

Project Return to Sender (a coalition of Haitian, Haitian American, and U.S. and European environmental justice and environmental groups) succeeds in returning a load of incinerator ash to the United States, which was dumped on a beach at Gonaives, Haiti, 15 years earlier in 1987.

Paul Mohai and David Kershner publish "Race and Environmental Voting in the U.S. Congress" in the journal *Social Science Quarterly*, demonstrating that members of the CBC have consistently voted more pro-environmentally than have their Republican or Democratic congressional colleagues during a two-decade period.

Power in Asians Organizing (PAO) is founded as APEN's second organizing project in Oakland, California, to organize a multiethnic Asian constituency for environmental justice. PAO and LOP work together and choose housing as its next campaign, particularly looking at housing affordability and community displacement as issues to broaden the environmental justice movement.

The New Jersey Environmental Justice Alliance (NJEJA) is formed with 40 organizations from local community groups, traditional environmental groups, civil rights organizations, labor unions, and other groups.

The *Air of Injustice: African Americans and Power Plant Pollution* report is published in October, in coalition with Black Leadership Forum, the SOC for Economic and Social Justice, the Georgia Coalition for the Peoples' Agenda, and the Clear the Air Campaign.

The Latinos and the Environment Conference is organized by the University of Michigan's School of Natural Resources and Environment's Environmental Justice Initiative.

The Second People of Color Environmental Leadership Summit, or EJ Summit II, is convened from October 24 to 27, 2002, in Washington, DC. The event attracts more than 1,400 attendees.

California AB 2312 establishes an Environmental Justice Small Grant Program administered by Cal/EPA. The program provides grants up to $20,000.

California SB 1542 ensures that state regulators include low-income and minority communities in the decision-making for the siting of landfills. The bill requires that the California Integrated Waste Management Board provide environmental justice models and information to local jurisdictions for siting landfills by April 1, 2003.

The IOM landmark study, *Unequal Treatment: Confronting Racial and Ethnic Disparities in Health Care*, is published, helping to broaden the base of health philanthropy considering racial and ethnic disparities in quality of health services.

LOP wins the prestigious Leadership for a Changing World Award from the Ford Foundation.

WE ACT convenes a national conference entitled "Human Genetics, Environment and Communities of Color: Ethical and Social Implications."

WE ACT serves as first community-based editor of special monograph of *Environmental Health Perspectives*: "Advancing Environmental Justice Through Community-Based Participatory Research."

EPA Region 2 conducts first assessment of Northern Manhattan's air quality. Data gathered are used to promulgate national fine particulate standard for $PM_{2.5}$.

On November 25, the United States Conference of Catholic Bishops (USCCB) makes its first and largest environmental justice grant ($40,000) ever to a Black Catholic organization in the United States, the Knights of Peter Claver, Inc. (KPC).

The Atlanta-based GreenLaw, on behalf of Friends of the Chattahoochee and the Sierra Club, and the Coalition for the People's Agenda, launches its legal campaign against coal-fired power plants in Georgia.

The California Environmental Justice Alliance is organized. It is comprised of grassroots environmental justice organizations including Environmental Health Coalition, PODER, Communities for a Better Environment, APEN, Center for Community Action and Environmental Justice, and the CRPE.

2003
The New York State Department of Environmental Conservation adopts a policy requiring environmental justice reviews before the issuance of permits.

The West Virginia Department of Environmental Protection issues an environmental equity policy.

The U.S. Commission on Civil Rights issues its report, *Not in My Backyard: Executive Order 12898 and Title VI as Tools for Achieving Environmental Justice,* concluding that "minority and low-income communities are most often exposed to multiple pollutants and from multiple sources."

The U.S. Navy closes Camp García, the firing zone in Vieques, Puerto Rico, on May 1, after having used the area for target practice since the 1940s.

WE ACT's Peggy M. Shepard receives the Heinz Award for the Environment for her courageous advocacy and determined leadership in combating environmental injustice within urban America.

The University of California Sociology Professor David N. Pellow's *Garbage Wars: The Struggle for Environmental Justice in Chicago* wins the American Sociological Association C. Wright Mills Award.

Paul Mohai publishes "Dispelling Old Myths: African American Concern for the Environment" in the journal *Environment*, providing a comprehensive examination of African American concern for the environment during a three-decade period.

The Minority Environmental Leadership Development Initiative (MELDI) is launched at the University of Michigan's School of Natural Resources and Environment in January. MELDI's goal is to provide resources to enhance career and leadership development opportunities for people of color interested in environmental professions.

Cleanup of the Warren County, North Carolina, PCB landfill is completed at a cost of $17.1 million, and plans for the "Justice Park" on the site by Warren County government begin.

California AB 1497 passes requiring operators of solid waste facilities to receive regulatory approval before making "significant changes" to a waste facility's design or operation beyond the scope of the original permit.

California AB 1360 directs the Office of Environmental Health Hazard Assessment at Cal/EPA to develop "environmental indicators," or "scientific measurements of environmental conditions or trends."

California thermal power plant permitting requires applications for the siting of a thermal power plant to address disproportionate impacts "in a manner consistent with Section 650410.12 of the Government Code."

Mississippi passes the Hazardous Waste Facility statute, which has an anticoncentration provision.

Rhode Island's Industrial Property Remediation and Reuse Act mandates that the Rhode Island Department of Environmental Management "shall consider the effects that clean-ups would have on the population surrounding each site and shall consider the issues of environmental equity for low-income and racial minority populations."

The Maryland Commission of Environmental Justice and Sustainable Communities is tasked with examining environmental justice and sustainable communities' issues that may be associated with creating healthy, safe, economically vibrant, environmentally sound communities for all Marylanders in a manner that allows for democratic processes and community involvement.

The New Haven Environmental Justice Network, an affiliate of Connecticut Coalition for Environmental Justice, prevents the reopening of English Station power plant in New Haven; the event was the first instance in Connecticut state history in which an air pollution permit was denied.

The Physicians for Social Responsibility (PSR-LA) helps craft Cal/EPA's Environmental Justice Guidelines, a first of its kind in the United States.

The Chicago Historical Society, under the direction of its first African American president, creates a training program for KPC Chicago teen members to conduct an environmental justice oral history of African American Catholics in the city. KPC conducts an environmental health disparities survey of 350 adult members at their Northern District Conference meeting in Newark, New Jersey.

NAPA issues report *Addressing Community Concerns: How Environmental Justice Relates to Land Use Planning and Zoning.*

California Environmental Justice Alliance wins adoption of landmark environmental justice policies for Cal/EPA.

In March, PODER convinces the Austin City Council to downzone more than 600 properties zoned for industrial and commercial use in the Govalle/Johnston Terrace Neighborhood Plan area. This community plan was approved by the city council in the same month, making history by rezoning these more than 600 properties from industrial to less intense uses and uses more compatible with residential areas. Included in this rezoning were properties that were zoned industrial but the actual use was residential. While numerous properties have been rezoned, many facilities which store hazardous chemicals are still located next to schools and in residential areas. PODER will continue to organize for relocation.

In July, LVEJO receives the Green Demonstrations Program Award through the Illinois EPA and the Illinois Governor's Office.

2004
The American Bar Association Special Committee on Environmental Justice publishes *Environmental Justice for All: A Fifty-State Survey of Legislation, Policies, and Initiatives.*

New Jersey Governor James McGreevey signs the state's first environmental justice executive order.

Georgia passes the Anti-Concentration Law for Solid Waste Facilities, GA Code Ann. § 12-8-25 (2004).

The Los Angeles Harbor Hispanic Environmental Justice Organization, Coalition for a Safe Environment, and San Pedro residents win a victory when the California South Coast Air Quality Management District Arbitration Board finds San Pedro Kinder Morgan Fuel Storage Tank Facility guilty of not negotiating in good faith and cancels their permit to conduct future business permanently.

A March EPA Office of Inspector General report, *EPA Needs to Consistently Implement the Intent of the Executive Order on Environmental Justice*, sums up the treatment of environmental justice under the Bush administration.

On April 19, Norco, Louisiana, environmental justice leader Margie Eugene Richard makes history by becoming the first African American to win the prestigious Goldman Environmental Prize.

In October, Wangari Muta Maathai, a professor and environmental justice activist from Kenya, becomes the first African woman to win the Nobel Peace Prize. Professor Maathai founded the Green Belt Movement where, for nearly 30 years, she mobilized poor women to plant some 30 million trees.

The University of Michigan's School of Natural Resources and Environment's Environmental Justice Initiative organizes an international climate change conference.

Arkansas passes an Environmental Equity Act that addresses environmental justice issues in the siting of solid waste disposal facilities.

PADEP issues its Environmental Justice Public Participation Policy.

KPC receives funding from the USCCB, Illinois Humanities Council, and DePaul University's Vincentian Endowment grant to develop a faith-based environmental justice film focused on environmental health disparities in Chicago.

The Center for Justice, Tolerance & Community publishes *Building a Regional Voice for Environmental Justice* (University of California–Santa Cruz).

The Congressional Black Caucus Foundation, Inc. (CBCF) and Redefining Progress publish *African Americans and Climate Change: An Unequal Burden*.

Lynn Goldman and Christine M. Coussens, editors, Roundtable on Environmental Health Sciences, Research, and Medicine, publish *Environmental Health*

Indicators: Bridging the Chasm of Public Health and the Environment, Workshop Summary (Washington, DC: National Academies Press).

Michael K. Dorsey publishes *The Promise and Threat of Climate Justice: Geographies of Resistance in the Context of Uneven Development* (Social Science Research Network).

2005
The Oakland-based Environmental Justice Coalition for Water releases its report *Thirsty for Justice: A Blueprint for California Water*.

The New Jersey Work Environment Council organizes a successful campaign that leads to the adoption of an administrative order by the New Jersey DEP that allows workers and union representatives to participate in investigations of facilities that use extremely hazardous chemicals. This is the first agreement of its kind in the nation and will help protect workers and fenceline communities from toxic dangers.

North Carolina passes a solid wastes permitting statute requiring local demographics to be considered in the selection of or approval of landfills.

The John D. and Catherine T. MacArthur Foundation names Sustainable South Bronx leader Majora Carter as one of the 2005 MacArthur Fellows.

Congress passes an amendment to the EPA's appropriations bill directing the agency not to spend any congressionally appropriated funds in a manner that contravenes Executive Order 12898 or delays its implementation.

The GAO issues *Environmental Justice: EPA Should Devote More Attention to Environmental Justice When Developing Clean Air Rules*.

More than 45 environmental justice and mainstream environmental groups oppose the EPA's plan to drop mention of race from its draft *Environmental Justice Strategic Plan*.

Twenty-five Democrats in the Senate and House send a letter to the EPA criticizing it for its failure to apply the Executive Order 12898 in its flawed "strategic plan for environmental justice."

In August, MELDI holds a National Diversity Summit at the University of Michigan's School of Natural Resources and Environment in Ann Arbor. MELDI published and distributed *The Paths We Tread*, a book of profiles of more than 70 people of color who have had outstanding careers in the environmental field.

The Cal/EPA Air Resources Board selects the Hispanic community of Wilmington for a 2-year Children's Environmental Risk Reduction Program and Cumulative Impact Assessment.

On August 28, Hurricane Katrina devastates New Orleans and the Louisiana, Mississippi, and Alabama Gulf Coast.

Summit 2005: Diverse Partners for Environmental Progress is held in Wakefield, Virginia.

In December, the Associated Press publishes the study *More Blacks Live With Pollution*.

Sierra Club Books publishes Robert D. Bullard's *The Quest for Environmental Justice: Human Rights and the Politics of Pollution*, a follow-up to his 1996 *Unequal Protection: Environmental Justice and Communities of Color* anthology.

The Hawaii state legislature passes resolution authorizing the Environmental Council to create a state environmental guidance.

The Illinois EPA creates an environmental justice advisory group.

California SB 1110 requires California OPR to develop advisory guidelines for addressing environmental justice matters in city and county general plans.

New Mexico Governor Bill Richardson signs the Environmental Justice Executive Order 2005-056.

Hartford Park Tenants Ass'n v. R.I. Dep't of Envtl. Management, 2005 R.I. Super. LEXIS 148 (R.I. Super. Ct. 2005) was a school siting lawsuit in Providence, Rhode Island, filed to keep two schools from opening because they were built on top of a city dump. The suit did not stop the schools from opening, but court orders were issued to the state to create a stakeholder group to develop proposals on a variety of subjects for legislation, regulations, and policies concerning public participation on contaminated site cleanups and environmental justice.

PSR-LA hosts a groundbreaking summit on the subject of chemical policy reform in California, bringing together environment, women's health, and environmental justice advocates.

Citizens for Environmental Justice, Corpus Christi, Texas, receives the Congressional Hispanic Caucus Institute Award for Outstanding Achievements in Environmental Justice.

The Center for Law in the Public Interest (Robert Garcia, Executive Director and Christopher T. Hicks, Policy Director) submit public comments regarding the EPA's "Framework for Integrating Environmental Justice," and "Environmental Justice Strategic Plan Outline."

Mossville Environmental Action Now (MEAN) brings the first-ever environmental human rights legal challenge against the U.S. government for establishing an environmental regulatory system that deprives people of color of their fundamental human rights to life, health, racial equality, and a healthy environment.

LOP in Richmond, California, wins implementation of the nation's first multilingual warning system in Contra Costa County.

WE ACT and NRDC file lawsuit against the EPA that is upheld in U.S. District Court charging the EPA with inadequate protection of children from rat poison exposure.

The National Research Council and Institute of Medicine of the National Academies issues a new report edited by Bernard Lo and Mary Ellen O'Connell entitled: *Ethical Considerations for Research on Housing-Related Health Hazards Involving Children* (Washington, DC: National Academies Press).

Redefining Progress publishes *Climate Change and Extreme Weather Events: An Unequal Burden on African Americans*, Issue Brief, No. 2 (Oakland, CA: CBCF, Center for Policy Analysis and Research).

The GAO publishes *Environmental Justice: EPA Should Devote More Attention to Environmental Justice When Developing Clear Air Rules.*

ACAT's community-based health researchers and academic partners David O. Carpenter et al. publish an article, "Polichlorinated Biphenyls in Serum of the Siberian Yupik People From St. Lawrence Island, Alaska," in the *International Journal of Circumpolar Health*, Volume 64, No. 4, pp. 322–335, an article regarding the disproportionately high body burden of PCBs in the Yupik people of St. Lawrence resulting from military contamination and long-range transport of chemical contamination into the Arctic.

In October, the Connecticut Coalition for Environmental Justice holds its First Annual Environmental Justice Conference, which was attended by 100 activists from throughout the state.

Environmental Health Coalition sponsors the first state law to ban the sale of lead-contaminated candies. It also collaborated with the California Attorney General's office to win more than $1 million from a Proposition 65 lawsuit against Mars and Hershey for selling lead-tainted candies. The funds are being used to provide technical assistance and certification to smaller, mostly Mexican candy companies enabling them to produce lead-safe candies.

2006
The Concerned Citizens of Agriculture Street Landfill, after 13 years of litigation, wins their class-action lawsuit to be relocated and bought out from their contaminated community.

The Indiana Department of Environmental Management issues new environmental justice policy.

More than 50 environmental organizations, unions, and academic institutions participate for more than a year to release the abstract of the top 18 recommendations in six environmental categories in *Green Los Angeles.*

Environmental justice scholars Manuel Pastor, Jr., Robert D. Bullard, James K. Boyce, Alice Fothergill, Rachel Morello-Frosch, and Beverly Wright publish *In the Wake of the Storm: Environment, Disaster, and Race After Katrina* (Russell Sage Foundation, May 15, 2006).

Paul Mohai and Robin Saha publish "Reassessing Racial and Socioeconomic Disparities in Environmental Justice Research" in the journal *Demography,* Volume 43, No. 2, pp. 383–399. demonstrating that newer methods that better match where people live and hazardous sites are located reveal far greater racial disparities around hazardous waste sites than previously reported.

On September 18, the EPA's Office of Inspector General issues another study, *EPA Needs to Conduct Environmental Reviews of Its Program, Policies, and Activities,* chastising the agency for falling down on the job when it comes to implementing environmental justice.

In September, Dr. Beverly Wright, director of DSCEJ at Dillard University, is honored with the Special Gulf Coast Award for outstanding leadership in the aftermath of Hurricane Katrina by the Robert Wood Johnson Community Health Leadership Program.

The Oakland-based Pacific Institute releases a Ditching Dirty Diesel Collaborative Report titled *Paying With Our Health: The Real Cost of Freight Transport in California.* The report presents new data and insight from an environmental justice perspective and includes 14 community organizations and a union.

The environmental justice organizations Communities for a Better Environment, the Coalition for a Safe Environment, and California Environmental

Rights Alliance lead a campaign in which the California South Coast Air Quality Management District Board votes unanimously to adopt the most stringent oil refinery antiflaring rules in California and U.S. history.

The 32-acre Los Angeles State Historic Park at the Cornfield opens in September, after the community stops a proposal to build warehouses there by the city of Los Angeles and wealthy developers. It is the last vast open space in downtown Los Angeles.

Beginning on Sunday, September 24, a coalition of more than 70 environmental justice, social justice, public health, human rights, and workers' rights groups launch the National Environmental Justice for All Tour to highlight the devastating impact of toxic contamination on people of color and in poor communities across the United States.

The DSCEJ at Dillard University holds the Race, Place, and the Environment After Katrina: Looking Back to Look Forward Symposium in New Orleans, from October 19 to 21. More than 250 people attend the 3-day symposium.

In December, the EPA announces its decision to finalize gutting changes to the Toxics Release Inventory (TRI) program. Changes announced by the EPA will exempt nearly 3,000 facilities that release up to 2,000 pounds of toxic chemicals from issuing detailed reports and also will exempt companies that manage up to 500 pounds of the most dangerous substances, including mercury and lead.

In December, the Indigenous World Uranium Summit (individuals, tribes, and organizations from indigenous nations and from Australia, Brazil, Canada, China, Germany, India, Japan, the United States, and Vanuatu) draft and approve a Declaration calling for a ban on uranium mining, processing, enrichment, fuel use, weapons testing and deployment, and nuclear waste dumping on indigenous lands. The ban is justified on the basis of the extensive record of "disproportional impacts" of the nuclear fuel chain on the health, natural resources, and cultures of indigenous peoples. The Declaration calls attention to "intensifying nuclear threats to Mother Earth and all life," and asserts that nuclear power—the primary use for uranium—is not a solution to global warming.

An Alabama Executive Order creates the Alabama Commission on Environmental Initiatives.

The California Global Warming Solutions Act of 2006 (AB 32) is passed. The law imposes a statewide greenhouse gas cap and reduction measures and directs the California Air Resources Board to undertake measures to safeguard environmental justice communities and their ability to provide meaningful input.

Hawaii passes environmental study legislation that charges the University of Hawaii with reviewing the state environmental impact statement system, particularly whether existing law adequately addresses the effects of proposed actions on cultural practices of native communities.

In May, environmental justice advocates win an important victory when the Hastings Amendment is adopted into the House Interior and EPA appropriations bill.

In May, PG&E Hunters Point in San Francisco ceases operation.

In May, longtime environmental justice and human rights activist Damu Smith dies. At the time, Damu was the Executive Director of the NBEJN.

Lois Marie Gibbs at the Center for Health, Environment and Justice (CHEJ) publishes the Center's 25th anniversary issue of the *Journal of the Grassroots Environmental Movement*.

After a 5-year campaign, APEN and the Stop Chinatown Evictions Committee successfully save 50 units of affordable housing in Oakland, California's Chinatown while also securing funds to build 50 additional, low-income senior apartment rental units in Chinatown.

PAO leaders in Oakland, California, receive a landmark Community Benefits Agreement issued by the city to ensure stringent environmental cleanup of a brownfield site that results in 465 new units of affordable housing and open space for surrounding communities and its residents.

WE ACT and UPROSE (United Puerto Rican Organization of Sunset Park) are appointed to New York City Mayor's Sustainability Advisory Board, which helps produce PlaNYC 2030, a development plan for New York City that sets priorities for the refurbishment of city infrastructure.

In August, the Children's Environmental Health Network launches a 3-year project to educate leaders in three key communities—pediatric and other health professions, environmental justice, and public health—about the impact of environmental hazard exposures on the health and welfare of children, and to encourage leaders in these communities to promote awareness of the issues of children's environmental health.

The film *Struggles for Environmental Justice and Health in Chicago* along with a peer-reviewed educational guide is completed and distributed to 3,000 KPC members at their national convention.

Sylvia Hood Washington, Heather Goodall, and Paul Rosier publish *Echoes From the Poisoned Well: Global Memories of Environmental Injustice* (Roman & Littlefield).

Tides Foundation publishes *Changing the Social Climate: How Global Warming Affects Economic Justice* (San Francisco, CA).

Rachel Morello-Frosch and Russell Lopez publish "The Riskscape and the Color Line: Examining the Role of Segregation in Environmental Health Disparities," *Environmental Research*, Volume 102, No. 2, pp. 181–196.

Manuel Pastor, Jr., Rachel Morello-Frosch, and James L. Sadd publish "Breathless: Schools, Air Toxics, and Environmental Justice in California," *Policy Studies Journal*, Volume 34, No. 3, pp. 337–362.

In March, PODER becomes lead organizer of the "Annual Cesar E. Chavez March." Cesar Chavez demonstrated the need for all working people to support those who are oppressed and exploited.

Led by ACAT and Pesticide Action Network North America, 86 nongovernmental environmental health and justice organizations in 18 countries sign a letter sent to the governments of Mexico, Canada, and the United States to eliminate production and use of lindane, a pesticide that harms the health of farmworkers and communities in North America. Mexico banned all uses of lindane and Canada banned agricultural uses. In 2006, U.S.-based groups prompted the EPA to withdraw agricultural uses of lindane in the United States.

In November, PODER members educate voters on the $55 million affordable housing bond initiative that voters approved. PODER presented reports and testified before boards and commissions about gentrification and the need for affordable housing.

In December, PODER convinces the city of Austin to purchase the 6-acre site known as Oak Springs and appoint PODER as lead group to manage property. The natural springs are protected and numerous trees were saved from destruction.

2007
On January 24, Congressman Alcee Hastings (D-FL) and the CBCF hold Environmental Justice Policy Forum on Executive Order 12898 in Washington, DC.

The 2-square-mile Baldwin Hills Park, the largest urban park designed in the United States in more than a century, opens in the historic African American heart of Los Angeles. Community efforts defeated efforts to site a power plant and garbage dump there.

In February, the advocacy work of the Labor Community Strategy Center/Bus Riders Union pays off such that in the Omnibus Appropriations Bill it passed, the U.S. Senate included a $9.8 million first installment for the 12-mile bus-only lanes project along Wilshire Boulevard in California.

In March, the United Church of Christ releases *Toxic Wastes and Race at Twenty, 1987–2007* report at the National Press Club in Washington, DC. The report is authored by Robert D. Bullard, Paul Mohai, Robin Saha, and Beverly Wright.

On April 10, the EPA Working Group conducts environmental justice reviews to assess the extent to which its programs, policies, and activities address environmental justice concerns.

On June 7, the EPA Office of Environmental Justice launches its Environmental Justice Collaborative Problem-Solving Program where ten community-based organizations receive $100,000 to undertake a local project on environmental and health issues.

On June 21, the African American Forum on Race and Regionalism completes a report for the President's Council of Cleveland. Angela Glover Blackwell, Robert D. Bullard, Deeohn Ferris, and john a. powell are the authors of *Regionalism: Growing Together to Expand Opportunity to All* (Cleveland, OH: President's Council of Cleveland, June 2007).

On June 13, South Carolina passes Environmental Justice Bill H-3933 into law.

On June 14, the EPA releases *Environmental Justice: The Power of Partnerships— The Collaborative Problem-Solving Model at Work*, a documentary video that chronicles the story of a low-income African-American community in Spartanburg, South Carolina.

In June, EPA Region 3 Office collaborates with several partners to develop the first formalized, controlled demolition practices designed to reduce exposure to lead dust, protecting residents living around the project's perimeter from lead emissions.

In June, the 74th Oregon Legislative Assembly enacts Senate Bill 420 that creates an Environmental Justice Task Force.

On July 25, the U.S. Senate Subcommittee on Superfund and Environmental Health holds first-ever environmental justice hearing on oversight of the EPA's environmental justice programs in Washington, DC.

In July, MEAN, Advocates for Environmental Human Rights, and the Subra Company release the report, *Industrial Sources of Dioxin Poisoning in Mossville, Louisiana: A Report Using the Government's Own Data.*

In August, Youth United for Community Action, Environmental Justice Working Group, Gila River Alliance for a Clean Environment, Greenaction for Health and Environmental Justice, tribal members of the Gila River Indian Community, and other allies shut down Romic Environmental Technologies Corporation in East Palo Alto, California. Additionally, around the same time, Gila River Alliance for a Clean Environment, Greenaction for Health and Environmental Justice, Youth United for Community Action and other allies protested, supported, and pushed the Tribal Council of Gila River Indian Community to deny the renewal of operations to Romic Environmental Technologies Corporation—Southwest. The Tribal Council's denial subsequently led the EPA to deny Romic's renewal permit and ultimately close the facility.

On November 1, Michigan Governor Jennifer Granholm issues Executive Order 2007-23, "Promoting Environmental Justice." The Environmental Justice Leadership Forum on Climate Change, a new effort focused on influencing national climate change policies and bringing the voice of people of color into the dialogue around solutions, is formed.

Detroiters Working for Environmental Justice (DWEJ) joins the DSCEJ at Dillard University and launches a comprehensive Green Jobs Workforce Development Training Program.

Arbor Hill Environmental Justice Corporation hosts the Second National Leadership Summit sponsored by the U.S. Department of Health and Human Services Office of Minority Health.

NJEJA organizes a statewide environmental justice tour of New Jersey for foundation program officers in spring 2007.

Thousands of activists gather at the U.S. Social Forum 2007 in Atlanta, Georgia, under the banner "Another World Is Possible."

Harambee House, Inc./Citizens for Environmental Justice help form Savannah Environmental Collaborative, a group of 25 diverse partners working in the Hudson Hill and Woodville neighborhoods, which are surrounded by 17 industries.

APEN helps found Oakland Rising, a formation of six community-based organizations that have come together to build progressive political power in Oakland, California.

The Public Law Research Institute at the University of California's Hastings College of Law publishes *Environmental Justice for All: A Fifty-State Survey of Legislation, Policies and Cases*, 3rd edition (April 2007).

GreenLaw and the Turner Environmental Law Clinic at the Emory University Law School publish *Putting the Law to Work in Our Communities: A Citizen's Guide to Environmental Protection and Justice in Georgia* (Atlanta, Georgia).

San Diego County Regional Airport Authority Reform Act of 2007 (SB 10) is introduced by state Senator Christine Kehoe. The act establishes the governing body and structure of the authority and assigns various powers and duties to the authority regarding the establishment and operation of airports within the County.

In California, SB 375 (Steinberg) requires that the 18 metropolitan planning regions in California demonstrate that planning scenarios will result in carbon emissions reductions. It builds on the California Global Warming Solutions Act of 2006 (AB 32) by stipulating that curbing sprawl will be a mandatory part of curbing greenhouse gas emissions.

Healthy Heart and Lung Act (AB 233) will make California's air cleaner by addressing the need for enhanced enforcement of diesel emission regulations which protect public health and reduce toxic exposure.

The Hazardous Waste Cleanup (SB 32) authorizes local governments to investigate and clean up small parcels of property contaminated with hazardous waste.

The California Alternative and Renewable Fuel, Vehicle Technology, Clean Air, and Carbon Reduction Act of 2007 (AB 118) creates the Alternative and Renewable Fuel and Vehicle Technology Program which provides loans, grants, and other funding measures to develop and deploy innovative technologies that transform California's fuel and vehicle types to help attain the state's climate change polices.

Michigan HB 5247 (Lemmons) is introduced in the House to amend the National Resources and Environmental Protection Act to require that notices of certain cleanup activities and related public hearings be published in at least one ethnic or minority-owned media.

In Oregon, SB 420 (Gordly) establishes an Environmental Justice Task Force with 12 members appointed by the governor.

In May, the South Carolina legislature passes HB 3933, a Joint Resolution to create the multiagency South Carolina Environmental Justice Advisory Committee to the Department of Health and Environmental Control.

The Haida Village of Hydaburg and ACAT, with a coalition of conservation and fishing organizations, blocks multiple attempts by the timber industry to spray harmful herbicides from helicopters on Alaska forests using grassroots organizing methods. These actions protected the health of streams and coastal areas that the Haida people depend on for their traditional foods and culture (yearly 2001–2007).

In September, PODER forced the closing of the polluting Holly Street Power Plant that was negatively impacting the health of the Latino community. The plant had noise levels that exceed federal Housing and Urban Development (HUD) standards for residential areas, in addition to elevated electromagnetic field emissions (EMFs). The plant was the largest stationary source of nitrogen oxide in the Austin, Texas, area, and several fires at the site raised additional public health and safety concerns. PODER's Young Scholars for Justice have conducted community health surveys and participated in press conferences to voice community concerns. Ongoing community pressure led the City Council to close the plant on September 30, 2007.

In October, PODER convinces the Capital Area Metropolitan Planning Organization to vote not to toll existing highways in East Austin, Texas. Low-income workers would have been double taxed and sure to face hardship as a result of the toll.

2008
In March, the Los Angeles Harbor Commission approves a Clean Truck Program designed to achieve long-term sustainability, accelerate the replacement of high-polluting trucks with cleaner trucks, lessening the impact of harbor pollution on the adjacent community of color.

Alternatives for Community & Environment (ACE) helps to pass a green jobs bill with their partners (Boston Green Justice Coalition and Massachusetts Green Jobs Coalition).

In May, Connecticut passes its first Environmental Justice Law (Public Act No 08-94), which recognizes 25 distressed municipalities and more than 50 other low-income neighborhoods as environmental justice communities. It required enhanced informational processes to increase community participation in state environmental permitting, and also required negotiation of environmental benefits for environmental justice communities when there is the establishment or expansion of a major polluting facility in these locations.

In May, a delegation of environmental justice leaders residing in Louisiana's "Cancer Alley" testify before the UN Special Rapporteur on Racism. Dienne Doudou embarks on an official fact-finding mission on racism to the United States.

In May, a Race, Place, and Environment After Hurricane Katrina Symposium is opened by the DSCEJ at Dillard University in New Orleans.

DWEJ partners with the Sustainable Business Forum of Southeast Michigan to develop the Detroit Sustainability Center, an institution which will provide a focal point for sustainable development.

Citizens for Environmental Justice, located in Corpus Christi, Texas, conducts monitoring study of a fenceline community (the first ever in the country) that finds high levels of benzene in the blood and urine of adults and children tested.

NJEJA organizes a spring conference on the siting of schools on contaminated land. The conference is held in Trenton, New Jersey.

CRPE achieves a victory on buffer zones to protect Tulare County School children and rural residents from pesticides. This is a major step in protecting children, farmworkers, and rural residents from pesticide drift.

Residents in Hinkley, California, a rural town featured in the movie *Erin Brockovich*, wins another environmental case, this time against the county, for its approval of a proposed open-air sewage sludge compost facility.

CRPE Air Project Director Brent Newell receives Breathe California's Clean Air Award in honor of his "extraordinary efforts to combat global warming" through his successful campaign to regulate air pollution from agricultural sources.

WE ACT convenes the Environmental Justice Leadership Forum on Climate Change.

Illinois EPA adopts the film *Struggles for Environmental Justice and Health in Chicago* as a training tool for its workers and for communities across the state.

GreenLaw, Newfields, LLC, and the University of Georgia School of Law Land Use Clinic publish *Health, Environment, and Quality of Life Impacts: Newtown Community, Gainesville, GA* in July.

CHEJ celebrates the 30th anniversary of Love Canal, where an environmental crisis occurred in 1978 in a neighborhood in Niagara Falls, New York.

CHEJ launches the BE SAFE initiative and campaign that advances a precautionary approach to environmental decision-making at all levels of government.

California Green Collar Jobs Act of 2008 requires the California Workforce Investment Board to establish a special committee called the Green Collar Jobs Council.

San Joaquin Valley Clean Air Attainment Program (AB 252) (Arambula) provides funding for air pollution control programs. The San Joaquin Clean Air Attainment Program authorizes the San Joaquin Valley Air Pollution Control District to increase fees on motor vehicles under specified conditions for incentive-based programs to achieve motor vehicle emissions reductions.

On November 4, Senator Barack H. Obama is elected president of the United States.

In January, the last of the 175 homes in the Celotex area are remediated from polycyclic aromatic hydrocarbons to a community-negotiated level of 0.01 parts per million (acceptable state of Illinois level).

From January to April, the Chicago Metropolitan Agency for Planning and LVEJO host three community visioning sessions that lead to communities' demand to restore 31st Street bus service by the Chicago Transit Authority.

In the summer, LVEJO and Transit Campaign convince the Chicago Transit Authority to apply for federal funding to reinstate service on the 31st Street bus that would close a 7-mile no-transit gap through Chicago's southwest side.

The Organización en California de Líderes Campesinas, Inc. (Líderes Campesinas) honor CRPE's Director of Organizing Lupe Martinez and Assistant Director of Organizing Gustavo Aguirre for their outstanding advocacy on behalf of farmworkers.

Caroline Farrell, Assistant Director of the CRPE, is named one of five rising stars in public interest by OMB Watch.

Environmental Health Coalition leads the fight for adoption of the Children's Right to Lead Safe Housing Ordinance by the San Diego City Council; the ordinance would required lead hazard control in rental units and lead-safe practices to protect workers.

Environmental Health Coalition leads a successful campaign for the adoption of a Climate Change Initiative by the city of Chula Vista, which will result in an 80% reduction of 1990 carbon dioxide levels by 2010.

The Environmental Health Coalition celebrates the conclusion of the historic, binational toxic site cleanup at Metales y Derivados, an abandoned battery recycler in Tijuana. The Environmental Health Coalition and Colonia residents successfully submitted a binational citizen complaint to the Commission on Environmental Cooperation, which declared that the site posed a serious threat to the health of the neighboring community and the environment.

2009

On January 20, Senator Barack H. Obama is sworn in as the 44th president of the United States, the first African American to hold this office.

On January 23, Lisa P. Jackson is confirmed by the U.S. Senate as U.S. Environmental Protection Agency Administrator.

In January, the S. 642 Bill codifies Executive Order 12898 (relating to environmental justice) to require the administrator of the EPA to fully implement the recommendations of the inspector general of the agency and the comptroller general of the United States.

In March, Citizens for Environmental Justice in Corpus Christi, Texas, receives a Community Service Award from a fenceline community.

New Jersey Governor Jon S. Corzine signs Executive Order 131 (on February 5), directing all state entities involved in decisions that affect environmental quality and public health to provide opportunities for input by representatives of low-income and minority groups. The order further creates the Environmental Justice Advisory Council to make recommendations to the State Commissioner of the

Department of Environmental Protection regarding issues of environmental justice and equality.

In April, the Labor/Community Strategy Center publishes the policy report *The Bus Riders Union Transit Model: Why a Bus Centered System Will Best Serve U.S. Cities.*

In April, the Chicago Transit Authority is approved for $1.1 million to begin new 31st Street bus service under the Job Access Reverse Commute Program.

In May, an international coalition of environmental justice and health groups (International POPs Elimination Network) prompt the 164 nations who are parties to the Stockholm Convention to add nine new chemicals under provisions of the legally binding treaty for global phaseout. ACAT published a new report highlighting the particular threats of persistent chemicals to northern indigenous peoples and a call for the phaseout of these chemicals as a necessary measure to protect health and cultural survival.

In May, NAPA publishes an independent evaluation of the CARE program. The CARE model provides a solid and tested framework for engaging communities and other stakeholders. The CARE model involves decades of thought and effort by the EPA's career staff, especially those working in environmentally overburdened and economically disadvantaged communities.

In May, President Barack Obama proposes allotting $1.25 billion in the FY 2010 budget to settle discrimination lawsuits by thousands of Black farmers against the USDA. Nearly $1 billion in damages were paid out on almost 16,000 claims, but nearly 75,000 additional Black farmers filed their claims after the deadline.

In June, the city of Cincinnati, Ohio, passes a groundbreaking environmental justice ordinance, which is the first of its kind where a municipality can use their police powers to enforce environmental justice in the form of an "environmental justice permit."

In June, the Royal Dutch Shell Oil Company agrees to pay $15.5 million to settle a lawsuit filed against them by the son of Ken Saro-Wiwa, a Nigerian environmental activist who, along with eight others, was executed in 1995 by the military regime that ruled Nigeria at the time. However, the company denied any liability for the deaths, stating that the payment was part of a reconciliation process.

In June, the Interfaith Center on Corporate Responsibility, a national group of social responsible investors, conducts a fact-finding mission on environmental justice along the Louisiana's "Cancer Alley."

In June, the DSCEJ holds the first meeting of the Public Policy Task Force, called "The State of Recovery in New Orleans."

In July, a judge orders Chevron to stop work on its controversial oil refinery expansion in Richmond, California. The plaintiffs to push this through the courts were West County Toxics Coalition, Communities for a Better Environment, and APEN.

NJEJA organizes a conference called "The People's Assembly" that focuses on how several communities in New Jersey fought or are fighting various environmental injustices. The conference is held in Trenton, New Jersey, in late spring.

Colorado state legislature passes HB 09-1233, "Recognition of *Acequias*." The law reestablishes the norms and practices of acequia customary law in certain south-central Colorado watersheds.

WE ACT convenes Advancing Climate Justice: Transforming the Economy, Public Health and Our Environment Conference in New York, New York.

The Oregon Senate Bill 420 that created an Environmental Justice Task Force is passed.

Maryland passes SB 529 and SB 4/HR 1054, which require the Maryland Department of Environment, in consultation with the Environmental Justice

Commission and the Department of Planning, to develop maps that identify environmentally stressed communities within the state.

Luke Cole and the CRPE are given the American Bar Association's Award for Excellence in Environmental, Energy, and Resource Stewardship.

In November, PODER and the Govalle/Johnston Terrace Neighborhood Contact Team work with the city of Austin's Health and Human Services offices, Parks and Recreation Department, and the County Health District on a redevelopment plan for a 22-acre site located in East Austin on the Levander Loop. The City Council passed a resolution on November 19 supporting the conceptual plan for the campus located at Levander Loop, which includes new affordable housing, Health and Human Services offices, an Art in Public Places project, Parks and Recreation facilities, a community garden, and a new animal shelter.

In an unprecedented victory for public health, the California Energy Commission votes unanimously to deny the Peaker Plant expansion proposed by the plant's owner, MMC—an expansion of a polluting power plant that would have sacrificed the health of hundreds of low-income families that live and work in nearby Chula Vista neighborhoods. The Environmental Health Coalition was an official party to the California Energy Commission proceedings and organized opposition to the expansion.

2010
In January, the EPA for the first time proposed a geographically focused air toxics program to address the needs of communities that are disproportionately affected by toxic air pollution.

In January, EPA Administrator Jackson announced that expanding environmentalism and environmental justice are one of the top seven priorities for the EPA.

In January, the EPA, Office of Air Quality Planning and Standards, DSCEJ, Dillard University, and NIEHS, Worker Education and Training Program, host the Environmental Justice, Air Quality, Goods Movement, and Green Jobs: Evolution and Innovation Conference in New Orleans.

In February, the Environmental Justice Resource Center at Clark Atlanta University held The State of Black Atlanta Summit 2010 and published the report *State of Black Atlanta: Exploding the Myth of Black Mecca.*

In February, the University of California Hastings College of Law Public Law Research Institute published *Environmental Justice for All: A Fifty-State Survey of Legislation, Policies and Cases,* 4th edition.

In February, the Obama administration denies the Bay Area Rapid Transit (BART) district $70M in stimulus funds, citing civil rights failures. Title VI violations found in the investigation were spearheaded by a complaint from civil rights, transportation, and environmental advocates.

In February, the EPA phases out prevalent toxic chemical decaBDE, a major victory for children's health and the environment.

In March, the National Center for Environmental Economics, National Center for Environmental Research, National Health and Environmental Effects Research Laboratory, Office of Children's Health Protection, and Office of Environmental Justice host "Strengthening Environmental Justice and Decision Making: A Symposium on the Science of Disproportionate Environmental Health Impacts" in Washington, DC.

In March, the EPA hosts "Symposium to Strengthen Research and Policy on Environmental Justice" in Washington, DC. Participants included leaders from across the country including researchers, academics, policymakers, nongovernmental organizations, government officials, tribal leaders, environmental justice activists, and community experts.

In March, African American residents of Mossville—a community just west of Lake Charles, Louisiana—won a hearing before the Inter-American Commission on Human Rights on charges that the U.S. government has violated their rights to privacy and racial equality in not forcing local chemical plants to stop polluting, marking the first time the international organization has agreed to hear complaints of environmental racism against the United States by its own citizens.

In March, ACE and Working Group release the new report *Environmental Justice and the Green Economy: A Vision Statement and Case Studies for Just and Sustainable Solutions.*

In March, Clean New York hosts its first *Women's Health and the Environment Symposium.*

In March, the University of Washington, Vancouver Center for Social and Environmental Justice releases its *2010 Clark County Equity Report.*

In April, the EPA's Pollution Right-to-Know Program gets revived after 10 years of neglect from the Bush administration. The EPA is now proposing to revitalize the TRI—the bedrock public right-to-know program that tracks toxic pollution from thousands of businesses. The EPA's proposals would expand the number of chemicals reported to the program. This would be the first expansion since 1999.

In April, The California State Court of Appeal upholds environmental justice in Richmond, California, declaring the environmental impact report for Chevron Corporation refinery expansion inadequate.

In May, IEN and Movement Generation host a gathering of 25 grassroots leaders in Occidental, California, and Climate Justice Now! North America Network is formed to help define climate justice from the perspective of those most affected (grassroots, base building, indigenous communities, and communities of color), and who share a commitment to putting forth real solutions that are materially and culturally necessary to ensure justice through the epic ecological and economic transition of climate change.

In May, the Movement Strategy Center publishes its new report entitled *Dare to Change: Environmental Justice Leadership for Climate Justice, Sustainable Communities and a Deep Green Economy.*

In June, the Lawyers' Committee for Civil Rights Under Law releases its new report *Now Is the Time: Environmental Injustice in the U.S. and Recommendations for Eliminating Disparities.*

From June 22 to 26, nearly 20,000 leaders from across the nation attend the U.S. Social Forum in Detroit, Michigan.

In June, CHEJ and other community advocates continue to urge the EPA for rigorous, child-protecting school siting standards for the location of new schools.

In June, Kettleman City, California, advocacy organizations (People for Clean Air and Water and Kids Protecting Our Planet) petition Caltrans and U.S. DOT to investigate Kings County officials for alleged civil rights violations and racial discrimination in the approval of a hazardous waste landfill expansion near Kettleman City.

In July, the EPA releases an interim guidance document to help agency staff incorporate environmental justice into the agency's rulemaking process. The rulemaking guidance is an important and positive step toward meeting EPA Administrator Lisa P. Jackson's priority to work for environmental justice and protect the health and safety of communities who have been disproportionately impacted by pollution.

On September 22, 2010, for the first time in more than a decade, the Interagency Working Group on Environmental Justice (EJ IWG) was reconvened in a meeting held at the White House, by U.S. Environmental Protection Agency Administrator Lisa P. Jackson and White House Council on Environmental Quality Chair Nancy Sutley.

On December 15, the Obama administration convenes environmental justice leaders at an historic White House environmental justice forum. The participants at the forum includes five cabinet secretaries, senior officials from several federal agencies (Council on Environmental Quality Chair Nancy Sutley, EPA Administrator Lisa P. Jackson, Attorney General Eric Holder, Secretary of the Interior Ken Salazar, Secretary of Labor Hilda Solis, Secretary of Health and Human Services Kathleen Sebelius, and Secretary of Homeland Security Janet Napolitano), and more than 100 environmental justice leaders from across the United States. The focus of the forum was as follows: (1) How investments in the clean energy economy are expanding green job opportunities in environmental justice communities and beyond; (2) How existing legal authorities are being used to more fully engage communities that have been left out and left behind; (3) How the federal government is addressing environmental and health disparities in communities throughout the country; and (4) How low-income communities can work with federal, state, and local governments to prepare for the environmental and health impacts of climate change. This environmental justice forum held by President Obama indicates that he is committed to ensuring that all Americans have strong protection from environmental and health hazards.

References

1. Robert D. Bullard, *The Quest for Environmental Justice: Human Rights and the Politics of Pollution* (San Francisco: Sierra Club Books, 2005).

2. Public Law Institute, *Environmental Justice for All: A Fifty State Survey of Legislation, Policies and Cases*, 3rd ed. (San Francisco: University of California Hastings College of Law, 2007), p. 3.

3. Public Law Institute, *Environmental Justice for All: A Fifty State Survey of Legislation, Policies and Cases*, 4th ed. (San Francisco: University of California Hastings College of Law, 2009).

4. Karen Springen, "The View From Altgeld Gardens: At the Chicago Apartment Block Where Obama Worked as a Community Organizer, Remembering a 'God-Sent' Young Man," *Newsweek*, November 5, 2009; and Barack Obama, *Dreams of My Father: A Story of Race and Inheritance* (New York: Three Rivers Press, 1995; re-released 2004).

5. Robert D. Bullard, Paul Mohai, Robin Saha, and Beverly Wright, *Toxic Wastes and Race at Twenty: 1987–2007* (Cleveland, OH: United Church of Christ Witness & Justice Ministries, 2007), pp. 16–37.

4

Community Leaders Singled Out for National Awards, 1968–2009

MUCH OF THE WORK around environmental health and racial equity still goes unnoticed by the larger society. For decades, the leaders of this new movement did great work but received little national recognition. In the 1970s and 1980s, few of these leaders made the six o'clock news or received much media coverage, and even fewer won national awards and honors for their hard work. However, this began to change in the 1990s—with more leaders beginning to be singled out for prestigious national awards: the Heinz Award, the Goldman Environmental Prize, the MacArthur "Genius" Fellowship, the Ford Foundation Leadership for a Changing World Award, the Robert Wood Johnson Community Health Leaders Award, among others.

It is no accident that the majority of the leaders receiving national awards are women, since they carry more than their share of the load. The awardees presented in this report represent the tip of the iceberg, however. The hard work and dedication of these individuals and thousands of other unsung leaders built a national movement around environmental health and racial equity.

Each entry below contains a general biographical description for each one of the award recipients. This list also includes all available contact information including street address, phone number, fax number, e-mail address, and organization and award Web site URLs when available.

Susana Almanza

Susana Almanza is one of the founding members of People Organized in Defense of Earth and her Resources (PODER), founded in May 1991. Almanza and the other PODER founding members recognized the need for an organization to address the social, cultural, economic, and environmental impacts of industrial development on East Austin's communities of color. PODER's 16 years of activism has included involvement in numerous dynamic campaigns, programs, and projects, generating publicity and policies locally as well as throughout Texas and around the world. Among numerous victories and successes, one of the organization's proudest achievements was the 1991–1993 East Austin Tank Farm Campaign, in which residents (predominately African American and Latinos) who were being exposed to toxic pollutants successfully obtained an agreement to relocate gasoline storage facilities. PODER also continues to build the next generation of leaders through the Young Scholars for Justice Leadership Development Program. Almanza is a co-recipient of the 2002 Ford Foundation's Leadership for a Changing World Award.

Susana Almanza
Executive Director and Cofounder
PODER
P.O. Box 6237
Austin, TX 78762-6237
Phone: 512-472-9921
Fax: 512-472-9922
E-mail: poder_tx@sbcglobal.net
Web site: http://www.poder-texas.org
Award Web site: http://www.leadershipforchange.org/awardees/awardee.php3?ID=60

Bradley Angel

Bradley Angel is an international leader in the environmental health and justice movement, working with communities to stop pollution threats and to promote pollution prevention, clean technologies, and safe jobs. He is the cofounder of Greenaction, which works to address health and environmental justice issues within urban, rural, and indigenous communities. Since 1987, Angel has worked with hundreds of diverse low-income and working-class communities and native nations impacted and threatened by pollution. He has played a leading role in helping communities win some of the most important struggles in the history of the environmental justice movement. Some of those victories include defeating a hazardous waste incinerator planned to be sited near the farming community of Kettleman City, California; stopping a proposed nuclear waste dump on land sacred to several tribes in Southern California and Arizona; and preventing a hazardous waste dump in Mexico on lands sacred to the Tohono O'odham tribe. Prior to cofounding Greenaction, Angel was the Southwest Toxics Campaign Coordinator for Greenpeace USA from 1986 through 1997. He also served as Codirector of the San Francisco Nuclear Weapons Freeze Campaign in 1985. In December 2008, he was one of five worldwide recipients of the Lannan Foundation's Cultural Freedom Award for his environmental justice work over the years.

Bradley Angel
Executive Director
Greenaction
1095 Market Street, Suite 712
San Francisco, CA 94103
Phone: 415-248-5010
Fax: 415-248-5011
E-mail: bradley@greenaction.org
Web site: http://www.greenaction.org
Award Web site: http://www.lannan.org/lf/cf/awards-list/by-last-name/12596

Atum Azzahir

Atum Azzahir helps citizens create a safer and healthier environment in her community through an "invisible college" that trains Citizen Health Action Teams (CHAT groups) to solve their problems. The CHAT groups broaden the definition of health to include personal and economic development, adequate housing, safe homes and streets, education, employment and job satisfaction, and spiritual well-being. The program created a new multicultural Wellness Center that offers classes in nutrition and exercise, as well as health care services. Azzahir was a recipient of the 1996 Community Health Leaders Award from the Robert Wood Johnson Foundation.

Atum Azzahir
Executive Director
Powderhorn-Phillips Wellness & Cultural Health Practices Center
1527 East Lake Street
Minneapolis, MN 55407

Phone: 612-721-5745
E-mail: atum@ppcwc.org
Web site: http://www.ppcwc.org
Award Web site: http://www.communityhealthleaders.org/leaders/leader/atum_azzahir

Edward Bautista

As a teenager, Edward Bautista watched his South Brooklyn neighborhood of Red Hook unravel. Red Hook had once been a thriving waterfront community of 25,000 residents, but the rise of containerized shipping and the subsequent loss of local contracts led to 40 years of decline. As the shipping industry left, jobs disappeared, buildings were condemned, and families—including Bautista's own—were displaced. In 1977, city officials began, then suspended, a reconstruction project behind Bautista's house, exposing the community to an open sewer for over a year. Several buildings in the neglected neighborhood collapsed, killing four residents and much of the neighborhood's spirit. Bautista remembers how, as a boy of 13, he watched neighbors organize to save the community. Despite his youth, he joined in, attending meetings and carrying petitions. But the grassroots effort ended when local politicians seized control of the campaign and the city condemned dozens more buildings. Replacement housing was built but was unaffordable for most of the low-income Puerto Rican residents that the construction displaced. Bautista was one of the recipients of the 2003 Ford Foundation's Leadership for a Changing World Award.

Edward Bautista
Director of Community Planning
New York Lawyers for the Public Interest
151 West 30th Street, 11th Floor
New York, NY 10001-4007
Phone: 212-244-4664, ext. 229
Fax: 212-244-4570
E-mail: ebautista@nylpi.org
Web site: http://www.nylpi.org
Award Web site: http://www.leadershipforchange.org/awardees/awardee.php3?ID=103

Robert D. Bullard

Robert D. Bullard, PhD, Edmund Asa Ware Distinguished Professor of Sociology and founding director of the Environmental Justice Resource Center at Clark

Atlanta University, has received numerous awards, honors, and recognitions over the past three decades. His research, writings, scholarship, expert testimony, and activism have been used to advance environmental justice, human rights, and healthy communities for all. In 2000, he received the Excellence in Diversity and Environmental Stewardship Award from the Environmental Careers Organization in Boston, Massachusetts. In 2005, the American Sociological Association Environmental and Technology Section selected his *Dumping in Dixie: Race, Class, and Environmental Quality* (Westview Press 2000) book as one of the "Top Ten" books in environmental sociology, and the International Sociological Association named the book to its "Books of the Century." In July 2007, he was featured in *CNN News'* "People You Should Know." That same year, he was honored with the William Foote Whyte Distinguished Career Award by the Sociological Practice Section of the American Sociological Association. In 2008, *Newsweek* named him one of 13 "Environmental Leaders of the Century," and Green America (formerly Co-op America) presented him with its Lifetime Achievement Building Economic Alternatives Award. In 2010, The Grio named him to the list of "100 History Makers in the Making," and Green Harmony named him one of "Ten African American Green Heroes."

Robert D. Bullard
Director and Edmund Asa Ware Distinguished Professor of Sociology
Environmental Justice Resource Center
Clark Atlanta University
223 James P. Brawley Drive
Atlanta, GA 30314
Phone: 404-880-6911
Fax: 404-880-8132
E-mail: rbullard@cau.edu
Web site: http://www.ejrc.cau.edu/Welcome.html
Award Web site: http://www.cnn.com/2007/US/07/17/pysk.bullard/index.html; http://www.newsweek.com/id/130264; http://www.coopamerica.org/pdf/CAQ76.pdf

Majora Carter

Majora Carter simultaneously addresses public health, poverty alleviation, and climate change as one of the nation's pioneers in successful green-collar job training and placement systems. She founded Sustainable South Bronx in 2001 to achieve environmental justice through economically sustainable projects informed by community needs. Her work has garnered numerous awards and accolades, including a MacArthur "Genius" Fellowship in 2005. She was one of *Essence* magazine's "25 Most Influential African-Americans" in 2007. *Newsweek* named her one of 13 "Environmental Leaders of the Century" in 2008, and she has been one of the *New York Post*'s "Most Influential NYC Women" for the past 2 years. She is a board member of the Wilderness Society and SJF Ventures and hosts a special National Public Radio series called "The Promised Land." As president of the Majora Carter Group, LLC, her work now includes advising cities, foundations, universities, businesses, and communities around the world on unlocking their green-collar economic potential to benefit everyone.

Majora Carter
President and CEO
Majora Carter Group
901 Hunts Point Avenue, 2nd Floor
The Bronx, NY 10474
Phone: 718-874-7313
Fax: 718-701-4952
E-mail: info@majoracartergroup.com
Web site: http://www.majoracartergroup.com
Award Web sites: http://www.macfound.org/site/c.lkLXJ8MQKrH/b.1076861/apps/nl/content2.asp?content_id={DD826DBF-DAE6-4730-A35C-8AA6FF8AF3DE}&notoc=1; http://www.christianpost.com/article/20071120/top-25-most-influential-african-americans/index.html; http://www.newsweek.com/id/130264

Bill Gallegos

A leader in California's environmental justice movement, Bill Gallegos is the executive director of Communities for a Better Environment (CBE). He is an outstanding individual whose lifework demonstrates that although the arc of history is long, it bends toward justice. With nearly 30 years of experience as a social justice activist and leader, as director of CBE Gallegos now heads one of the foremost environmental justice organizations in the United States. He is currently a member of the California Environmental Justice Advisory Committee working to help implement California's new greenhouse gas legislation; he is also a leader of GREEN LA, a coalition of Los Angeles' leading environmental and environmental justice organizations working to make the city "the greenest big city in the

United States." Gallegos's continuing efforts are highly esteemed in the environmental and social justice community. It is his work, dedication, and passion that deserves honor and recognition as he paves the way for local, national, and global change in the environmental arena. Gallegos received the 2009 Changemaker Award from the Liberty Hill Foundation.

Bill Gallegos
Executive Director
Communities for a Better Environment
Huntington Park Office
5610 Pacific Boulevard, Suite 203
Huntington Park, CA 90255
Phone: 323-826-9771
Fax: 323-588-7079
E-mail: billgallegos@cbecal.org
Web site: http://www.cbecal.org
Award Web site: http://www.libertyhill.org/donor/dinner_honorees09.html

Lois Marie Gibbs

Lois Marie Gibbs serves as executive director of The Center for Health, Environment and Justice (CHEJ), and speaks with communities nationwide and internationally about toxic chemicals and children's unique vulnerability to environmental exposures. CHEJ has convened several nationwide coalitions of grassroots groups to implement collaborative strategies around persistent toxic chemicals like dioxin, children's environmental health, and the Precautionary Principle. Gibbs has been recognized extensively for her critical role in the grassroots environmental justice movement. The many awards she has received include the 1990 Goldman Environmental Prize, *Outside Magazine*'s "Top Ten Who Made A Difference Honor Roll" in 1991, the 1998 Heinz Award, and the 1999 John Gardner Leadership Award from the Independent Sector; in 2003, she was nominated for the Nobel Peace Prize, and in 2008, *Newsweek* named her one of 13 "Environmental Leaders of the Century." She has received an honorary PhD from the State University of New York—Cortland College and another from Haverford College in May 2006. She also sits on numerous boards and advisory committees. Gibbs lives in Virginia with her husband and one of her four children.

Lois Marie Gibbs
Executive Director
The Center for Health, Environment and Justice
P.O. Box 6806
Falls Church, VA 22040-6806
Phone: 703-237-2249
E-mail: chej@chej.org
Web site: http://www.chej.org
Award Web site: http://www.heinzawards.net/recipients/lois-gibbs; http://www.news
week.com/id/130264; http://www.goldmanprize.org/node/103

Sylvia Herrera

Sylvia Herrera is a native of East Austin, Texas, is a founding member of PODER, and resides in one of the neighborhoods adjacent to the East Austin Tank Farm. She is responsible for coordination of environmental health information for PODER's programs and the Nahui Ollin-Healthy Communities and the Young Scholars for Justice projects. Herrera received her PhD in kinesiology and health education from the University of Texas at Austin. She is presently on the board of the State of Texas Environmental Health Institute, the Holly Power Plant Closure Committee, and the Johnston High School Campus Advisory Council. Herrera is a co-recipient of the 2002 Ford Foundation's Leadership for a Changing World Award.

Sylvia Herrera
Health Coordinator and Cofounder
PODER
P.O. Box 6237
Austin, TX 78762-6237
Phone: 512-472-9921
Fax: 512-472-9922
E-mail: poder_tx@sbcglobal.net
Web site: www.poder-texas.org
Award Web site: http://www.leadershipforchange.org/awardees/awardee.php3?ID=60

Sarah James

Sarah James is a Neets'aii Gwich'in Indian, a member of the northernmost Native American tribe in North America, located in Arctic Village, Alaska. Gwich'in is

James's first language. She grew up traditionally, following the caribou migration. As a Gwich'in, she was born with motivation to care for her land. "Loss of the caribou would mean the end of my people, much like the loss of the buffalo resulted in the decimation of many indigenous cultures in the Great Plains over a century ago," she says. But James did not choose to become a leader for the Gwich'in; that choice was made for her. For almost 20 years, James quietly served her people as a community health aide, in a log cabin with no running water, and founder of a preschool. Then, in 1988, the elders and spiritual leaders of the entire Gwich'in nation—encompassing 15 villages and several million acres of remote land in northeastern Alaska and Canada—chose her to become the public spokesperson for preserving the caribou, the land they travel, and the Gwich'in culture. James was one of the recipients of the 2001 Ford Foundation's Leadership for a Changing World Award.

Sarah James
Spokesperson
Gwich'in Steering Committee
P.O. Box 51
Arctic Village, AK 99722
Phone: 907-587-5315
Fax: 907-587-5316
E-mail: sarahjamesav@hotmail.com
Award Web site: http://www.leadershipforchange.org/awardees/awardee.php3?ID=15

Charlotte Keys

Charlotte Keys lost her county job and her life was threatened when, as a county clerk, she discovered and publicly discussed lawsuits filed by several workers against Reichold Chemical. After she learned about the severe health problems plaguing the old and young in her community—problems traced to a 1977 explosion at Reichold's plant—Keys created Jesus People Against Pollution to mobilize her community to demand health and environmental justice. Keys was a recipient of the 2001 Community Health Leaders Award from the Robert Wood Johnson Foundation.

Charlotte Keys
Founder and Executive Director
Jesus People Against Pollution

P.O Box 765
Columbia, MS 39429
Phone: 601-736-7099
E-mail: keysjpap@aol.com
Award Web site: http://www.communityhealthleaders.org/leaders/leader/charlotte_keys

Grace Kong

Grace Kong is the daughter of Laotian immigrants. Her parents, while struggling to live day-to-day and provide for their family, taught her the core values of treating everyone with dignity and of working for a just and compassionate society for all people. In 1995, the Asian Pacific Environmental Network launched the Laotian Organizing Project to help members of the Richmond, California, Laotian community struggle for environmental justice and social change. Among the organization's community-building activities: conducting a survey project on contaminated seafood consumption, managing land available to Laotian families for communal gardening to ensure food security, and supporting political campaigns against anti-immigrant statewide initiatives. The group's youth organizing arm, the Asian Youth Advocates, has worked with adolescents, especially girls, to develop leadership and environmental awareness. The teenagers have developed and administered surveys and have photographed, mapped, and documented toxic hazards in their neighborhoods. Kong was one of the recipients of the 2002 Ford Foundation's Leadership for a Changing World Award.

Grace Kong
Community Organizer
Laotian Organizing Project
220 25th Street
Richmond, CA 94804
Phone: 510-236-4616
Fax: 510-236-4572
E-mail: may@apen4ej.org
Web site: www.apen4ej.org
Award Web site: http://www.leadershipforchange.org/awardees/awardee.php3?ID=54

Ray E. López

Ray E. López works with East Harlem residents to help combat environmental conditions affecting their health, including insect infestation, mold, and poor air quality. He helps families control asthma triggers in their homes, reducing costly emergency room visits and school absences. He also developed solutions to the growing bedbug infestation in New York City, including wrapping duct tape around the edge of a cleaned mattress as a kind of sticky moat to prevent reinfestation. These approaches have directly helped hundreds of East Harlem residents resolve their own personal environmental health issues and created a ripple effect as they help relatives and neighbors. Under López's leadership, LSA (Little Sisters of the Assumption) Family Health Service has become widely recognized for its environmental interventions, receiving the U.S. Environmental Protection Agency's Region 2 Environmental Quality Award for its asthma program, which López oversees. López was a recipient of the 2008 Community Health Leaders Award from the Robert Wood Johnson Foundation.

Ray E. López
Director
Environmental Health Program
Little Sisters of the Assumption Family Health Service
333 East 115th Street
New York, NY 10029-2210
Phone: 646-672-5236
Fax: 212-987-4430
E-mail: rlopez@lsafhs.org
Web site: http://www.littlesistersfamily.org
Award Web site: http://www.communityhealthleaders.org/leaders/leader/ray_lopez

Vernice Miller-Travis

Vernice Miller-Travis is the principal of the environmental consulting group Miller Travis & Associates. She was a key convener of an effort to bring the voices of the environmental justice constituency into dialogue with the Obama/Biden transition team and the new administration. She was invited to the White House to witness President Obama signing two memoranda of understanding on raising automobile fuel efficiency standards. As a program officer of the Ford Foundation, she launched their environmental justice portfolio for grantmaking in the United States. She is also cochair of the EPA's Working Group on School Air Monitoring to the National Environmental Justice Advisory Council, and serves as vice chair of the Maryland State Commission on Environmental Justice and Sustainable Communities, where she leads an effort to encourage state and local governments to consider the environmental and public health dimensions of local land-use and zoning decisions. She is a cofounder of West Harlem Environmental Action, a 20-year-old community-based environmental justice organization in New York City, and she is a founding member of The National Black Environmental Justice Network. She is the recipient of the 2009 Damu Smith Environmental Achievement Award.

Vernice Miller-Travis
Principal Consultant
Miller Travis & Associates
104 Jewett Place
Bowie, MD 20721
Phone: 301-537-2115
E-mail: vmt_3@msn.com

Harold Mitchell

After a 1997 survey of his Spartanburg, South Carolina, community by the U.S. Environmental Protection Agency (EPA) found no contaminants, Mitchell conducted an investigation of his own and presented his report at a community meeting. Harold Mitchell built a coalition and, in 1998, founded ReGenesis, a community-based environmental justice organization with more than 1,400 members. ReGenesis works with 124 partners ranging from nonprofits, private sector, and government agencies to raise public awareness and reverse the health impacts that industrial toxic wastes have had on the Spartanburg region. After ReGenesis presented its citizen research to the EPA, the agency conducted tests in 1999, found toxic metals and contaminants, and designated Spartanburg a Superfund site. Responding to the report, International Mineral and Chemical Corp—which had sold the property after the fertilizer plant closed—repurchased the property, covered several acres with a canopy to ensure that toxic particles did not get into the air, and dismantled the old plant. Moore was one of the recipients of the 2002 Ford Foundation's Leadership for a Changing World Award.

Harold Mitchell
C.E.O.
ReGenesis
710 South Church Street, #2

Spartanburg, SC 29306
Phone: 864-583-2712
Fax: 864-583-2713
E-mail: regenesi@bellsouth.net
Award Web site: http://www.leadershipforchange.org/awardees/awardee.php3?ID=57

Richard E. Moore

The near-death of a baby from toxic well water was the catalyst for Richard Moore's environmental activism. Moore and his family live in a working-class community in Albuquerque, New Mexico, that is also home to the city's sewage treatment plant. Pollutants from the plant and other industrial sites contaminated well water with nitroglycerine and nitrites. As a founding member of the South West Organizing Project, Moore helped launch the first successful campaign in New Mexico to clean contaminated groundwater. Today, he is executive director of the Southwest Network for Environmental and Economic Justice, an umbrella group with 57 organizations and a thousands-strong membership in the Southwest, West, and across the border in Mexico. Moore was one of the recipients of the 2005 Ford Foundation's Leadership for a Changing World Award.

Richard E. Moore
Executive Director
Southwest Network for Environmental and Economic Justice
P.O. Box 7399
Albuquerque, NM 87194
Phone: 505-242-0416
Fax: 505-242-5609
E-mail: richardm@sneej.org
Web site: http://www.sneej.org
Award Web site: http://www.leadershipforchange.org/awardees/awardee.php3?ID=321

Father Vien Nguyen

The New Orleans Vietnamese American community is the third largest in the United States and Father Nguyen has been described as its "cornerstone." He has dedicated his life to preserving and strengthening this new community of modest means. When Hurricane Katrina hit, Nguyen opened the two-story rectory and school under his charge to shelter poor and elderly residents who could not evacuate, and he organized boat rescues for people stranded in their homes. Shortly after the hurricane, he traveled 10,000 miles to Vietnamese American evacuees in Texas, Louisiana, and Arkansas to ensure that they received the relief services they needed and to facilitate their return to New Orleans. Also, he organized the community to prevent the use of a nearby landfill as a dumping ground for dangerous contaminated debris from the storms. Nguyen was a recipient of the 2006 Community Health Leaders Award from the Robert Wood Johnson Foundation.

Father Vien Nguyen
Pastor
Mary Queen of Vietnam Community Development Corporation
14001 Dwyer Boulevard
New Orleans, LA 70129
Phone: 504-255-9250
E-mail: ntv3@aol.com
Award Web site: http://www.communityhealthleaders.org/leaders/leader/vien_nguyen

Florence Robinson

For more than a decade, Florence Robinson waged virtually a one-woman war against toxic wastes. Her battlefield has been "Cancer Alley," an 80-mile strip of land along the Mississippi River between New Orleans and Baton Rouge, Louisiana, where low-income, minority communities exist side by side with large industries. Since she accepted a position as professor of biology at her alma mater, Southern University, in the early 1970s, Robinson has lived in the small community of Alsen, near Devil's Swamp. Once an idyllic spot, Alsen was home to many newly freed slaves who, settling there after the Civil War, enjoyed cool, clean water and plentiful harvests. That ended in 1964 when an industrial "borrow" pit was opened in Alsen to dispose of hazardous waste. The area was further fouled by 11 nearby petrochemical plants, a commercial hazardous waste incinerator, and several waste landfills. Robinson shares the 1998 Heinz Award in the Environment for her tireless fight against industrial polluters who foul the land and threaten the health of communities with chemical and other hazardous wastes.

Florence Robinson
North Baton Rouge Environmental Association
421 Springfield Road
Baton Rouge, LA 70807
Phone: 504-775-0341

Fax: 504-774-2928
E-mail: robinsof@rtk.net
Award Web site: http://www.heinzawards.net/recipients/florence-robinson

Anne Rolfes

For more than 8 years, Anne Rolfes, founder of the Louisiana Bucket Brigade, has worked with residents in Louisiana to mitigate the impact of polluted air and contaminated soil. Rolfes advocates for pollution control, health protections, and fair compensation so longtime residents living on or near contaminated areas can relocate. Members of the Bucket Brigade have learned to collect and test soil and air samples and amass data that clearly show the link between the contamination and myriad health problems suffered by residents who live near oil refineries and chemical plants. Rolfes has led the largest collection of community-gathered air samples in the United States and documented hundreds of violations of state and federal air quality standards. This former Peace Corps worker's environmental advocacy work began in Nigeria, where she helped Ogoni refugees in the Niger Delta cope with a devastating environmental and health crisis. Rolfes was a recipient of the 2007 Community Health Leaders Award from the Robert Wood Johnson Foundation.

Anne Rolfes
Founding Director
Louisiana Bucket Brigade
4226 Canal Street
New Orleans, LA 70119
Phone: 504-484-3433
E-mail: annerolfes@hotmail.com
Web site: http://labucketbrigade.org
Award Web site: http://www.communityhealthleaders.org/leaders/leader/anne_rolfes

Juan E. Rosario

In 1989, Juan Rosario joined Misión Industrial de Puerto Rico, an environmental organization founded in 1969. In the capital city of San Juan, he helped assemble a wide alliance of groups from a half-dozen communities to stop construction of a massive municipal garbage incinerator, which was expected to burn more than 1,000 tons of waste a day. The alliance included communities in the Puerto Nuevo area of the city, various churches, and labor-union leaders. It brought together Catholics and Methodists—many of whom had never been in each other's church although they worshiped within walking distance from one another. Rosario was one of the recipients of the 2004 Ford Foundation's Leadership for a Changing World Award.

Juan E. Rosario
Community Organizer
Misión Industrial de Puerto Rico, Inc.
P.O. Box 363728
San Juan, PR 00936-3728
Phone: 787-462-5088
Fax: 787-754-6462
E-mail: amaneser@coqui.net
Award Web site: http://www.leadershipforchange.org/awardees/awardee.php3?ID=217

Juan Carlos Ruiz

Juan Carlos Ruiz came to the United States as a political exile from Peru and has continued his commitment to social justice ever since. He has played a leadership role in organizing local communities around the creation of school-based clinics and crime prevention. In Mount Rainier, Maryland, a city where the rates of childhood lead poisoning are five times the national average, Ruiz has successfully mobilized a coalition of parents and health providers to advocate for prevention initiatives. Ruiz was a recipient of the 1999 Community Health Leaders Award from the Robert Wood Johnson Foundation.

Juan Carlos Ruiz
National Community Capacity Consultants
4120 29th Street
Mount Rainier, MD 20712
Phone: 414-758-0600
E-mail: juancarlos@core.com
Award Web site: http://www.communityhealthleaders.org/leaders/leader/juan_ruiz

Peggy M. Shepard

Peggy Shepard is executive director and cofounder of WE ACT for Environmental Justice located in Harlem, New York. Founded in 1988, WE ACT was

New York's first environmental justice organization, created to improve environmental health and quality of life in communities of color. A recipient of the 2003 Heinz Award for the Environment and the 2008 Jane Jacobs Medal for Lifetime Achievement from the Rockefeller Foundation, she is a former Democratic district leader who represented West Harlem from 1985 to 1993 and served as president of the National Women's Political Caucus–Manhattan from 1993 to 1997. Shepard received the Dean's Distinguished Service Award in 2004 from the Columbia Mailman School of Public Health. In November 2000, Shepard received a Union Square Award, administered by the Fund for the City of New York, for her grassroots leadership and advocacy.

Peggy M. Shepard
Executive Director
WE ACT for Environmental Justice
271 West 125th Street, Suite 308
New York, NY 10027-4424
Phone: 212-961-1000, ext. 306
Fax: 212-961-1015
E-mail: peggy@weact.org
Web site: http://www.weact.org/Home/tabid/162/Default.aspx
Award Web sites: http://www.rockfound.org/about_us/news/2008/050508jj_medal.shtml;
http://www.heinzawards.net/recipients/peggy-shepard

Wilma Subra

Wilma Subra is an analytical chemist who puts her expertise to work helping residents in communities who are either protesting the existence of a nearby industry that is exposing them to toxic chemicals or trying to block the construction of one adjacent to their homes. The daughter of an inventor, Subra learned technical skills from a young age working in her father's laboratory before studying to be a chemist. To finance the pro bono technical assistance she provides to community groups, Subra does commercial work as a chemist analyzing the chemical makeup of hot sauces and other condiments manufactured in southern Louisiana. She works out of a small laboratory on a back road across from a field of sugarcane in New Iberia, Louisiana. Subra won the MacArthur "Genius" Fellowship for her work providing technical assistance to community groups in 1999 and was one of three finalists in the environmental category of the 2004

Volvo for Life Award. Subra is known as "St. Wilma" among residents of some of the communities she has helped.

Wilma Subra
President
Subra Company
P.O. Box 9813
New Iberia, LA 70562
Phone: 337-367-2216
Fax: 337-367-2217
E-mail: subracom@aol.com
Award Web sites: http://www.macfound.org/site/c.lkLXJ8MQKrH/b.1142725/k.2948/
Fellows_List__July_1999.htm; http://www.volvocars.com/us/footer/about/
VolvoForLifeAwards/Pages/default.aspx

Shelia Webb

Shelia Webb, the first African American and nonphysician to head the New Orleans Health Department, revitalized the city's neighborhood clinics by convincing the federal government to restore funding. She also expanded programs providing well baby care, promoting childhood immunization, and addressing environmental health problems of the city's poorest residents. In 2000, Webb received the Community Health Leaders Award from the Robert Wood Johnson Foundation.

Shelia Webb
Director
Center for Empowered Decision Making
1515 Poydras Street, Suite 1060
New Orleans, LA 70112
Phone: 504-620-0024
E-mail: swebb@excelth.com
Award Web site: http://www.communityhealthleaders.org/leaders/leader/shelia_webb

Beverly Wright

Having worked for more than two decades on environmental justice in other communities located in Louisiana's "Cancer Alley," Wright was forced by Hurricane Katrina to turn her Center's attention to her own community. Shortly before Hurricane Katrina, Beverly Wright's mother and only brother died. Then the storm destroyed her home and office. Wright looked beyond her personal tragedy and loss and focused instead on environmental issues that threatened low-lying areas and the health of the mostly minority and low-income people who live in New Orleans. In early 2006, she initiated a project that involved collaboration with the United Steel Workers Union and with volunteer, faith-based, and neighborhood organizations: a pilot cleanup effort on Aberdeen Road in New Orleans East. More than 180 volunteers showed up for training and work. Tainted soil was safely removed from each yard and replaced with new topsoil and sod as part of the Deep South Center for Environmental Justice at Dillard University's "A Safe Way Back Home" project. It resulted in a cleaner street, the return of residents, and many requests from other communities for a similar program. In 2006, Wright received the Community Health Leaders Award from the Robert Wood Johnson Foundation. In 2009, she received the Heinz Award for her environmental work.

Beverly Wright
Executive Director
Deep South Center for Environmental Justice at Dillard University
8000 Crowder Boulevard, Suite C
New Orleans, LA 70127
Phone: 504-240-3394
Fax: 504-816-4032
E-mail: bhwright@aol.com
Award Web sites: http://www.communityhealthleaders.org/leaders/leader/beverly_wright;
http://www.heinzawards.net/recipients/beverly_wright

5

University-Based Programs

OVER THE YEARS, WE have seen environmental health and racial equity move from community-based struggles around health to research and academic programs on college and university campuses.[1] In three decades, environmental health and racial equity concepts and paradigms have become commonplace in academia.[2] The environmental health and racial equity framework has had a positive impact on a range of academic disciplines: sociology, environmental studies, ethics and religious studies, natural resources, urban planning, law, public health, and dozens of others.

The following list represents university-based environmental health and racial equity centers, legal clinics, and academic degree–granting programs. The list was compiled using several sources, including the Internet, foundations' grantee lists and databases, and several national and regional environmental directories.

In 1990, there was only one environmental justice textbook, *Dumping in Dixie: Race, Class, and Environmental Quality*, adopted widely as required text by colleges and universities.[3] One of the recommendations in *Dumping in Dixie* was the need for environmental justice centers to be created at historically black colleges and universities, most of which are located in the Deep South. In 1992, the Deep South Center for Environmental Justice at Xavier University, a historically Black Catholic university located in New Orleans, Louisiana, was established. Two years later, the Environmental Justice Resource Center at Clark Atlanta University, another historically Black college and university (HBCU), was established in Atlanta, Georgia. Other environmental justice centers and programs would follow.

Today, there are 13 university-based environmental health and racial equity centers. Of the 13 centers, four are located at HBCUs. There are also 22 legal clinics that focus on environmental health and racial equity as core areas (one located at a HBCU), and six academic programs that grant degrees in environmental justice, including one legal program. Each entry below contains basic information on the organization, mostly compiled from the organization's Web site. This list also includes a main contact person and all available contact information including street address, phone number, fax number, e-mail address, and Web site URL when available.

University-Based Centers

Center for Environmental Equity and Justice

The Center for Environmental Equity and Justice (CEEJ) is an information resource center that seeks to increase the community, faith-based organizations, state and local government, and any other interested parties awareness of environmental justice issues primarily in the state of Florida and throughout the country. The Center assists, trains, and educates people about environmental justice.

Richard Gragg
Director
Center for Environmental Equity and Justice
1515 Martin Luther King Boulevard
Florida Agricultural and Mechanical University
Frederick S. Humphries Science Research Center
Tallahassee, FL 32306
Phone: 850-599-8193
Fax: 850-412-7785
E-mail: richard.gragg@famu.edu
Web site: http://www.famu.edu/index.cfm?environmentalscience&CEEJ

Center for Environmental Justice and Children's Health

Focused on environmental justice-related teaching, research, and service, the Center for Environmental Justice and Children's Health is a multidisciplinary group of Notre Dame faculty, students, and friends dedicated to addressing environmental injustice. Working pro bono, Center faculty and students focus on three main tasks. They (1) perform risk assessments and environmental-impact analyses in poor, minority, or other vulnerable communities; (2) help educate and empower potential victims of environmental injustice; and (3) promote victims' ability both to understand the risks they face and to give or withhold informed consent to the siting or continued operation of risky facilities that may threaten their health.

Kristin Shrader-Frechette
Director and O'Neill Family Endowed Professor
Center for Environmental Justice and Children's Health
Department of Biological Sciences and Department of Philosophy
100 Malloy Hall
University of Notre Dame
Notre Dame, IN 46556
Phone: 574-631-2647
Fax: 574-631-8209
E-mail: kristin.shrader-frechette.1@nd.edu
Web site: http://www.nd.edu/~kshrader

Center for Labor Research and Education

As part of the Institute for Research on Labor and Employment, the UCLA Center for Labor Research and Education plays a unique role as a bridge between the University and the labor community in Southern California. This role has grown in the past few years with the dramatic changes that have overtaken the Southern California economy.

Kent Wong
Director
Center for Labor Research and Education
UCLA Labor Center
P.O. Box 951478
10945 LeConte Avenue
Suite 1103
Los Angeles CA 90095-1478
Phone: 310-794-5983
Fax: 310-794-6410
E-mail: kentwong@ucla.edu
Web site: http://www.labor.ucla.edu

Deep South Center for Environmental Justice

The Deep South Center for Environmental Justice (DSCEJ) was developed in 1992 in collaboration with community environmental groups and universities within the region to address environmental justice issues. The DSCEJ provides opportunities for communities, scientific researchers, and decision-makers to collaborate on programs and projects that promote the rights of all people to be free from environmental harm as it impacts health, jobs, housing, education, and a general quality of life.

Beverly Wright
Director
Deep South Center for Environmental Justice
Dillard University
2601 Gentilly Boulevard
New Orleans, LA 70122
Phone: 504-816-4005
Fax: 504-816-4032
E-mail: bhwright@aol.com
Web site: http://www.dscej.org/index.html

Environmental Justice Project

The University of California–Davis Environmental Justice Project defines environmental justice broadly, to encompass environmental issues as they pertain to race, as well as to class and gender, in California's Central Valley.

Julie Sze
Director
Environmental Justice Project
The Barn, 122B
University of California–Davis
One Shields Avenue
Davis, CA 95616-8527
Phone: 530-752-5643
Fax: 530-754-9141
E-mail: sze@ucdavis.edu
Web site: http://ej.ucdavis.edu/index.html

Environmental Justice Resource Center at Clark Atlanta University

The Environmental Justice Resource Center was formed in 1994 to serve as a research, policy, and information clearinghouse on issues related to environmental justice, race and the environment, civil rights and human rights, facility siting, land-use planning, brownfields, transportation equity, suburban sprawl and smart growth, energy, global climate change, and climate justice. The overall goal of the Center is to assist, support, train, and educate people of color, students, professionals, and grassroots community leaders with the goal of facilitating their inclusion into the mainstream of decision-making. The Center is multidisciplinary in its focus and approach. It serves as a bridge between the social and behavioral sciences, health professionals, natural and physical sciences, engineering, management, and legal disciplines to prevent and solve environmental and health problems. The Center's programs build on the work that its staff has been engaged in for more than two decades.

Robert D. Bullard
Director and Asa Edmund Ware Distinguished Professor of Sociology
Environmental Justice Resource Center
Clark Atlanta University
223 James P. Brawley Drive
Atlanta, GA 30314
Phone: 404-880-6911
Fax: 404-880-8132
E-mail: rbullard@cau.edu
Web site: http://www.ejrc.cau.edu

Hunter College City University of New York Program in Urban Public Health

The Program in Urban Public Health (UPH) is committed to educating public health professionals who can promote health and prevent disease among diverse urban populations. UPH is devoted to developing public health personnel that employers in the New York City metropolitan region and beyond are looking to hire to help maintain a healthy population. UPH is also working to contribute new knowledge to solving the health problems faced by urban populations, as well as applying existing knowledge to these issues. UPH combines the expertise of a number of different academic disciplines. The core areas include epidemiology and biostatistics, social and behavioral dimensions of health, environmental health and safety, health policy, administration, and management. Some related areas of specialization include public health nutrition, reproductive and family health, gerontology, aging and longevity, and public health demography.

Jack Caravanos
Hunter College Program in Urban Public Health

Environmental and Occupational Health
425 East 25th Street (between FDR and 1st Avenue)
10th Floor, West Building
New York, NY 10010
Phone: 212-481-7569
E-mail: jcaravan@hunter.cuny.edu
Web site: http://www.hunter.cuny.edu/uph/welcome-page

Institute for Urban Research at Morgan State University

The Institute for Urban Research is the primary social science research and train-ing arm of Morgan State University. The Institute has a core staff of experienced researchers who seek to improve the response of governmental, nongovernmen-tal, private, and other institutions to the challenges of poverty, unemployment, poor health, truancy, and other urban and regional problems.

Raymond Winbush
Director
Institute for Urban Research
Morgan State University
Montebello Complex
Room D-216/217
1700 East Cold Spring Lane
Baltimore, MD 21251
Phone: 443-885-4800
E-mail: rwinbush@usit.net
Web site: http://iur.morgan.edu/index.html

Labor Occupational Health Program

The Labor Occupational Health Program, established in 1974, is a community outreach program at the University of California–Berkeley. The Program's staff of educators and technical experts are dedicated to improving health and safety in the workplace. It provides information, training, and other assistance to unions, workers, joint labor-management groups, community organizations, health pro-fessionals, government, and schools.

Barbara Plog
Associate Director
Labor Occupational Health Program

University of California–Berkeley
2223 Fulton Street
Berkeley, CA 94720-5120
Phone: 510-642-5507
Fax: 510-643-5698
E-mail: baplog@berkeley.edu
Web site: http://www.lohp.org

Northeastern Environmental Justice Research Collaborative

The Northeastern Environmental Justice Research Collaborative is a multidisciplinary research collaborative made up of scholars, activists, and policymakers engaged in the study of political ecology and environmental justice initiatives. Based at Northeastern University in Boston, Massachusetts, the Collaborative works on a wide range of local, regional, national, and international topics and issues. Professor Daniel Faber, a longtime researcher and advocate for environmental justice, serves as director.

Daniel Faber
Director and Associate Professor of Sociology
Northeastern Environmental Justice Research Collaborative
Department of Sociology and Anthropology
509 Holmes Hall
Northeastern University
Boston, MA 02115
Phone: 617-373-2878
Fax: 617-373-2688
E-mail: d.faber@neu.edu
Web site: http://www.socant.neu.edu/research/justice_research

Northwest Indiana Environmental Justice Resource Center

Indiana University Northwest is one of ten universities nationwide that received a grant from the U.S. Environmental Protection Agency to establish an environmental justice resource center. While not a legal clinic, the Center will help Midwest municipalities like East Chicago, Gary, and Hammond to educate residents about the pollution in their communities. Local residents can easily learn about the environmental hazards in their communities. At this new resource center, they will be able to determine the air and water quality in their neighborhoods and compare it with other areas locally and throughout the country.

Tim Sutherland
Director
Northwest Indiana Environmental Justice Resource Center
Indiana University Northwest
3400 Broadway
Library, Room 232B
Gary, IN 46408
Phone: 219-981-5612 or 219-980-6946
Fax: 219-980-6558
E-mail: sutherla@iun.edu
Web site: http://www.iun.edu/~enviroj

The Program for Environmental and Regional Equity

Established in 2007, the University of Southern California (USC) Program for Environmental and Regional Equity (PERE) is a research unit headed by Professor Manuel Pastor and situated within the USC College of Letters, Arts and Sciences. PERE conducts research and facilitates discussions on issues of environmental justice, regional inclusion, and immigrant integration. PERE's work is rooted in the new three Rs: rigor, relevance, and reach. The Program conducts high-quality research in focus areas that are relevant to public policy concerns and reaches those directly affected communities that most need to be engaged in the discussion. In general, PERE seeks and supports direct collaborations with community-based organizations in research and other activities, trying to forge a new model of how university and community can work together for the common good.

Manuel Pastor
Program for Environmental and Regional Equity
USC Center for Sustainable Cities
Kaprielian Hall 462
University of Southern California
3620 South Vermont Avenue
Los Angeles, CA 90089-0255
Phone: 213-740-5604
Fax: 213-740-5680
E-mail: mpastor@college.usc.edu
Web site: http://college.usc.edu/geography/ESPE/pere.html

Washington State University Center for Social and Environmental Justice

The Center for Social and Environmental Justice acts to fulfill Washington State University's land grant mission by engaging community capacities to address poverty, inequality, discrimination, and unequally borne environmental dangers. To eliminate poverty, inequality, and environmental degradation, the intersections of racism, sexism, classism, and heterosexism must be addressed. The Center supports interdisciplinary approaches to positive cultural, political, social, economic, and environmental change. University, nonprofit, nongovernmental, grassroots, and tribal groups will all benefit from overcoming multiple barriers in order to achieve solutions that are sustainable and effective. Center Codirector Noël Sturgeon and his Center colleagues believe the most useful collaborations will be suggested and initiated by nonuniversity groups articulating their needs and directing research or service projects.

Noël Sturgeon
Codirector
Center for Social and Environmental Justice
Washington State University
P.O. Box 644007
Pullman, WA 99164-4007
Phone: 509-335-1794
Fax: 509-335-4377
E-mail: sturgeon@wsu.edu
Web site: http://libarts.wsu.edu/csej

Legal Clinics

Earth Advocacy Clinic at Barry University Law School

The Earth Advocacy Clinic, which complements the Barry University Law School's Dominican history of concern for the environment, provides Barry law students with hands-on legal practice experience on environmental issues, represents clients who may have difficulties seeking adequate legal representation on these issues, and contributes to the betterment of the environment. The clinic focuses on litigation, client counseling, regulatory work, lay education, and research as it relates to environmental issues.

Jeanne Zokovitch Paben
Assistant Professor of Law
Director, Earth Advocacy Clinic
Barry University
11300 NE 2nd Avenue
Miami Shores, FL 33161
Phone: 321-206-5761
E-mail: jzokovitch@mail.barry.edu
Web site: http://www.barry.edu/universityRelations/pressreleases/details.aspx?ID=14235

Center for Earth Jurisprudence

The mission of the Center for Earth Jurisprudence (CEJ) is to advance legal principles, laws, and governance that reflect a transformative Earth-centered perspective and support the well-being of all. With offices in South and Central Florida, the CEJ is sponsored jointly by Barry and St. Thomas Universities. The Center works closely with both law schools and is the first of its type in the United States. Its mission is to re-envision law and governance in ways that support and protect the health and well-being of the entire Earth community.

Patricia Siemen, OP, JD
Director
Center for Earth Jurisprudence
16401 Northwest 37th Avenue
Miami Gardens, FL 33054
Phone: 305-623-2389
Fax 305-623-2390
E-mail: psiemen@stu.edu
Web site: http://earthjuris.org

Chicago Environmental Law Clinic

The Chicago Environmental Law Clinic is a collaboration between the Chicago Legal Clinic and Chicago-Kent College of Law. The mission of the Chicago Environmental Law Clinic is to enable people who are confronting urban environmental problems to have equal access to environmental justice. The Clinic offers environmental law students the opportunity to learn by serving people who would be unrepresented in environmental matters that directly affect the health, safety, and welfare of their families and communities. The Clinic does not impose an environmental agenda or ideology on its clients, but rather provides legal education, advocacy, and volunteer services in response to community-directed concerns.

Keith Harley
Director
Chicago Environmental Law Clinic
Chicago-Kent College of Law
Illinois Institute of Technology
205 West Monroe, 4th Floor
Chicago, IL 60606
Phone: 312-726-2938
Fax: 312-726-5206
E-mail: kharley@kentlaw.edu
Web site: http://www.kentlaw.edu/academics/peel/CELC-profile.html

American Indian Law Clinic at the University of Colorado Law School

The American Indian Law Clinic, established in 1992 as one of the first of its kind, provides quality legal representation to low-income clients with specific Indian law-related problems. Many in the Denver region have limited access to legal assistance and that access is further restricted when the issue involves Indian law. They have nowhere to turn when certain rights, some guaranteed by treaty, are denied. The Clinic's student attorneys provide hundreds of hours of pro bono legal work to assist these people with direct legal assistance when possible, or by acting as a referral source when unable to help directly.

Jill E. Tompkins
Clinical Professor of Law and Director of the Indian Law Clinic
Indian Law Clinic
University of Colorado Law School
105T Wolf Law Building
404 UCB
Boulder, CO 80309-0404
Phone: 303-735-2194
E-mail: jill.tompkins@colorado.edu
Web site: http://lawweb.colorado.edu/profiles/profile.jsp?id=58

Environmental Law Clinic at Columbia University

The New York City metropolitan region and the United States overall present a nearly inexhaustible supply of environmental troubles. At the urban core and in outlying areas, communities face diverse challenges such as alarmingly high asthma rates, scarce open-space resources, brownfield redevelopment, and sprawl. Students in the Environmental Law Clinic represent local, regional, and national environmental and community organizations working to solve critical environmental challenges facing the metropolitan region. Clinic students represent clients on a broad array of issues including clean water, wetlands preservation, endangered species, environmental justice, "smart growth," and clean air.

Edward Lloyd
Director
Environmental Law Clinic
Columbia University
838 Jerome Greene Hall
435 West 116th Street
New York, NY 10027
Phone: 212-854-4376
E-mail: elloyd@law.columbia.edu
Web site: http://www.law.columbia.edu/focusareas/clinics/environment

Environmental and Land Use Law Clinic at Nova Southeastern University

The Environmental and Land Use Law Clinic at Nova Southeastern University is a program and opportunity for third-year law students to work on real-world cases for government agencies, private law firms, and public interest firms across the country. It offers unique and varied opportunities to practice in South Florida, a region that is home to the Everglades and on the cutting edge of land use and environmental law. The "in-house" Clinic offers the opportunity to work for the Everglades Law Center, a public interest law firm whose representation of national, statewide, and local environmental groups on major federal, state, and local issues concerning the protection and restoration of the Florida Everglades and Florida Keys exposes students to the laws, players, processes, and other realities of high-profile complex public policy advocacy and litigation.

Richard Grosso
Director
Environmental and Land Use Law Clinic
Shepard Broad Law School
Nova Southeastern University
3305 College Avenue
Fort Lauderdale, FL 33314
Phone: 954-262-6140

E-mail: grossor@nsu.law.nova.edu
Web site: http://www.nsulaw.nova.edu/index.cfm

Environmental and Natural Resources Law Program at Emory University

Emory's Environmental and Natural Resources Law Program provides students with a comprehensive educational experience in which to study a wide array of environmental law issues. Building on Emory's strong faculty and its location in the dynamic business and governmental center of Atlanta, Georgia, the program offers students classroom, skills-training, and extracurricular opportunities making it one of the nation's strongest programs in environmental law. The program boasts more than a dozen course offerings, four full-time faculty members, outstanding adjunct professors from law firms and federal agencies, eight field placements, and the Turner Environmental Law Clinic. In addition to the core curriculum, the program also covers recent environmental issues such as conservation, environmental justice, urban sprawl, federalism and devolution, international and comparative environmental issues, and biodiversity. The Clinic was established in 1998 with a Turner Foundation grant.

Larry Sanders
Interim Director
Turner Environmental Law Clinic
Emory University School of Law
1301 Clifton Road
Atlanta, GA 30322
Phone: 404-727-5542
Fax: 404-727-7851
E-mail: lsanders@emory.edu
Web site: http://www.law.emory.edu/programs-centers-clinics/environmental-law/turner-clinic.html

Environmental Law and Justice Clinic at Golden Gate University School of Law

The Environmental Law and Justice Clinic (ELJC) at Golden Gate University (GGU) School of Law was established in 1994 and was one of the first law clinics in the United States to focus on environmental justice. The Clinic's mission is to train GGU law students to be effective and ethical lawyers and to improve environmental conditions for communities of color and low-income people, located primarily in the San Francisco Bay Area and California. ELJC is staffed with students who, under close faculty supervision, represent community clients on environmental matters. ELJC clinicians are certified under State Bar of California rules to perform many of the tasks of an attorney: they interview and counsel clients, develop legal strategies, draft legal documents, appear at hearings, and negotiate with opposing parties. The EJLC also has an environmental scientist on staff.

Helen Kang
Acting Clinic Director
Environmental Law and Justice Clinic
Golden Gate University School of Law
536 Mission Street
San Francisco, CA 94105-2968
Phone: 415-442-6647
Fax: 415-896-2450
E-mail: hkang@ggu.edu
Web site: http://www.ggu.edu/school_of_law/academic_law_programs/jd_program/environmental_law/environmental_law_justice_clinic

Institute for Public Representation, Georgetown University Law Center

The Institute for Public Representation is a public interest law firm and clinical education program founded by Georgetown University Law Center in 1971. Attorneys at the Institute act as counsel for groups and individuals who are unable to obtain effective legal representation on matters that have a significant impact on issues of broad public importance. The Institute works in the areas of first amendment and media law, environmental law, civil rights, environmental justice, and general public interest matters.

Angela Campbell
Codirector
Institute for Public Representation
Georgetown University Law Center
600 New Jersey Avenue, Northwest
Washington, DC 20001
Phone: 202-662-9535
Fax: 202-662-9634
E-mail: gulcipr@law.georgetown.edu
Web site: http://www.law.georgetown.edu/clinics/ipr/environmental.html

New York University School of Law Environmental Law Clinic

The Environmental Law Clinic program emphasizes environmental policy and litigation from the public interest point of view. Clinic participants work under the supervision of attorneys at the Natural Resources Defense Council. Approximately 12 to 15 hours of work per week are required. This is a one-semester clinic that is offered in both the fall and the spring. A maximum of eight students per term are generally accepted for the clinic. Typical issues that students have worked on recently include protection of New York City's drinking water, fisheries crisis, energy efficiency, global warming, water pollution, and environmental justice litigation.

Sarah Chasis
Codirector
Environmental Law Clinic
New York University School of Law
40 Washington Square South
New York, NY 10012
Phone: 212-727-4424
E-mail: schasis@nrdc.org
Web site: http://www.law.nyu.edu/academics/clinics/semester/environmental/index.htm

Public Law Research Institute, University of California Hastings College of the Law

Organized at Hastings College of the Law in 1983 by Professor Julian Levi, the Public Law Research Institute analyzes legal issues that currently confront California's state and local governments. The Institute concentrates its legal research on topics identified by the California Research Bureau, a part of the California State Library. The Institute also responds to requests from other sources, including various state and local governmental offices. The range of topics varies from year to year, and is as broad as the spectrum of issues state and local governments confront. Past topics have included legislative responses to the AIDS crisis, corporate governance, election reform, welfare reform, economic development, crime control, health care reform, and more.

David Jung
Director
Public Law Research Institute
UC Hastings College of the Law
200 McAllister Street

San Francisco, CA 94102
Phone: 415-565-4671
E-mail: plri@uchastings.edu
Web site: http://www.uchastings.edu/centers/public-law/index.html

Rutgers School of Law–Newark, Environmental Law Clinic

The mission of the Environmental Law Clinic is to provide law students the opportunity to advocate for the public interest in environmental protection. The Environmental Law Clinic is currently undergoing restructuring. The Clinic plans to focus more on environmental justice advocacy concerning pollution, hazardous sites, and other environmental problems that directly affect communities and ecosystems in Newark and northern New Jersey.

Steve C. Gold
Director
Environmental Law Clinic
Rutgers School of Law–Newark
Rutgers University
123 Washington Street
Newark, NJ 07102-3046
Phone: 973-353-5561
E-mail: sgold@kinoy.rutgers.edu
Web site: http://law.newark.rutgers.edu/clinics/environmental-law-clinic

Texas Southern University Environmental Law and Justice Center

The Environmental Law and Justice Center is a public interest, environmental project founded in 1994 to lend the expertise and commitment learned from the civil rights and environmental movements to disenfranchised minority and low-income communities in Texas and neighboring states throughout the South that are burdened by various environmental abuses. The Center's director, staff, and student interns provide a full range of services, including but not limited to research, legal representation at state or federal administrative hearings and in state and federal court, training, outreach, and educational workshops.

Martina E. Cartwright
Clinical Instructor/Staff Attorney
Environmental Law and Justice Center
Texas Southern University

3100 Cleburne Street
Houston, TX 77004
Phone: 713-313-7011
E-mail: mcartwright@tmslaw.tsu.edu
Web site: http://www.tsu.edu/pages/993.asp

Tulane University Law School Environmental Law Clinic

Tulane University Law School started its Environmental Law Clinic in 1989 to offer students the real-world experience of representing people who otherwise could not afford to enforce their rights under state and federal environmental laws. Now the Clinic is part of a first-tier environmental law program and has become Louisiana's premier public interest environmental legal services organization. On behalf of their clients, Clinic students and supervising attorneys litigate environmental "citizen suits" to abate industrial pollution, appeal permits for environmental pollution or destruction of wetlands, challenge agency regulations that fall short of legislative mandates, and prod agencies to perform statutory duties.

Adam Babich
Director
Environmental Law Clinic
Tulane University Law School
6329 Freret Street
New Orleans, LA 70118
Phone: 504-865-5789
Fax: 504-862-8721
E-mail: ababich@tulane.edu
Web site: http://www.law.tulane.edu/tlsfaculty/profiles.aspx?id=298

The University of Arizona Rogers College of Law Indigenous Peoples Law Clinic

The University of Arizona Rogers College of Law's Indigenous Peoples Law Clinic, under the auspices of the Indigenous Peoples Law and Policy (IPLP) Program, provides domestic and international legal assistance to the indigenous peoples of the southwest and the world. To that end, the Indigenous Law Clinic had established a court-appointed guardian-ad-litem program for the Tohono O'odham Indian reservation which involved the representation of abused and neglected children before their tribal courts in dependency proceedings. The Law and Policy Program has hosted the United Nation's Special Rapporteur for

Human Rights in his conference to assess annual reports from indigenous leaders from around the globe.

Robert A. Hershey
Director
Indigenous Peoples Law Clinic-PLP Program
Rogers College of Law
University of Arizona
Rountree Hall Room 202
P.O. Box 210176
Tucson, AZ 85721
Phone: 520-621-5677
E-mail: hershey@law.arizona.edu
Web site: http://www.law.arizona.edu/depts/iplp/contact.cfm?page=contact

Frank G. Wells Environmental Law Clinic at University of California–Los Angeles

The School of Law's Frank G. Wells Environmental Law Clinic offers excellent opportunities for students to obtain hands-on experience in environmental law. Working with many nonprofit and government agency partners, the Clinic has been very successful at training environmental lawyers while helping to protect the environment. Students who take the six-unit environmental law clinical course work on large and small cases, involving both federal and state law.

Sean B. Hecht
Executive Director
Environmental Law Center
UCLA School of Law
405 Hilgard Avenue, Room 1475
Los Angeles, CA 90095-1476
Phone: 310-825-1097
Fax: 310-206-1234
E-mail: hecht@law.ucla.edu
Web site: http://www.law.ucla.edu/home/index.asp?page=1514

University of Maryland School of Law, Environmental Law Clinic

The Environmental Clinic is part of this school's nationally acclaimed environmental law program and is a primary way for students to fulfill the requirements for a certificate of specialization in that area of law. The Clinic is also an appropriate choice for students interested in an administrative, legislative, and litigation practice involving health and safety regulation at both the federal and state levels. The Clinic currently represents a historic African American community in Prince George's County that is fighting the construction of a new industrial operation in its community. This small neighborhood is already beset by more than its share of industrial activity, with the resulting environmental issues that are associated with these types of industry. Clinic students will be representing the community association in an appeal for a county zoning determination.

Jane F. Barrett
Law School Associate Professor and
Director
Environmental Law Clinic
University of Maryland School of Law
500 West Baltimore Street
Baltimore, MD 21201
Phone: 410-706-8074
E-mail: jbarrett@law.umaryland.edu
Web site: http://www.law.umaryland.edu/programs/environment/index.html

Tribal Environmental Law Project at the University of North Dakota

This project provides legal and policy assistance to tribal governments developing environmental programs intended to protect the health and welfare of tribal citizens, tribal natural resources, and the quality of reservations and ceded lands. The project also researches legal issues of general relevance to the authority of tribal governments to implement and administer civil regulatory programs.

James M. Grijalva
Director
Tribal Environmental Law Project
School of Law
University of North Dakota
215 Centennial Drive, Stop 9003
Grand Forks, ND 58202-9003
Phone: 704-777-2227
E-mail: grijalva@law.und.edu
Web site: http://www.law.und.edu/npilc/nalp

University of Oregon Environmental and Natural Resources Law Program

Oregon Law was the first public law school in the nation to establish an environmental law program. The school's professors, students, and alumni have played leading roles in the public environmental movement. The Environmental and Natural Resources Law Program draws tremendously talented and committed students, many of whom engage in environmental work. The program is part of a world-class research institution with a focus on environmental studies. Faculty members are some of the nation's leading scholars in the field of environmental law. Academic life is enriched by extracurricular activities that immerse students in scholarship and service opportunities in the environmental area.

Heather Brinton
Assistant Director
Environmental and Natural Resources Law Program
Bowerman Center for Environmental Law
University of Oregon
1515 Agate Street
Eugene, OR 97403-1221
Phone: 541-346-1395
E-mail: enr@uoregon.edu
Web site: http://enr.uoregon.edu/program

Vermont Law School Environmental and Natural Resources Law Clinic

Vermont Law School Environmental and Natural Resources Law Clinic's powerful and effective advocacy has produced significant accomplishments and raised visibility of environmental issues, including winning a major victory for the endangered gray wolf; protecting wetlands and tributaries; standing up for the health of individuals threatened by the mining operations of a major, multinational company; and defending a sacred tribal site.

David Mears
Director
Environmental and Natural Resources Law Clinic
Vermont Law School
164 Chelsea Street
P.O. Box 96
South Royalton, VT 05068

Phone: 802-831-1627
E-mail: dmears@vermontlaw.edu
Web site: http://www.vermontlaw.edu/Academics/Environmental_Law_Center.htm

Washington University in St. Louis, Interdisciplinary Environmental Clinic

The Interdisciplinary Environmental Clinic at Washington University in St. Louis provides pro bono legal and technical services to environmental and community organizations in the greater St. Louis, Missouri, area, while simultaneously offering a unique education experience for students from across the University. The interdisciplinary structure of the Clinic—involving students from several schools of the University in advocacy representation of clients—is unique among environmental law clinics. Student attorneys (second- and third-year law students) and student consultants (graduate students and upper-level undergraduates in engineering, environmental studies, medicine, social work, and business) work in interdisciplinary teams under faculty supervision. They offer legal and technical assistance on environmental and community health problems to individuals and organizations that cannot afford to pay for such services. Clinic teams work on issues relating to air and water quality, lead poisoning, environmental justice, habitat destruction, and wetlands.

Maxine Lipeles
Director
Interdisciplinary Environmental Clinic
School of Law
Washington University in St. Louis
One Brookings Drive
St. Louis, MO 63130
Phone: 314-935-5837
E-mail: milipele@wulaw.wustl.edu
Web site: http://law.wustl.edu/intenv

Yale University Environmental Protection Law Clinic

The Yale Environmental Protection Law Clinic is designed to introduce students to the fields of environmental advocacy and policymaking by exploring a variety of environmental law and policy questions and the tools environmental professionals use to address them. While the Clinic supplements students' hands-on experience with seminars on environmental law and policy, the core of the program is the work students do for their clients: teams of three to four students work with client organizations on real-world projects, with the goal of producing a major work product for the client by the end of the semester.

Dale Bryk
Director
Yale Environmental Law Clinic
Yale University
Mailing address: 205 Prospect Street, New Haven, CT 06511
Office address: 301 Prospect Street, New Haven, CT 06511
Telephone: 203-432-8256
Fax: 203-432-0237
E-mail: dale.bryk@yale.edu
Web site: http://www.yale.edu/elc/index.htm

Academic Degree–Granting Programs

Environmental Justice Advocates Program

The Environmental Justice Advocates' (EJA) mission is to advocate for and support, through direct action and the law, communities' efforts toward environmental justice. EJA is a Lewis & Clark Law School student group, established by the students themselves in 2000, that pursues environmental justice through direct action and scholarship. Environmental justice is the idea that the income, race, or ethnicity of communities should not correlate to their quality of living environment, nor should members of these communities be asked to sacrifice their jobs or homes to gain a safe living environment. Pursuit of environmental justice must be rooted in the communities where the problems (and solutions) are; knowledge is an effective tool for change. Since then, EJA has been actively involved in air quality testing and community building in Northeast Portland, Oregon, provided legal assistance to neighborhood organizations facing freeway expansion along the I-5 corridor, and supported union efforts to prevent farmworker exposure to toxic fumes. In addition, the group worked with law faculty, especially the environmental and natural resource law faculty, to integrate environmental justice tenets into Lewis & Clark's existing curriculum. They have successfully lobbied for adjunct professors to teach an environmental justice survey course and a seminar class once a year.

Lewis & Clark University
Lewis & Clark Law School
10015 Southwest Terwilliger Boulevard
Portland, OR 97219
Phone: 503-768-6600
Fax: 503-768-6205
E-mail: eja@lclark.edu
Web site: http://www.lclark.edu/law/student_groups/environmental_justice_advocates/index.php

Environmental Justice BA/JD

St. Thomas University has developed a unique, interdisciplinary program to prepare students for the practice of environmental law in the twenty-first century. Environmental lawyers, whether in private practice, government, or public interest, must have a sound grounding in the technical issues and concepts that form the basis for environmental regulatory programs and which frequently arise in environmental litigation, transactions, and site cleanups. The environmental justice curriculum provides the aspiring environmental attorney with the ability to understand the science and technology that is essential to assessing and developing solutions to environmental problems. Unlike other programs at other universities, the environmental justice curriculum bridges the gap between the technical and legal training in a sequence of specially designed courses focusing on environmental justice.

St. Thomas University
School of Theology and Ministry
16401 Northwest 37th Avenue
Miami Gardens, FL 33054
Phone: 305-628-6658
E-mail: theology@stu.edu
Web site: http://www.stu.edu/BAJDEnvironmentalJustice/tabid/1097/Default.aspx

Environmental Justice Program

The University of Michigan School of Natural Resources and Environment's (SNRE's) environmental justice faculty has been at the forefront of environmental justice teaching, research, scholarship, and activism. In the early 1990s, the five faculty members who established the program worked together to recruit students, develop environmental justice courses, conduct research on the topic, and publish in the field. As a result, SNRE became the first school to put in place an environmental justice program that offered undergraduate and graduate degree specializations in the topic. Today, the school has one of the largest clusters of environmental justice faculty and students nationwide. Twelve SNRE faculty members are affiliated with the program. There are several other environmental justice faculty around the university with whom SNRE students can also work. SNRE's environmental justice faculty is very diverse and that diversity enhances the learning experience in the program.

University of Michigan
School of Natural Resources and Environment
Dana Building, 440 Church Street
Ann Arbor, MI 48109-1041
Phone: 734-764-2550
Fax: 734-763-8965
E-mail: bbryant@umich.edu
Web site: http://www.snre.umich.edu/degree_programs/environmental_justice/overview

Gender, Justice and Environmental Change Program

The Gender, Justice and Environmental Change Program at Michigan State University offers graduate students a supportive and rigorous academic environment for exploring these issues as well as credentials demonstrating specialized training in the field. The certification of the specialization will appear on the student's transcript. The specialization is intended to provide graduate students from different disciplinary backgrounds with the analytical and methodological tools to address environmental issues from gender relations and social justice perspectives; provide students with a global perspective on environmental issues by drawing out local–global linkages; foster the growth of research, service, and interdisciplinary collaboration in the fields of gender and environmental studies; and increase awareness among faculty, students, and the public of the linkages between gender and the environment, both domestically and internationally. The program is flexible and multidisciplinary in design and faculty and student participation. Students in natural science fields use the specialization to integrate gender and justice concerns with their regular program. Students in social sciences are exposed to the background, concepts, and methods of environmental studies necessary to communicate with natural scientists and policymakers.

Michigan State University (International)
Office of International Development
202 International Center
East Lansing, MI 48824-1035
Phone: 517-432-9184
Fax: 517-353-8765
E-mail: oid@msu.edu
Web site: http://www.oid.msu.edu/capabilities/envirojustice.htm

Social Responsibility Masters Program

The Social Responsibility Masters Program at St. Cloud University integrally connects social justice, peace, and environmental studies. The Program investigates the root causes of local and global problems, and develops practical skills for socially responsible careers and citizenship at the local, state, national, and global levels. Students learn to apply skills in critical analysis, investigation, research, writing, advocacy, organizing, educating, and implementing socially responsible policies and practices. Personal skills in peace, compassion, activism, and personal change for a better world are an integral part of the program.

St. Cloud State University
720 4th Avenue South
St. Cloud, MN 56301-4498
Phone: 320-308-3124
E-mail: socialresponsibility@stcloudstate.edu
Web site: http://www.stcloudstate.edu/socialresponsibility/default.asp

References

1. Bunyan Bryant, *Environmental Justice: Issues, Policies, and Solutions* (Washington, DC: Island Press, 1995).

2. Luke W. Cole and Sheila R. Foster, *From the Ground Up: Environmental Racism and the Rise of the Environmental Justice Movement* (New York: New York University Press, 2000).

3. Robert D. Bullard, *Dumping in Dixie: Race, Class, and Environmental Quality* (Boulder, CO: Westview Press, 1990).

6

Selected Groups Working on Environmental Justice, Health, and Racial Equity

THE FOLLOWING IS A list of Environmental Justice Groups (105), Environmental Justice Networks (17), and Environmental Justice Youth Groups (12) that work on health issues. This list was compiled using several sources including the *People of Color Environmental Groups Directory*, the Multicultural Environmental Leadership Development Initiative (MELDI) *Directory of Environmental Justice Groups*, foundations' grantee lists and databases, state and regional environmental directories, and groups identified using the "snowball" method (i.e., asking a core group of respondents to identify other groups they know working on environmental justice and health; groups identified were then asked to identify other groups; the process was repeated to arrive at the current list).

The 1992 *People of Color Environmental Groups Directory* listed 300 organizations. Today, there are more than 3,000 people-of-color environmental justice organizations, and can be found in nearly every state. From Puerto Rico to Alaska, these groups are shaping public policy and making their voices heard in community meetings and with those who serve on school boards, city councils, and state legislatures. The groups listed in this report represent a small sample of the many grassroots groups, regional and national organizations, and networks that are working on environmental and health equity.

Health and Environmental Justice Groups
Advocates for Environmental Human Rights

Advocates for Environmental Human Rights is a nonprofit, public interest law firm whose mission is to provide legal services, community organizing support, public education, and campaigns focused on defending and advancing the human right to a healthy environment and to advocate for the human rights of internally displaced Gulf Coast hurricane survivors.

Monique Harden
Codirector and Attorney
Advocates for Environmental Human Rights
650 Poydras Street, Suite 2523
New Orleans, LA 70130
Phone: 504-799-3060
Fax: 504-799-3061
E-mail: mharden@ehumanrights.org
Web site: http://www.ehumanrights.org

Alaska Community Action on Toxics

Alaska Community Action on Toxics (ACAT) is a statewide organization established in 1997 and dedicated to achieving environmental health and justice. The organization works to eliminate the production and release of harmful chemicals by industry and military sources; ensure community right-to-know; achieve policies based on the Precautionary Principle; and support the rights and sovereignty of indigenous peoples. ACAT has four program areas: military toxics and health, northern contaminants and health, pesticide right-to-know, and water quality protection.

Pamela K. Miller
Alaska Community Action on Toxics
505 West Northern Lights Boulevard, Suite 205
Anchorage, AK 99503
Phone: 907-222-7714
Fax: 907-222-7715
E-mail: pkmiller@akaction.net
Web site: http://www.akaction.org/ACAT_Staff.htm

Albany, Georgia, Tools for Change, Inc.

Albany, Georgia, Tools for Change, Inc.'s mission is to empower residents of the College Park, College Heights, and the Country Club Estates communities in Albany, Georgia, with respect to effectively enhancing their physical, emotional, and mental health and well-being by improving communication, information, and access to health resources and eliminating environmental toxins and pollutants.

Rebecca Reid
Executive Director
Albany State University
504 College Drive, Peace Hall
Albany, GA 31705
Phone: 229-432-1338
E-mail: breid01@bellsouth.net
Web site: http://www.agtfconline.org

Alliance for Healthy Homes

The Alliance for Healthy Homes is a national, nonprofit, public interest organization working to prevent and eliminate hazards in our homes that can harm the health of children, families, and other residents. These hazards include lead, mold, carbon monoxide, radon, pests, and pesticides.

Patrick MacRoy
Executive Director
Alliance for Healthy Homes
50 F Street Northwest, Suite 300
Washington, DC 20001
Phone: 202-347-7610
E-mail: pmacroy@afhh.org
Web site: http://www.cehrc.org/index.htm

Alternatives for Community & Environment

Alternatives for Community & Environment (ACE) builds the power of communities of color and lower-income communities in New England to eradicate environmental racism and classism and achieve environmental justice. ACE believes that everyone has the right to a healthy environment and to be decision-makers regarding issues that affect their communities.

Kalila Barnett
Executive Director
Alternatives for Community and Environment
2181 Washington Street, Suite 301
Roxbury, MA 02119
Phone: 617-442-3343
Fax: 617-442-2425
E-mail: kalila@ace-ej.org
Web site: http://www.ace-ej.org

Arbor Hill Environmental Justice Corporation

The mission of the Arbor Hill Environmental Justice Corporation is to serve the community as an environmental and public health advocate, conduct environmental testing, and rehabilitate green and open space.

Aaron Mair
Executive Director
Arbor Hill Environmental Justice Corporation
200 Henry Johnson Boulevard
Albany, NY 12210
Phone: 518-474-4059
E-mail: aaronmair@yahoo.com
Web site: http://www.ahej.org

Bayview Hunters Point Health and Environmental Resource Center

The Health and Environmental Resource Center (HERC) incorporates the community first objective of "community involvement" in its program philosophy. HERC will utilize the African American Health Initiative's innovative, Afrocentered approaches to motivate men to take a more active role in improving their health, the health of their families and neighborhoods. This will occur through opening community dialogue, taking a stand on issues, and pooling strengths, resources, and energy in order to reach men who may be hesitant to focus on their own health.

Dr. Betty McGee
Bayview Hunters Point Health and Environment Resource Center
828 Innes Avenue, Unit #110
San Francisco, CA 94124
Phone: 415-401-6810, ext. 302
Fax: 415 401-6812

E-mail: bmcgee_us@yahoo.com
Web site: http://www.bayviewherc.org/index.htm

Beyond Pesticides

Beyond Pesticides (formerly known as the National Coalition Against the Misuse of Pesticides) was founded in 1981 on the principle that people from all walks of life can join together and effect changes to protect human health and the environment from the daily assault of toxic pesticides. Beyond Pesticides works with allies in protecting public health and the environment to lead the transition to a world free of toxic pesticides. The organization seeks to effect change through local action, by assisting individuals and community-based organizations to stimulate discussion on the hazards of toxic pesticides, while providing information on safer alternatives.

Jay Feldman
Executive Director
Beyond Pesticides
701 E Street Southeast, #200
Washington, DC, 20003
Phone: 202-543-5450
E-mail: jfeldman@beyondpesticides.org
Web site: http://www.beyondpesticides.org

Black Mesa Water Coalition

The Black Mesa Water Coalition (BMWC) is dedicated to preserving and protecting Mother Earth and the integrity of indigenous peoples' cultures, with the vision of building sustainable and healthy communities. It also strives to empower young people while building these sustainable communities. BMWC was formed in 2001 by a group of young intertribal, interethnic people dedicated to addressing issues of water depletion, natural resource exploitation, and health promotion within Navajo and Hopi communities.

Enei Begaye
Codirector
Black Mesa Water Coalition
1823 North Center Street
Flagstaff, AZ 86004
Phone: 928-213-5909

E-mail: eneibegaye@mac.com
Web site: http://www.blackmesawatercoalition.org/index.html

Boston Public Health Commission

The Boston Public Health Commission (BPHC) is the oldest health department in the country. Their mission is to protect, promote, and preserve the health and well-being of all Boston residents, particularly the most vulnerable individuals. BPHC strives to fulfill its mission through a wide range of health initiatives that target preventable disease and injury. Through the years, BPHC has made great strides when it comes to infant mortality, childhood immunization, cancer, heart disease, and tuberculosis, to name a few. BPHC's Environmental Health Division protects the health of Bostonians and visitors to the city through environmental monitoring and prevention activities, inspections, and emergency response to environmental hazards, provides outreach and education, and enforcement of regulatory laws. Teaming with Boston University School for Public Health and Harvard University School of Public Health, Boston Housing Authorities and tenant groups, BPHC is working to improve the environment in public housing (pest control, asthma reduction, reduction of lead exposure).

Dr. Barbara Ferrer
Executive Director
Boston Public Health Commission
1010 Massachusetts Avenue, 2nd Floor
Boston, MA 02118
Phone: 617-534-5395
Fax: 617-534-5358
E-mail: info@bphc.org
Web site: http://www.bphc.org/Pages/Home.aspx

Calexico New River Committee

Frustrated by the lack of progress, and recognizing that the ultimate solution to cleaning up the New River pollution would involve complex international negotiations that could take further decades to accomplish, concerned citizens and officials in the Calexico area established the Calexico New River Committee in 2001. The Committee, which is dedicated to eliminating the negative impact of the New River in Calexico and the rest of Imperial County, has successfully consolidated community and political support behind the New River Public Health Protection Project.

Miguel Figueroa
Executive Director
Calexico New River Committee
P.O. Box 2374
Calexico, CA 92231
Phone: 760-357-8389
Fax: 760-357-8779
E-mail: info@calexiconewriver.com
Web site: http://www.calexiconewriver.com

California Environmental Rights Alliance

The California Environmental Rights Alliance (CERA) works to achieve environmental justice and improve community health. CERA believes all people have the right to a safe and healthful environment. It supports policies that fix problems in our most polluted communities. Also, it provides advice and technical assistance to communities of color and low-income neighborhoods.

Joseph K. Lyou
Executive Director
California Environmental Rights Alliance
P.O. Box 116
El Segundo, CA 90245-0116
Phone: 310-536-8237
Fax: 866-442-7905
E-mail: jlyou@envirorights.org
Web site: http://www.envirorights.org

California Communities Against Toxics

California Communities Against Toxics (CCAT) advocates for environmental justice, pollution prevention, and world peace. CCAT was formed in 1989 at the Santa Isabel Church in East Los Angeles. The organization has been very successful in stopping the siting of new polluting facilities in communities of color and in gaining recognition of the environmental injustice of pollution in California. CCAT is one of the oldest and most successful environmental justice networks in the country. Its work has united Native Nations, inner-city people of color, and the rural poor in a coalition that has stopped every major attempt to roll back environmental regulations in California for the past decade.

Jane Williams
Executive Director
California Communities Against Toxics
P.O. Box 845
Rosamond, CA 93560
Phone: 661-510-3412
Fax: 661-947-9793
E-mail: info@stoptoxics.org
Web site: http://www.stoptoxics.org

Californians for Pesticide Reform

Californians for Pesticide Reform (CPR) is a statewide coalition of more than 185 organizations, founded in 1996 to shift fundamentally the way pesticides are used in California. CPR's mission is to protect public health, improve environmental quality, and expand a sustainable and just agriculture system by building a diverse movement across California to change statewide and local pesticide policies and practices. CPR has built a diverse, multi-interest coalition to challenge the powerful political and economic forces opposing change.

David Chatfield
Executive Director
Californians for Pesticide Reform
49 Powell Street, Suite 530
San Francisco, CA 94102
Phone: 415-981-3939
Fax: 415-981-2727
E-mail: dchatfield@igc.org
Web site: http://www.pesticidereform.org/index.php

Center for Community Action and Environmental Justice

The Center for Community Action and Environmental Justice (CCAEJ) is a 501(c) (3) nonprofit organization with its main office located in Riverside, California. The Center's goal is to bring groups of people together to find opportunities for cooperation, agreement, and problem solving. CCAEJ works with community groups in developing and sustaining democratically based, participatory organizations that promote involvement of a diverse segment of the community in ways that empower.

Penny Newman
Executive Director

Center for Community Action and Environmental Justice
P.O. Box 33124
Riverside, CA 92519
Phone: 951-360-8451
Fax: 951-360-5950
E-mail: penny.n@ccaej.org
Web site: http://www.ccaej.org

Center for Empowered Decision Making

The Center for Empowered Decision Making (CEDM), established in early 2001, is the official working arm of the Healthy New Orleans Partnership. The center was created to support the fulfillment of the vision and objectives of the New Orleans Community Public Health Systems Improvement Plan. The organization's work plan includes community voices forums, community capacity building, leadership training, and development of a comprehensive resource directory and Web site.

Shelia Webb
Center for Empowered Decision Making
1515 Poydras Street, Suite 1060
New Orleans, LA 70112
Phone: 504-620-0024
E-mail: swebb@excelth.com
Web site: http://www.ctrfedm.org

Center for Environmental Health

The Center for Environmental Health protects people from toxic chemicals and promotes business products and practices that are safe for public health and the environment.

Michael Green
Executive Director
Center for Environmental Health
2201 Broadway, Suite 302
Oakland, CA 94612
Phone: 510-655-3900
Fax: 510-655-9100
E-mail: michael@ceh.org
Web site: http://www.ceh.org/index.php

Center for Health, Environment and Justice

The Center for Health, Environment and Justice (CHEJ) is the only national environmental organization that was founded and is led by a grassroots leader. Lois Gibbs founded CHEJ after winning the nation's first community relocation of 900 families as a result of a leaking toxic waste dump in Love Canal, New York. Through this effort she also woke up the nation to recognize the link between people's exposures to dangerous chemicals in the community setting and serious public health impacts.

Lois Marie Gibbs
Executive Director
Center for Health, Environment and Justice
P.O. Box 6806
Falls Church, VA 22040-6806
Phone: 703-237-2249
E-mail: chej@chej.org
Web site: http://www.chej.org

Center on Race, Poverty & the Environment

The Center on Race, Poverty & the Environment (CRPE) is an environmental justice litigation organization dedicated to helping grassroots groups across the United States attack head-on the disproportionate burden of pollution borne by poor people and people of color. CRPE provides organizing and technical and legal assistance to help community groups stop immediate environmental threats.

Caroline Farrell
Acting Executive Director
Center on Race, Poverty & the Environment
47 Kearny Street, Suite 804
San Francisco, CA 94108
Phone: 661-586-2621
E-mail: cfarrell@crpe-ej.org
Web site: http://www.crpe-ej.org

Chelsea Collaborative

The mission of the Chelsea Collaborative is to empower Chelsea residents and Chelsea organizations to enhance the social, environmental, and economic health of the community and its people. The Collaborative carries out its mission through community organizing, technical assistance, program development, and information dissemination.

Gladys Vega
Executive Director
Chelsea Collaborative
300 Broadway
Chelsea, MA 02150
Phone: 617-889-6080
Fax: 617-889-0559
E-mail: gladysv@chelseacollab.org
Web site: http://www.chelseacollab.org

Childhood Lead Action Project, Inc.

Since 1992, the Childhood Lead Action Project has worked to eliminate childhood lead poisoning through education, parent support, and advocacy. The Project is the only organization in Rhode Island devoted exclusively to this critical issue. Childhood lead poisoning remains the most pervasive, yet preventable environmental health problem in Rhode Island. It is one of the most insidious indicators of environmental injustice—children of color continue to have alarming rates of poisoning. Over the years, the Childhood Lead Action Project has come to be recognized as a leading education and information resource by the community and as a catalyst for social change.

Roberta Hazen Aaronson
Executive Director
Childhood Lead Action Project, Inc.
1192 Westminster Street
Providence, RI 02909
Phone: 401-274-2652, ext. 182
E-mail: roberta@leadsafekids.org
Web site: http://www.leadsafekids.org/matriarch/default.asp

Citizens Campaign for the Environment

The Citizens Campaign for the Environment (CCE) was formed in 1985 by a small group of concerned citizens who recognized the need to provide public involvement in the course of advancing stronger environmental policy. Today, after 20 years as a not-for-profit, nonpartisan advocacy organization, CCE has grown to an 80,000-member organization with offices in New York (Farmingdale, White Plains, Albany, Syracuse, and Buffalo) and New Haven, Connecticut. CCE continues to work to empower the public by providing members with opportunities to participate in the political process and thereby advance a progressive environmental agenda.

Adrienne Esposito
Executive Director
Citizens Campaign for the Environment
466 Westcott Street, 2nd Floor
Syracuse, NY 13210
Phone: 315-472-1339
Fax: 315-472-1179
E-mail: aesposito@citizenscampaign.org
Web site: http://www.citizenscampaign.org/index.asp

Citizens' Environmental Coalition

The Citizens' Environmental Coalition (CEC) coordinates the Alliance for a Toxic Free Future, a coalition of community, environmental, labor, health, and environmental justice groups working to prevent harm from toxic chemicals. In 2008, CEC implemented campaigns to prevent pollution and promote environmental health, zero waste, green purchasing, green buildings, green jobs, brownfield, and radioactive waste cleanup.

Barbara Warren
Executive Director
Citizens' Environmental Coalition
33 Central Avenue
Albany, NY 12210
Phone: 518-462-5527
E-mail: warrenba@msn.com
Web site: http://www.cectoxic.org/index.html

Citizens League for Environmental Action Now

The Citizens League for Environmental Action Now (CLEAN) is working to clean up the air and improve the overall quality of the environment. CLEAN offers solutions to improve Houston's, Texas air quality that will benefit Houston socially and economically. The organization encourages the public to speak out on these issues.

Jane Dale Owen
President
Citizens League for Environmental Action Now
720 North Post Oak Road, Suite 265
Houston, TX 77024
Phone: 713-524-3000
E-mail: info@cleanhouston.org
Web site: http://www.cleanhouston.org/index.htm

Citizens for Safe Water Around Badger

Citizens for Safe Water Around Badger (CSWAB) was organized in 1990 when the community learned private drinking water wells near Wisconsin's Badger Army Ammunition Plant were polluted with high levels of cancer-causing chemicals. The organization's founders believed community involvement could have prevented this tragedy and consequently organized CSWAB both to empower and to protect nearby residents and plant workers from further harm.

Laura Olah
Executive Director
Citizens for Safe Water Around Badger
E12629 Weigand's Bay South
Merrimac, WI 53561
Phone: 608-643-3124
Fax: 608-643-0005
E-mail: info@cswab.org
Web site: http://www.cswab.org

The City Project

The mission of The City Project is to achieve equal justice, democracy, and livability for all. The City Project carries out its mission by influencing the investment of public resources to achieve results that are equitable, enhance human health and the environment, and promote economic vitality for all communities. Focusing on parks and recreation, playgrounds, schools, health, and transit, the organization helps bring people together to define the kind of community in which they want to live and raise children.

Robert García
President and Counsel
The City Project

1055 Wilshire Boulevard, Suite 1660
Los Angeles, CA 90017
Phone: 213-977-1035
Fax: 213-977-5457
E-mail: rgarcia@cityprojectca.org
Web site: http://www.cityprojectca.org/index.php

Clean New York

Although harm to the natural environment affects everyone, women and children bear the brunt of these health impacts. Clean New York is an environmental justice organization committed to empowering all women to be strong voices for change. To demonstrate to policymakers, opinion leaders, and businesses that women's decisions—whether political or economic—are tied to support for environmental ethics, responsibility, health, and justice, the organization supports women of all ages and from all walks of life in advocating on their own behalf for environmental health protection. Clean New York reaches out to women-led and -oriented organizations across the state to educate and activate the enormous untapped potential of this key constituency. Although harm to the natural environment affects everyone, women and children bear the brunt of these health impacts.

Bobbi Chase Wilding
Organizing Director
Clean New York
323 Bonnyview Lane
Schenectady, NY 12306
Phone: 518-708-3875
Fax: 518-234-8421
E-mail: clean.bobbi@gmail.com
Web site: http://www.clean-ny.org

Coalition to End Childhood Lead Poisoning

The Coalition to End Childhood Lead Poisoning is a national 501(c)(3) nonprofit organization that creates, implements, and promotes programs and policies to eradicate childhood lead poisoning and further healthy homes. The coalition was originally founded in 1986 as Parents Against Lead, a grassroots volunteer effort. Today, the coalition is a nationally recognized policy, advocacy, and direct service organization headquartered in Baltimore, Maryland.

Ruth Ann Norton
Executive Director
Coalition to End Childhood Lead Poisoning
2714 Hudson Street
Baltimore, MD 21224
Phone: 410-534-6447
Fax: 410-534-6475
E-mail: ranorton@leadsafe.org
Web site: http://www.leadsafe.org/index.cfm

Colonias Development Council

Twenty years ago, the Colonias Development Council emerged as a local, grassroots group in cooperation with the Office of Catholic Social Ministry to help farmworkers in New Mexico. The Council became an independent 501(c)(3) nonprofit in 1994 to develop multi-issue, self-help community-based organizations to respond to common needs in Colonia communities. The group's work is characterized by a long-term commitment to facilitating the processes for community organizing and leadership development in order to achieve social change.

Dr. Diana Bustamante
Executive Director
Colonias Development Council
Concilio para el Desarrollo de las Colinas
1050 Monte Vista
Las Cruces, NM 88001
Phone: 575-647-2744
Fax: 575-647-1462
E-mail: diana@colonias.org
Web site: http://www.colonias.org/splash-english.html

Communities for a Better Environment

Communities for a Better Environment (CBE) is a social justice organization with a focus on environmental health and justice. It organizes in working-class communities of color because these communities suffer the most from environmental pollution and toxics. CBE works in urban communities in Northern and Southern California among low-income African Americans, Latinos, and other nationalities who are bombarded by pollution from freeways, power plants, oil refineries, seaports, airports, and chemical manufacturers.

Bill Gallegos
Executive Director
Communities for a Better Environment
Oakland Office
1440 Broadway, Suite 701
Oakland, CA 94612
Phone: 510-302-0430, ext. 11
Fax: 510-302-0437
E-mail: billgallegos@cbecal.org
Web site: http://www.cbecal.org/index.html

Community Coalition for Environmental Justice

Located in South Seattle, Washington, the Community Coalition for Environmental Justice strives to achieve environmental and economic justice in low-income communities and communities of color and to support youth leadership.

Katie Manuel
Executive Director
Community Coalition for Environmental Justice
1620 18th Avenue, Suite 10
Seattle, WA 98122
Phone: 206-720-0285
Fax: 206-720-5241
E-mail: katiem@ccej.org
Web site: http://www.ccej.org/index.html

Connecticut Coalition for Environmental Justice

The Connecticut Coalition for Environmental Justice is an organization that was established in Hartford in the summer of 1997. It was formed in response to community concerns about the siting of yet another fossil-fueled power generator in South Hartford as a result of the closure of Connecticut's nuclear power plants.

Dr. Mark Mitchell
Director
Connecticut Coalition for Environmental Justice
P.O. Box 2022
10 Jefferson Street
Hartford, CT 06145-2022

Phone: 860-548-1133
Fax: 860-548-9197
E-mail: mark.mitchell@environmental-justice.org
Web site: http://www.environmental-justice.org

Detroiters Working for Environmental Justice

Detroiters Working for Environmental Justice (DWEJ) is organized to empower individuals, communities, and community organizations in Southeast
Michigan to educate, advocate, and organize for cleaner, healthier communities and environments. Since 1994, DWEJ has been has been a voice for
environmental justice in Michigan. Historically, minority and low-income
populations have suffered disproportionately from environmental pollution,
often because they have the least capacity to respond. Therefore, DWEJ is
dedicated to empowering urban residents to take a meaningful role in the
decision-making process surrounding environmental concerns in their own
communities.

Donele Wilkins
Executive Director
Detroiters Working for Environmental Justice
P.O. Box 14944
Detroit, MI 48214
Phone: 313-833-DWEJ (3935)
Fax: 313-833-3955
E-mail: dwdwej@aol.com
Web site: http://www.dwej.org/board.htm

Ditching Dirty Diesel

Cofounded by the Pacific Institute in 2004, the Ditching Dirty Diesel (DDD)
Collaborative is comprised of Bay Area individuals and organizations working
to reduce diesel pollution, particularly in low-income communities of color. The
DDD Collaborative works to connect diesel-reduction advocates and build their
capacity, support community-based organizations as they grow, affect systemic
and long-term policy change, and raise public awareness.

Jason Morrison
Program Director

Pacific Institute
654 13th Street
Preservation Park
Oakland, CA 94612
Phone: 510-251-1600
Fax: 510-251-2203
E-mail: jmorrison@pacinst.org
Web site: http://www.pacinst.org

East Yard Communities for Environmental Justice

East Yard Communities for Environmental Justice (EYCEJ) is an environmental health and justice nonprofit organization working toward a safe and healthy environment for communities that are disproportionately suffering the negative impacts of industrial pollution.

Angelo Logan
East Yard Communities for Environmental Justice
Executive Director
2317 Atlantic Boulevard
City of Commerce, CA 90040
Phone: 323-263-2113
Fax: 323-263-2114
E-mail: alogan@eycej.org
Web site: http://www.eycej.org

Ella Baker Center for Human Rights

The Ella Baker Center for Human Rights is a strategy and action center working for justice, opportunity, and peace in urban America. Based in Oakland, California, the Center promotes positive alternatives to violence and incarceration through four cutting-edge campaigns.

Jakada Imani
Executive Director
Ella Baker Center for Human Rights
344 40th Street
Oakland, CA 94609
Phone: 510-428-3939
Fax: 510-428-3940
E-mail: contact@ellabakercenter.org
Web site: http://www.ellabakercenter.org/page.php?pageid=1

Environmental Community Action, Inc.

Environmental Community Action, Inc's (ECO-Action's) work is based on the intersection of three issues: threats to human health, environmental degradation, and social injustice. ECO-Action's mission is to help communities organize to confront environmental health threats. ECO-Action serves the general population, but the organization focuses its assistance on communities that are in need of it the most rural residents, people with limited formal education, people with few resources, women, and people of color.

Yomi Noibi
Executive Director
Environmental Community Action, Inc.
250 Georgia Avenue, Suite 309
Atlanta, GA 30312-3046
Phone: 404-584-6499
E-mail: yomi@eco-act.org
Web site: http://www.eco-act.org

Environmental Health Coalition

The Environmental Health Coalition (EHC) is one of the oldest and most effective grassroots organizations in the United States, using social change strategies to achieve environmental justice. EHC is dedicated to achieving environmental and social justice and believes that justice is accomplished by empowered communities acting together to make social change. It organizes and advocates to protect public health and the environment threatened by toxic pollution. EHC supports broad efforts that create a just society, which fosters a healthy and sustainable quality of life.

Diane Takvorian
Executive Director
401 Mile of Cars Way, Suite 310
National City, CA 91950
Phone: 619-474-0220, ext. 112
Fax: 619-474-1210
E-mail: diane@environmentalhealth.org
Web site: http://www.environmentalhealth.org

Environmental Health Watch

Since 1980, Environmental Health Watch (EHW) has played a unique role in Northeast Ohio, helping the public and policy-makers address critical health concerns related to the urban and industrial environment. EHW helps devise, assess, demonstrate, and promote programs to prevent and reduce exposures to harmful substances indoors and outdoors that cause or aggravate serious health conditions. EHW's program activities are in four functional areas: (1) information and direct services, (2) training and technical consulting, (3) research and demonstration, and (4) policy development and advocacy. Activities are concentrated in two substantive areas: (1) indoor environments and (2) outdoor environments.

Stuart Greenberg
Executive Director
Environmental Health Watch
3500 Lorain Avenue
Cleveland, OH 44113
Phone: 216-961-4646
Fax: 216-961-7179
E-mail: sgreenberg@ehw.org
Web site: http://www.ehw.org

Environmental Justice Advocates of Minnesota

Environmental Justice Advocates of Minnesota (EJAM) evolved from a 2003 Minneapolis Urban League (MUL) meeting focusing on health disparities in communities of color. This meeting served as the foundation for a coalition of community members and organizations coming together to focus on environmental justice and health disparities. Issues that came up at the meeting were coal plant pollution, need for neighborhood legal advocacy assistance, lead poisoning, and health disparities. Since then, the MUL has hosted monthly EJAM meetings to define mission, goals, and scope of the newly formed coalition, which consists of North Minneapolis community members, MUL, NAACP, Sierra Club North Star Chapter, Metropolitan Area African American Chamber of Commerce, Institute for Agricultural and Trade Policy, Women's Cancer Resource Center, Council on Black Minnesotans, Indigenous Women's Network, African American Tobacco Network, Synergy Publishing, Alliance for Metropolitan Stability, and members of area churches, public schools, and the medical community.

Michael Neumann
Executive Director
Environmental Justice Advocates of Minnesota
2100 Plymouth Avenue
Minneapolis, MN 55411

Phone: 612-436-5402
E-mail: mkneumann@comcast.net
Web site: http://www.ejamn.org

Environmental Justice Coalition for Water

The Environmental Justice Coalition for Water (EJCW) is a network of more than 50 grassroots and intermediary organizations. EJCW works to empower community members to become strong voices for water justice in their communities.

Miriam Torres
Project Coordinator
Environmental Justice Coalition for Water
1201 Martin Luther King Jr. Way
Oakland CA, 94612
Phone: 510-286-8400
Fax: 510-444-2502
E-mail: Miriam@ejcw.org
Web site: http://www.ejcw.org/index.html

Environmental Justice and Health Union

The mission of the Environmental Justice and Health Union (EJHU) is to identify tools to help environmental justice activists and environmental health professionals work together to stop environmental disease in low-income communities of color in the United States.

Max Weintraub
Director
Environmental Justice and Health Union
528 61st Street, Suite A
Oakland, CA 94609
E-mail: ejhu@ejhu.org
Web site: http://www.ejhu.org/about_us.html

Esperanza Environmental Justice Project

Since 1998, this project has conducted health surveys, helped to organize communities to fight a Browning Ferris Industries landfill, held informational summits about the local electrical company and air pollution, and more.

Graciela Sánchez
Executive Director

Esperanza Environmental Justice Project
Esperanza Peace and Justice Center
922 San Pedro
San Antonio, TX 78212
Phone: 210-228-0201
Fax: 210-228-0000
E-mail: graciela@esperanzacenter.org
Web site: http://www.esperanzacenter.org/poderenvironmental.htm

Farm Labor Organizing Committee

The Farm Labor Organizing Committee, AFL-CIO, (FLOC) is both a social movement and a labor union. The organization's immediate constituency is migrant workers in the agricultural industry, but it is also involved with immigrant workers, Latinos, local communities, and national and international coalitions concerned with justice. FLOC's vision emphasizes human rights as the standard and self-determination as the process. FLOC struggles for full justice for those who have been marginalized and exploited for the benefit of others, and the organization has sought to change the structures of society to enable these people a direct voice in their own conditions.

Baldemar Velasquez
President
Farm Labor Organizing Committee, AFL-CIO
1221 Broadway Street
Toledo, OH 43609
Phone: 419-243-3456
E-mail: info@floc.com
Web site: http://www.floc.com

Farm Worker Pesticide Project

The Farm Worker Pesticide Project (FWPP) works directly with farmworkers and their families to reduce and eliminate their exposures to pesticides. To that end, FWPP provides resources and information to farmworkers and their advocates about pesticides, unites diverse groups and individuals behind a joint strategy to address the farmworker pesticide problems, and participates in that strategy as an advocate, organizer, educator, and researcher.

Carol Dansereau
Executive Director

Farm Worker Pesticide Project
7500 Greenwood Avenue North
Seattle, WA 98103
Phone: 206-729-0498
E-mail: cdansereaufwpp@earthlink.net
Web site: http://www.fwpp.org

Farmworker Association of Florida

The Farmworker Association of Florida, Inc. (FWAF) is a membership organization of over 6,330 farmworker families from predominately Mexican, Haitian, African American, Guatemalan, and Salvadoran communities, which was founded in 1983 and incorporated in May 1986. The goal is to build a strong, multiracial, economically viable organization of farmworkers in Florida empowering farmworkers to respond to and gain control over the social, political, economic, and workplace issues that affect their lives. An elected board of directors sets policy, guarantees implementation of work plans, and monitors finances. FWAF members work mainly in the following agriculture product markets: ferns, foliage, citrus, vegetables, and mushrooms. To date there are members in more than 11 counties, including: Orange, Lake, Sumter, Seminole, Volusia, Putnam, Dade, Hendry, Collier, Lee, and Osceola. The South Florida organizing projects were initiated in 1992. Because of this expansion, the Association's board voted to change its name from the Farmworker Association of Central Florida to the Farmworker Association of Florida.

Jeannie Economos
Coordinator
Pesticide Safety and Environmental Health Project
Farmworker Association of Florida
1264 Apopka Boulevard
Apopka, FL 32703
Phone: 407-886-5151
Fax: 407-884-6644
E-mail: farmworkerassoc@aol.com
Web site: http://www.farmworkers.org/fwafpage.html

Forrest County Environmental Support Team

The Forrest County Environmental Support Team (FCEST) is a strong community voice for the predominately African American east side of Hattiesburg, Mississippi.

FCEST uses community-driven education and training, participatory research, and partnering with faith-based, academic environmental programs and health centers to achieve its goal of eliminating environmental injustice and health disparities, while advancing programs to include the African American community in the emerging green economy. The organization's major focus has been on creosote contamination that threatens the health and environment of nearby residents.

Sherri Jones
Executive Director
Forrest County Environmental Support Team
P.O. Box 374
Hattiesburg, MS 39403-0374
Phone: 601-441-4646
E-mail: sjfcest48@yahoo.com
Web site: http://www.usm.edu/environmentaljustice/index.html

Fort Ord Environmental Justice Network

The Fort Ord Environmental Justice Network (FOEJN) was formed in 1995 as an outgrowth of community concerns over the cleanup and reuse efforts of the former Fort Ord U.S. Army base. Since its inception, FOEJN has advocated for the participation of disenfranchised communities in the activities and decisions made regarding the cleanup of toxins, contaminated groundwater, 8,000 acres of military munitions, and other contaminants that cause adverse health affects to impacted residents.

LeVonne Stone
Executive Director
Fort Ord Environmental Justice Network
P.O. Box 361
Marina, CA 93933
Phone: 831-582-0803
E-mail: ejustice@mbay.net
Web site: http://www.foejn.org

Global Community Monitor

Global Community Monitor (GCM) is an environmental justice and human rights nonprofit that empowers industrial communities to re-create a clean, healthy and truly sustainable environment. GCM was created to provide hands-on tools for impacted communities to monitor their own neighborhoods. Based on community knowledge and new data, industrial neighborhoods can increase their power to reduce health threats on their own terms.

Denny Larson
Executive Director
Global Community Monitor
P.O. Box 1784
El Cerrito, CA 94530
Phone: 510-233-1870
E-mail: denny@gcmonitor.org
Web site: http://www.gcmonitor.org

Glynn Environmental Coalition

For more than 20 years, the Glynn Environmental Coalition (GEC) has worked diligently to make Glynn County a safe and healthy place to raise families by assuring a clean environment and healthy economy for coastal Georgia. Serving as environmental advocates, GEC is committed to protecting and preserving the homes within Glynn County—one of the most environmentally unique ecosystems on earth—although the organization's work has had implications nationwide. The need is great, as Glynn County is home to 17 identified hazardous waste sites, four Superfund sites, and four actively polluting industries. Community awareness of health risks associated with these polluters and toxic waste sites led to the formation of the GEC in 1990.

Daniel Parshley
Project Manager
Glynn Environmental Coalition
P.O. Box 2443
Brunswick, GA 31521-2443
Phone: 912-466-0934
Fax: 912-634-0234
E-mail: gec@glynnenvironmental.org
Web site: http://www.glynnenvironmental.org

Greenaction for Health and Environmental Justice

Greenaction for Health and Environmental Justice mobilizes community power to win victories that change government and corporate policies and practices to protect health and promote environmental justice.

Bradley Angel
Executive Director
Greenaction for Health and Environmental Justice
One Hallidie Plaza, Suite 760
San Francisco, CA 94102
Phone: 415-248-5010
Fax: 415-248-5011
E-mail: bradley@greenaction.org
Web site: http://www.greenaction.org/org/mission.shtml

Gwich'in Steering Committee

The Gwich'in Steering Committee was formed in 1988 in response to imminent plans to open the Sacred Place Where Life Begins, the coastal plain (also known as the 1002 area) of the Arctic National Wildlife Refuge, to leasing for oil drilling.

Sarah James
Gwich'in Steering Committee
P.O. Box 51
Arctic Village, AK 99722
Phone: 907-587-5315
Fax: 907-587-5316
E-mail: sarahjamesav@hotmail.com
Web site: http://www.gwichinsteeringcommittee.org/index.html

Harambee House, Inc./Citizens for Environmental Justice

The Harambee House is a community center that focuses on political, socioeconomic, and community empowerment.

Mildred McCain
Harambee House, Inc./Citizens for Environmental Justice
1115 Habersham Street
Savannah, GA 31410
Phone: 912-233-0907
E-mail: cfej@bellsouth.net
Web site: http://www.theharambeehouse.com

Honor the Earth

Honor the Earth is a Native-led organization established in 1993 to address the two primary needs of the Native environmental movement: the need to break the geographic and political isolation of Native communities and the need to increase financial resources for organizing and change.

Winona LaDuke
Executive Director
2104 Stevens Avenue South
Minneapolis, MN 55404
Phone: 612-879-7529
E-mail: wlhonorearth@earthlink.net
Web site: http://www.honorearth.org

Improving Kids Environment, Inc.

Improving Kids Environment (IKE) is a nonprofit advocacy organization dedicated to reducing environmental threats to children's health. IKE will help children reach their full potential by working with citizens, nonprofit organizations, governments, businesses, and others to identify environmental threats to children's health; ensure that parents and other guardians have access to information about these threats and how to prevent them; support organizations that remove, reduce, and communicate these threats; and promote practical means to remove or reduce environmental threats to children's health.

Janet McCabe
Executive Director
Improving Kids Environment, Inc.
3951 North Meridian Street, Suite 160
Indianapolis, IN 46208
Phone: 317-902-3610
Fax: 866-234-8505
E-mail: mccabe@ikecoalition.org
Web site: http://www.ikecoalition.org

Ironbound Community Corporation

The Ironbound Community Corporation (ICC) is a nonprofit community-based organization rooted in the diverse Newark, New Jersey, neighborhood called Ironbound. Founded in 1969 by community residents, ICC's major role has been to work with neighborhood people to develop and operate programs and services to meet the needs of the area and improve the quality of life for individuals, families, and the general community.

Joseph DellaFave

Executive Director
Ironbound Community Corporation
179 Van Buren Street
Newark, NJ 07105
Phone: 973-589-3353
Fax: 973-589-3637
E-mail: info@ironboundcc.org
Web site: http://www.ironboundcc.org

IPM Institute of North America, Inc.

The IPM Institute of North America is a nonprofit organization formed in 1998 to foster recognition and rewards in the marketplace for goods and service providers who practice integrated pest management (IPM). IPM is an approach to managing pests that protects health and the environment and improves economic returns. IPM practitioners in agriculture and communities learn pest biology and use that knowledge to reduce pest control costs and hazards.

Dr. Thomas Green
President
IPM Institute of North America, Inc.
4510 Regent Street
Madison, WI 53705
Phone: 608-232-1410
Fax: 608-232-1440
E-mail: ipmworks@ipminstitute.org
Web site: http://www.ipminstitute.org/index.htm

Jesus People Against Pollution

Jesus People Against Pollution's mission is to work to obtain environmental justice for Columbia, Mississippi, and use this as a model for helping all communities suffering from toxic exposures to secure equal justice in their own community.

Charlotte Keys
Jesus People Against Pollution
P.O. Box 765
Columbia, MS 39429
Phone: 601-736-7099
E-mail: keysjpap@aol.com

Land Loss Prevention Project

The Land Loss Prevention Project (LLPP) was founded in 1982 by the North Carolina Association of Black Lawyers to curtail epidemic losses of Black-owned land in North Carolina. LLPP was incorporated in the state of North Carolina in 1983. The organization broadened its mission in 1993 to provide legal support and assistance to all financially distressed and limited-resource farmers and land-owners in North Carolina.

Savi Horne
Deputy Director
Land Loss Prevention Project
P.O. Box 179
Durham, NC 27702
Phone: 919-682-5969
Fax: 919-688-5596
E-mail: savi@landloss.org
Web site: http://www.landloss.org/index.php

Laotian Organizing Project

The Laotian Organizing Project (LOP) was started in 1995 to bring together the diverse Laotian ethnic and tribal groups in Contra Costa County, California, to respond to the needs of the community, work toward change, and provide a vehicle to build the community they envision. LOP has a membership base of 200 families and over 20 leaders.

Grace Kong
Community Organizer
Laotian Organizing Project
220 25th Street
Richmond, CA 94804
Phone: 510-236-4616
Fax: 510-236-4572
E-mail: may@apen4ej.org
Web site: http://www.apen4ej.org

Labor/Community Strategy Center

The Labor/Community Strategy Center is a "Think Tank/Act Tank" for regional, national, and international movement building founded in 1989 and based in Los Angeles, California. The Center's campaigns, projects, and publications are rooted in working-class communities of color and address the totality of urban life with a particular focus on civil rights, environmental justice, public health, global warming, and the criminal legal system.

Eric Mann
Executive Director
Labor/Community Strategy Center
3780 Wilshire Boulevard, Suite 1200
Los Angeles, CA 90010
Phone: 213-387-2800
Fax: 213-387-3500
Email: eric@thestrategycenter.org
Web site: http://www.thestrategycenter.org

Labor Occupational Health Program

The Labor Occupational Health Program is a community outreach program in the School of Public Health at the University of California–Berkeley whose work addresses today's workplace health and safety needs in nearly every industry, from health care to agriculture to construction. The staff of educators and technical experts provide information, training, and other assistance to unions, workers, community organizations, health professionals, joint labor-management groups, government, and schools.

Pam Tau Lee
Labor Occupational Health Program
University of California–Berkeley
2223 Fulton Street
Berkeley, CA 94720-5120
Phone: 510-642-5507
E-mail: ptlee@uclink4.berkeley.edu
Web site: http://globetrotter.berkeley.edu/EnvirPol/organizations/lohp.html

Literacy for Environmental Justice

Founded in 1998 by a coalition of youths, educators, and community leaders, Literacy for Environmental Justice addresses the ecological and health concerns of Bayview Hunters Point and the surrounding communities of Southeast San Francisco, California.

Malik Looper
Executive Director

Literacy for Environmental Justice
800 Innes Avenue, Suite 11
San Francisco, CA 94124
Phone: 415-282-6840
Fax: 415-282-6839
E-mail: info@lejyouth.org
Web site: http://www.lejyouth.org

Little Sisters of the Assumption Family Health Services, Inc.

The Little Sisters of the Assumption Family Health Service, Inc., founded in 1958, is a nonprofit community-based organization that works with the people of East Harlem, New York, to address the physical, emotional, educational, and spiritual dimensions of family health.

Ray E. López
Little Sisters of the Assumption Family Health Services, Inc.
333 East 115th Street
New York, NY 10029-2210
Phone: 646-672-5236
Fax: 212-987-4430
E-mail: rlopez@lsafhs.org
Web site: http://www.littlesistersfamily.org

Little Village Environmental Justice Organization

The Little Village Environmental Justice Organization (LVEJO) has worked with parent organizers going door-to-door to find out the concerns of the community. Based on that foundation of organizing, LVEJO campaigns were created and have evolved into its work today.

Kimberly Wasserman
Coordinator
Little Village Environmental Justice Organization
2856 South Millard Avenue
Chicago, IL 60623
Phone: 773-762-6991
E-mail: coordinator@lvejo.org
Web site: http://www.lvejo.org

Louisiana Bucket Brigade

The Louisiana Bucket Brigade is a 501(c)(3) environmental health and justice organization working with communities that neighbor the state's oil refineries and chemical plants. Its mission is to support communities' use of grassroots action to become informed, sustainable neighborhoods free from industrial pollution.

Anne Rolfes
Founding Director
Louisiana Bucket Brigade
4226 Canal Street
New Orleans, LA 70119
Phone: 504-484-3433
E-mail: annerolfes@hotmail.com
Web site: http://www.labucketbrigade.org

Mary Queen of Vietnam Community Development Corporation

The Mary Queen of Vietnam Community Development Corporation (MQVN CDC) was established by community leaders of the Mary Queen of Vietnam Church in May 2006 to assist Vietnamese Americans in New Orleans East rebuild their lives and their community. In the immediate aftermath of Hurricane Katrina, MQVN CDC played a leading role in providing emergency relief assistance as well as organizing Vietnamese American residents to play an active role in the rebuilding of the community surrounding the New Orleans East area.

Father Vien Nguyen
Pastor
Mary Queen of Vietnam Community Development Corporation
14001 Dwyer Boulevard
New Orleans, LA 70129
Phone: 504-255-9250
E-mail: ntv3@aol.com
Web site: http://www.mqvncdc.org

Misión Industrial de Puerto Rico, Inc.

For the people of Puerto Rico, pollution is not a disposable problem; island living imposes its own limits. What might be absorbed or hidden on a larger landmass can be immediately devastating on an island. Misión Industrial de Puerto Rico, Inc. believes that developing an ecologically sustainable economy is dependent on developing a sustainable sense of community.

Juan E. Rosario
Community Organizer
Misión Industrial de Puerto Rico, Inc.
P.O. Box 363728
San Juan, PR 00936-3728
Phone: 787-462-5088
Fax: 787-754-6462
E-mail: amaneser@coqui.net

Mississippi Center for Justice

The Mississippi Center for Justice opened its doors in 2003, giving Mississippi a critical capacity for social change: a home grown, nonprofit, public interest law firm that pursues racial and economic justice through advocacy for systemic change. The Mississippi Center for Justice carries out its mission through a "community lawyering" approach that advances specific social justice campaigns in partnership with national and local organizations and community leaders.

Martha Bergmark
President/CEO
Mississippi Center for Justice
5 Old River Place, Suite 203 (39202)
P.O. Box 1023
Jackson, MS 39215-1023
Phone: 601-352-2269
Fax: 601-352-4769
E-mail: mbergmark@mscenterforjustice.org
Web site: http://www.mscenterforjustice.org/index.php

Mossville Environmental Action Now

Mossville Environmental Action Now (MEAN) is a nonprofit corporation organized and based in Louisiana. MEAN is a membership organization dedicated to promoting environmental justice and protecting the residents of Mossville and Southwest Louisiana from toxic pollution.

Dorothy Felix
Vice President
Mossville Environmental Action Now
P.O. Box 891
Sulphur, LA 70663
Phone: 337-853-0035

E-mail: mossville4ej@yahoo.com
Web site: http://meannow.net

National Alliance for Hispanic Health/The Health and Environment Action Network

The Health and Environment Action Network (HEAN) is a project of the National Alliance for Hispanic Health and is funded through a grant from the W. F. Kellogg Foundation. HEAN is a national and locally driven effort committed to securing the right of all people to clean air and water. The network is currently active in four communities to document the nexus of environmental risk and health impacts, mobilize community solutions, and secure national and local action on the environmental risks that compromise the air, water, and health and well-being of communities.

Dr. Jane L. Delgado
President and CEO
National Alliance for Hispanic Health
1501 Sixteenth Street, Northwest
Washington, DC 20036
Phone: 202-797-4341
E-mail: jdelgado@hispanichealth.org
Web site: http://www.hispanichealth.org

National Hispanic Environmental Council

The National Hispanic Environmental Council (NHEC) is a national, non-profit, membership-based organization founded in 1996 and located just outside Washington, DC. NHEC seeks to educate, empower, and engage the community on environmental and sustainable development issues; encourage Latinos to actively work to preserve and protect the environment; provide a national voice for Latinos before federal, state, and nonprofit environmental decision-makers; and actively assist Latinos to pursue the many career, educational, and policy opportunities in the environment and natural resources field.

Roger Rivera
President and Founder
National Hispanic Environmental Council
106 North Fayette Street
Alexandria, VA 22314

Phone: 703-683-3956
Fax: 703-683-5125
E-mail: rogrivera@earthlink.net
Web site: http://www.nheec.org

Native Action

Native Action is a nonprofit, community empowerment organization located on the Northern Cheyenne Indian Reservation in Southeastern Montana. Founded in 1984 by members of the Northern Cheyenne Indian Tribe, Native Action has established itself as a leading model for citizen empowerment on Indian reservations. Native Action has been actively working for more than two decades to heal the wounds of the past century, correct the injustices and inequities of the present, and preserve the cultural heritage and land base of Native People.

Gail Small
Executive Director
Native Action
P.O. Box 409
Lame Deer, MT 59043
Phone: 406-477-6390
Fax: 406-477-6421
E-mail: gailsmall001@aol.com
Web site: http://www.nativeaction.org

New Jersey Work Environment Council

The New Jersey Work Environment Council (WEC) is an alliance of labor, community, and environmental organizations working together for safe, secure jobs and a healthy, sustainable environment. WEC links workers, communities, and environmentalists through training, technical assistance, grassroots organizing, and public policy campaigns to promote dialogue, collaboration, and joint action.

Rick Engler
Director
New Jersey Work Environment Council
142 West State Street, 3rd Floor
Trenton, NJ 08608
Phone: 609-695-7100
E-mail: rickengler@aol.com
Web site: http://www.njwec.org/index.cfm

New Mexico Environmental Law Center

New Mexico Environmental Law Center is a nonprofit, public interest law firm that provides free and low-cost legal services on environmental matters throughout New Mexico. Founded in 1987, the law center works with clients—often individuals, neighborhood associations, environmental organizations, tribes, and pueblos—seeking to protect the environment. The mission of the New Mexico Environmental Law Center is to protect New Mexico's natural environment and communities through legal and policy advocacy and public education.

Douglas Meiklejohn
Executive Director
New Mexico Environmental Law Center
1405 Luisa Street, Suite 5
Santa Fe, NM 87505
Phone: 505-989-9022
Fax: 505-989-3769
E-mail: dmeiklejohn@nmelc.org
Web site: http://www.nmenvirolaw.org/index.php/site/contact

New York Lawyers for the Public Interest

New York Lawyers for the Public Interest (NYLPI) is a nonprofit, civil rights law firm that strives for social justice. In partnership with member law firms, corporate law departments, and other organizations, NYLPI helps underrepresented people develop legal strategies to serve their vision for themselves and their communities. The "community lawyering" model drives much of NYLPI's work.

Eddie Bautista
New York Lawyers for the Public Interest
151 West 30th Street, 11th Floor
New York, NY 10001-4007
Phone: 212-244-4664, ext. 229
Fax: 212-244-4570
E-mail: ebautista@nylpi.org
Web site: http://www.nylpi.org

Newtown Florist Club

In the 1950s, Faye Bush helped organize the Newtown Florist Club, a group of African American housewives in a neighborhood of Gainesville, Hall County,

Georgia, who collected money to provide funeral wreaths for bereaved families in their community. Today, the group promotes youth development and organizes for social, economic, and environmental justice in Gainesville.

Faye Bush
Newtown Florist Club
P.O. Box 908403
Gainesville, GA 30501
Phone: 770-718-1343
Fax: 770-718-1388
E-mail: newtown193@aol.com
Web site: http://www.newtownfloristclub.com/2/index.php

Northeast Georgia Children's Environmental Health Coalition

The Northeast Georgia Children's Environmental Health Coalition is a network organized to address the growing concern of environmental toxicants in the lives of children. The major focus is to educate the community on links between environmental hazards and children's health, and at the same time promote prevention and precautionary action.

Jill McElheney
Vice Chair
The Northeast Georgia Children's Environmental Health Coalition
P.O. Box 275
Winterville, GA 30683
Phone: 706-742-7826
Fax: Call to notify
E-mail: jill@micahsmission.org
Web site: http://www.micahsmission.org/negcehc.html

Nuestras Raíces

Nuestras Raíces was founded in 1992 by the members of La Finquita community garden in South Holyoke, Massachussetts, to manage the garden and with the goal of developing a greenhouse in downtown Holyoke. Nuestras Raíces is building cultural pride as well as the ability of low-income Latinos in Holyoke to address environmental, economic development, substance abuse, and food security issues.

Daniel Ross
Executive Director

Nuestras Raíces
329 Main Street
Holyoke, MA 01040
Phone: 413-535-1789
E-mail: mdross@nuestras-raices.org
Web site: http://www.nuestras-raices.org

Organizing People-Activating Leaders

Organizing People-Activating Leaders (OPAL) is a community organization formed in September 2005 that works for environmental justice in the Portland, Oregon metro area. The organization supports ignored communities that fight against the oppression of pollution and social injustice. OPAL is concerned with the following issues: air quality and asthma, brownfields and contaminated sites, urban renewal and urban revitalization, land use and obesity, democratic justice and ignored communities, government accountability and diverse civic leadership, and community participation.

Kevin Raymond Odell
Executive Director
Organizing People-Activating Leaders
P.O. Box 4642
Portland, OR 97208
Phone: 503-997-3853
E-mail: kevin@opalpdx.org
Web site: http://www.opalpdx.org

People for Children's Health and Environmental Justice

People for Children's Health and Environmental Justice is a grassroots, environmental justice organization based in the Bay Area of California. The group serves low-to-moderate-income communities of color. Its mission is to safeguard communities' basic human rights to a safe and toxic-free environment, including clean drinking water and fish that are safe enough to be a regular part of a child's diet.

LaDonna Williams
People for Children's Health and Environmental Justice
P.O. Box 5653
Vallejo, CA 94591
1019 MacDonald Avenue
Richmond, CA 94801

Phone: 707-712-4088
E-mail: zzeria@aol.com

People Organized in Defense of Earth and her Resources

People Organized in Defense of Earth and her Resources' (PODER's) mission is redefining environmental issues as social and economic justice issues and collectively setting an agenda to address these concerns as basic human rights. PODER seeks to empower communities through education, advocacy, and action.

Susana Almanza
PODER
P.O. Box 6237
Austin, TX 78762
Phone: 512-472-9921
E-mail: poder.austin@gmail.com
Web site: http://www.poder-texas.org

People Organizing to Demand Environmental and Economic Rights

People Organizing to Demand Environmental and Economic Rights (PODER) is a grassroots, environmental justice organization based in San Francisco's Mission District. PODER's mission is to organize with Mission residents to work on local solutions to issues facing low-income communities and communities of color. PODER believes that the solutions to community problems depend on the active participation of all people in decision-making processes.

Antonio Díaz
Organizational Director
74 Valencia Street, Suite 125
San Francisco, CA 94103
Phone: 415-431-4210
Fax: 415-431-8525
E-mail: adiaz@podersf.org
Web site: http://www.podersf.org

Physicians for Social Responsibility–Los Angeles

Physicians for Social Responsibility–Los Angeles is a physician and health advocate-based membership organization working for policy and systems change to protect public health and the environment. As the physician and health professional voice for public health, the organization combines its commitment to science, public health, and social justice to create healthier communities.

Martha Dina Argüello
Executive Director
Physicians for Social Responsibility–Los Angeles
617 South Olive Street, Suite 810
Los Angeles, CA 90014-1629
Phone: 213-689-9170
Fax: 213-689-9199
E-mail: arguello@psrla.org
Web site: http://www.psrla.org/index.htm

Powderhorn Phillips Wellness and Cultural Health Practices Center

The Cultural Wellness Center engages people in using culture as a resource for taking responsibility for their own health and well-being. To achieve its mission of unleashing the power of citizens to heal themselves, the Center works with individuals, communities, families, professionals, and partners with academic institutions, government agencies, philanthropists, and other nonprofits.

Atum Azzahir
Powderhorn Phillips Wellness and Cultural Health Practices Center
1527 East Lake Street
Minneapolis, MN 55407
Phone: 612-721-5745
E-mail: atum@ppcwc.org
Web site: http://www.ppcwc.org

The Praxis Project

The Praxis Project is a national, nonprofit organization that builds partnerships with local groups to influence policymaking to address the underlying, systemic causes of community problems. Committed to closing the health gap facing communities of color, the organization forges alliances for building healthy communities.

Makani Themba-Nixon
Executive Director
The Praxis Project
1750 Columbia Road, Northwest, 2nd Floor
Washington, DC 20009

Phone: 202-234-5921
Fax: 202-234-2689
E-mail: mthemba@thepraxisproject.org
Web site: http://www.thepraxisproject.org

Redefining Progress

Redefining Progress is the nation's leading public policy think tank dedicated to smart economics. The organization finds solutions that ensure a sustainable and equitable world for future generations. While conventional models for economic growth discount such assets as clean air, safe streets, and cohesive communities, Redefining Progress integrates these assets into a more sustainable economic model. Working with government and advocacy groups, Redefining Progress develops innovative policies that balance economic well-being, environmental preservation, and social justice.

Y. Armando Nieto
Chief Executive Officer
Redefining Progress
1904 Franklin Street, Suite 600
Oakland, CA 94612
Phone: 510-444-3041
Fax: 510-444-3191
E-mail: anieto@rprogress.org
Web site: http://www.rprogress.org/index.htm

ReGenesis Health Care

ReGenesis Health Care (RHC) is a nonprofit organization that provides comprehensive, high-quality health care in a culturally appropriate manner. Any individual who needs health care or a place to call their medical home will be equally taken care of by board-certified physicians and qualified medical staff. RHC is one of 20 federally qualified community health centers in South Carolina and the only center of its kind in Spartanburg and Cherokee counties.

Harold Mitchell
Chief Executive Officer
ReGenesis Health Care
710 South Church Street, #2
Spartanburg, SC 29306
Phone: 864-583-2712

Fax: 864-583-2713
E-mail: regenesi@bellsouth.net

Rogers-Eubanks Coalition to End Environmental Racism

The Rogers-Eubanks Coalition to End Environmental Racism is an organization founded in 2007 to reverse the decision of the Orange County, North Carolina, Board of County Commissioners to place a regional solid waste transfer station in the Rogers-Eubanks community, to redress the injustices that affect the health and safety of residents in the neighborhoods which abut the Orange County Landfill, and to ensure that Rogers-Eubanks community residents and all North Carolinians have affordable access to safe drinking water, sanitary waste disposal, and safe communities.

Rev. Robert L. Campbell
Cochair
Rogers-Eubanks Coalition to End Environmental Racism
1711 Purefoy Drive
Chapel Hill, NC 27516
Phone: 919-933-6210
E-mail: rplcampbell@gmail.com
Web site: http://www.rogersroad.wordpress.com

Silicon Valley Toxics Coalition

The Silicon Valley Toxics Coalition is a diverse organization engaged in research, advocacy, and grassroots organizing to promote human health and environmental justice in response to the rapid growth of the high-tech industry.

Sheila Davis
Executive Director
Silicon Valley Toxics Coalition
760 North First Street
San Jose, CA 95112
Phone: 408-287-6707
Fax: 408-287-6771
E-mail: svtc@svtc.org
Web site: http://www.etoxics.org/site/PageServer?pagename=svtc_staff_and_board

Sixteenth Street Community Health Center

The Sixteenth Street Community Health Center has provided quality health care, health education, and social services on Milwaukee's, Wisconsin multicultural Southside since 1969. The Center is recognized as a leader in the community in terms of the excellent care provided as well as advocacy for public health issues. In 2008, Sixteenth Street provided health care services to 27,118 people; 25,185 of these people received medical care at 105,690 individual appointments; and 2,166 people received behavioral health services with 11,233 individual appointments.

Dr. John Bartkowski
1337 South Cesar C. Chavez Drive
Milwaukee, WI 53204-2714
Phone: 414-672-6220
Fax: 414-672-0191
Web site: http://www.sschc.org

South Bronx Clean Air Coalition

The South Bronx Clean Air Coalition is a nonprofit community-based organization engaged in organizing and educating the community on environmental issues, especially air contamination and toxics and waste management issues.

Carlos Alicea
Educator Program Development
South Bronx Clean Air Coalition
384 East 149th Street, Suite 330
New York, NY 10455
Phone: 718-585-6480
Fax: 718-585-6480
E-mail: calicea@pegasus.rutge rs.edu
Web site : http://www.icisnyu.org/south_bronx/Links.html

South Jersey Environmental Justice Alliance

The South Jersey Environmental Justice Alliance (SJEJA) is based in Camden, New Jersey, and several of its members are Camden residents. SJEJA intends to make Camden a significant focus of its activities because of the severity of the city's environmental problems. The general focus of SJEJA's work is in the eight counties that make up South Jersey. These counties include Atlantic, Burlington, Camden, Cape May, Cumberland, Mercer, Ocean, and Salem.

Roy Jones
Coordinator
South Jersey Environmental Justice Alliance

539 State Street, 3rd Floor
Camden, NJ 08102-1918
Phone: 856-365-9038
Fax: 856-365-0011
E-mail: sjenvironmentaljustice@yahoo.com
Web site: http://www.sjeja.org

Southwest Organizing Project

The Southwest Organizing Project (SWOP) is a statewide multiracial, multi-issue, community-based membership organization. Since 1980, SWOP has worked to make it possible for thousands of New Mexicans to begin to have a place and voice in social, economic, and environmental decisions that affect their lives.

Robby Rodriguez
Director
Southwest Organizing Project
211 10th Street
Albuquerque, NM 87102
Phone: 505-247-8832
Fax: 505-247-9972
E-mail: robby@swop.net
Web site: http://www.swop.net/mystore.htm

Southwest Research and Information Center

Southwest Research and Information Center (SRIC) was founded in 1971 for the purpose of providing information to the public on the effects of energy development and resource exploitation on the people and their cultures, lands, water, and air of New Mexico and the Southwest.

Don Hancock
SRIC Administrator
Southwest Research and Information Center
105 Stanford Southeast
P.O. Box 4524
Albuquerque, NM 87196
Phone: 505-262-1862
Fax: 505-262-1864
E-mail: info@sric.org.
Web site: http://www.sric.org

Southwest Workers Union

The Southwest Workers' Union is an organization of low-income workers and families, community residents, and youths, united in one organizational struggle for worker rights, environmental justice, and community empowerment.

Genaro Rendon
Director
Southwest Workers Union
P.O. Box 830706
San Antonio, TX 78283
Phone: 210-299-2666
Fax: 210-299-4009
E-mail: genaro@swunion.org
Web site: http://www.swunion.org/index.htm

Sustainable South Bronx

Sustainable South Bronx (SSBx) is a community organization dedicated to environmental justice solutions through innovative, economically sustainable projects that are informed by community needs. SSBx was created in 2001 to address policy and planning issues like land use, energy, transportation, water, waste, education, and, most recently, design and manufacturing.

Miquela Craytor
Executive Director
Sustainable South Bronx
890 Garrison Avenue, 4th Floor
Bronx, NY 10474
Phone: 646-400-5430
E-mail: ssbxinfo@gmail.com
Web site: http://www.ssbx.org/index.php

United Puerto Rican Organization of Sunset Park

The United Puerto Rican Organization of Sunset Park (UPROSE) is dedicated to the development of Southwest Brooklyn, New York, and the empowerment of its residents, primarily through broad and converging environmentally sustainable development and youth justice campaigns. Founded in 1966, UPROSE is Brooklyn's oldest Latino community-based organization. In 1996, the organization's mission shifted to organizing, advocacy, and developing intergenerational, indigenous leadership through activism around a host of environmental justice issues.

Elizabeth Yeampierre
Executive Director
Unite Puerto Rican Organization of Sunset Park
166A 22nd Street
Brooklyn, NY 11232
Phone: 718-492-9307
Fax: 718-492-9030
E-mail: elizabeth@uprose.org
Web site: http://www.uprose.org

Urban Ecology

Urban Ecology was founded in 1975 by visionary architects and activists who believed that cities should serve both people and nature. From the beginning, Urban Ecology has used urban planning, ecology, and public participation to help design and build healthier cities.

Milton Marks
Executive Director
Urban Ecology
582 Market Street, Suite 1020
San Francisco, CA 94104
Phone: 415-617-0158
Fax: 415-617-0016
E-mail: milton@urbanecology.org
Web site: http://www.urbanecology.org

Urban Habitat

Founded in 1989, Urban Habitat builds bridges between environmentalists, social justice advocates, government leaders, and the business community. Urban Habitat builds power in low-income communities and communities of color by combining education, advocacy, research and coalition-building to advance environmental, economic, and social justice in the Bay Area.

Juliet Ellis
Executive Director
Urban Habitat
436 14th Street, #1205
Oakland, CA 94612
Phone: 510-839-9510
Fax: 510-839-9610
E-mail: jre@urbanhabitat.org
Web site: http://urbanhabitat.org/uh/newfront

Virginia Organizing Project

The Virginia Organizing Project (VOP) is a statewide grassroots organization dedicated to challenging injustice by empowering people in local communities to address issues that affect the quality of their lives. VOP especially encourages the participation of those who traditionally have had little or no voice in our society. By building relationships with individuals and groups throughout the state, VOP helps and encourages them to work together, democratically and nonviolently, for change.

Joe Szakos
Executive Director
Virginia Organizing Project
703 Concord Avenue
Charlottesville, VA 22903-5208
Phone: 434-984-4655
Fax: 434-984-2803
E-mail: szakos@virginia-organizing.org
Web site: http://www.virginia-organizing.org/index.php

West County Toxics Coalition

The West County Toxics Coalition (WCTC) is a nonprofit, 501(c)(3), multiracial membership organization founded in 1986 to empower low- and moderate-income residents to exercise greater control over environmental problems that impact their quality of life in County Costa County, particularly West Contra Costa County (West County), in Northern California.

Henry Clark
West County Toxics Coalition
305 Chesley Avenue
Richmond, CA 94801
Phone: 510-232-3427
Fax: 510-232-4111
E-mail: henryc11@prodigy.net
Web site: http://www.westcountytoxicscoalition.org

West Harlem Environmental Action, Inc.

WE ACT for Environmental Justice (West Harlem Environmental Action, Inc.) is a nonprofit, community-based, environmental justice organization dedicated to building community power to fight environmental racism and improve environmental health, protection, and policy in communities of color. WE ACT accomplishes this mission through community organizing, education and training, advocacy and research, and public policy development.

Peggy M. Shepard
Executive Director
WE ACT for Environmental Justice
271 West 125th Street, Suite 308
New York, NY 10027-4424
Phone: 212-961-1000
Fax: 212-961-1015
E-mail: peggy@weact.org
Web site: http://www.weact.org/tabid/201/Default.aspx

Wilderness Inner-City Leadership Development

Wilderness Inner-City Leadership Development (WILD) is a program of the International District Housing Alliance since 1997. WILD is a leadership program for Asian and Pacific Islander immigrant and refugee youths and elders. It fosters leadership skills while instilling a social and environmental justice consciousness among its participants.

Sharyne Shiu Thornton
Executive Director
International District Housing Alliance
606 Maynard Avenue South, Suite 105
Seattle, WA 98104
Phone: 206-623-5132
Fax: 206-623-3479
E-mail: sharyne@apialliance.org
Web site: http://www.apialliance.org/about-us/contact/contact-us

Women's Voices for the Earth

Women's Voices for the Earth (WVE) is a national grassroots environmental justice organization. WVE's mission is to empower women, who historically have had little power in affecting environmental policy, to create an ecologically sustainable and socially just society. WVE works regionally and nationally to eliminate and/or substantially reduce environmental toxics impacting human health, and to increase women's participation in environmental decision-making. Currently, the organization's projects include a Mercury and Reproductive Justice Campaign to ban the sale, use, and disposal of mercury products in Montana; a Safe Cosmetics Campaign to protect the health and welfare of women working in the salon industry; and providing women across the country with technical and organizing support to address toxics issues in their local communities.

Erin Switalski
Acting Executive Director
Women's Voices for the Earth
Missoula Office
P.O. Box 8743
Missoula, MT 59807
Phone: 406-543-3747
Fax: 406-543-2557
E-mail: erin@womenandenvironment.org
Web site: http://www.womenandenvironment.org

Networks That Work on Health and Environmental Justice
Asian Pacific Environmental Network

The Asian Pacific Environmental Network (APEN) seeks to empower low-income Asian Pacific Islander communities to achieve environmental and social justice. APEN believes that the environment includes everything around us: where we live, work, and play. The organization strives to build grassroots organizations that will improve the health, well-being, and political strength of communities.

Roger Kim
Executive Director
Asian Pacific Environmental Network
310 8th Street, Suite 309
Oakland, CA 94607
Phone: 510-834-8920
Fax: 510-834-8926
E-mail: mroger@apen4ej.orgr
Web site: http://www.apen4ej.org/index.htm

Children's Environmental Health Network

The Children's Environmental Health Network is a national nonprofit organization whose mission is to protect the fetus and the child from environmental health hazards and promote a healthy environment.

Nsedu Obot Witherspoon
Executive Director
Children's Environmental Health Network
110 Maryland Avenue Northeast, Suite 505
Washington, DC 20002
Phone: 202-543-4033
Fax: 202-543-8797
E-mail: nobot@cehn.org
Web site: http://www.cehn.org

Coalition of Black Trade Unionists–Community Action and Response Against Toxics

The Coalition of Black Trade Unionists (CBTU) is part of the growing environmental justice movement that empowers community-based organizations to identify harmful or discriminatory conditions, mobilize their constituencies, and resolve local environmental health problems. In 1998, CBTU initiated an environmental action strategy. Several CBTU chapters have formed Community Action and Response Against Toxics teams, which—along with other safety and environmental allies—helps to educate and monitor issues such as illegal waste dumping and hauling in poor communities.

Carolyn Bell
Project Coordinator
Community Action and Response Against Toxics
CBTU National Office
1625 L Street Northwest
Washington, DC 20036
Phone: 202-429-1203
Fax: 202-429-1114
Web site: http://www.cbtu.org/justice.html

Comite de Apoyo a los Trabajadores Agricolas

Comite de Apoyo a los Trabajadores Agricolas (CATA), the Farmworkers Support Committee, is active in New Jersey, Pennsylvania, and the Delmarva Peninsula. CATA uses popular education methods to develop proactive farmworker leadership in workplaces and communities addressing issues including environmental justice and immigrant rights. CATA was instrumental in organizing the Kaolin Workers Union, the first group of Pennsylvania mushroom workers to secure a collective bargaining agreement.

Nelson Carrasquillo
General Coordinator
Comite de Apoyo a los Trabajadores Agricolas
P.O. Box 510
Glassboro, NJ 08028
Phone: 856-881-2507
Fax: 856-881-2027
E-mail: catanc@aol.com
Web site: http://www.cata-farmworkers.org/english%20pages/about.htm

Green for All

Green for All is a national organization working to build an inclusive green economy strong enough to lift people out of poverty. Green for All is dedicated to improving the lives of all Americans through a clean energy economy. The group works in collaboration with business, government, labor, and grassroots communities to create and implement programs that increase quality jobs and opportunities in green industry—all while holding the most vulnerable people at the center of the agenda.

Phaedra Ellis-Lamkins
Chief Executive Officer
Green for All
1611 Telegraph Avenue, Suite 600
Oakland, CA 94612
Phone: 510-663-6500
Fax: 510-663-6510
E-mail: officeofthepresident@greenforall.org
Web site: http://www.greenforall.org

Indigenous Environmental Network

Established in 1990, the Indigenous Environmental Network (IEN) was formed by grassroots indigenous peoples and individuals to address environmental and economic justice issues. IEN's activities include building the capacity of indigenous communities and tribal governments to develop mechanisms to protect sacred sites, land, water, air, natural resources, and the health of both indigenous people and all living thing; IEN also seeks s, and to build economically sustainable communities. IEN accomplishes this by maintaining an informational clearinghouse, organizing campaigns, direct actions and public awareness, building the capacity of community and tribes to address environmental and economic justice issues, and the development of initiatives to impact policy.

Tom Goldtooth
Executive Director
Indigenous Environmental Network
P.O. Box 485
Bemidgi, MN 56601
Phone: 218-751-4967
E-mail: ien@igc.org
Web site: http://www.ienearth.org/contactus.html

Indigenous Women's Initiatives

Indigenous Women's Initiatives (IWI) empowers indigenous women, their families, communities, and nations by applying indigenous values to contemporary settings and supporting projects that encourage sustainability by recognizing and strengthening leadership capacities across generations. IWI connects women involved in settings both rural and urban, university and civic with the Indigenous Women's Network at both national and international levels.

Agnes Williams
Coordinator
Indigenous Women's Initiatives
1272 Delaware Avenue
Buffalo, NY 14209
Phone: 716-332-6988
Fax: 716-332-6998
Email: info@iwinitiatives.org; iwinitiatives@aol.com
Web site: http://www.iwinitiatives.org/index.html

Joint Center for Political and Economic Studies/PLACE MATTERS

PLACE MATTERS is a nationwide initiative of the Joint Center for Political and Economic Studies, Health Policy Institute. The initiative is intended to improve the health of participating communities by addressing social conditions that lead to poor health. The organization's national learning community consists of 16 PLACE MATTERS teams responsible for designing and implementing health strategies for residents in 21 counties and three cities. The Health Policy Institute provides technical assistance to participating teams in the form of facilitation, Design Lab meetings (including providing national-level experts and peer-to-peer learning opportunities), technical assistance grants, and access to data. The PLACE MATTERS approach to reducing health disparities involves identifying the complex root causes of health disparities and defining strategies to address them. Addressing upstream causes of health (e.g., employment, education, poverty, and housing) is at the core of its work.

Dr. Brian D. Smedley
Vice President/Director, Health Policy Institute
PLACE MATTERS
Joint Center for Political and Economic Studies-HPI
1090 Vermont Avenue, 11th Floor
Washington, DC 20005-4928
Phone: 202-789-3530
Fax: 202-789-6390
E-mail: bsmedley@jointcenter.org
Web site: http://www.jointcenter.org/hpi/

Just Transition Alliance

The Just Transition Alliance was founded in 1997 as a coalition of environmental justice and labor organizations. Together with frontline workers and community members who live along the fenceline of polluting industries, the Alliance creates healthy workplaces and communities. The organization focuses on contaminated sites that should be cleaned up and on the transition to clean production and sustainable economies.

José T. Bravo
Executive Director
Just Transition Alliance
P.O. Box 210593
Chula Vista, CA 91921
Phone: 619-838-6694
E-mail: jtawest@yahoo.com
Web site: http://www.jtalliance.org/index.html

Michigan Network for Children's Environmental Health

The Michigan Network for Children's Environmental Health is a coalition of health professionals, health-affected groups, environmental organizations, and others dedicated to a safe and less-toxic world for Michigan's children. Through education, outreach, and advocacy, the Network seeks to protect Michigan's children from adverse impacts caused by exposure to widespread hazardous chemicals.

Genevieve K. Howe
Environmental Health Campaign Director
Ecology Center and Michigan Network for Children's Environmental Health
117 North Division Street
Ann Arbor, MI 48104
Phone: 734-761-3186, ext. 115
E-mail: gen@ecocenter.org
Web site: http://www.mnceh.org/home.php

National Black Environmental Justice Network

The National Black Environmental Justice Network (NBEJN) is a national preventive health and environmental/economic justice network with affiliates in 33 states and the District of Columbia. NBEJN members include some of the nation's leading African American grassroots environmental justice activists, community organizers, researchers, lawyers, public health specialists, technical experts, and authors addressing the intersection of public health, environmental hazards, and economic development within Black communities.

Payton Wilkins
Youth Coordinator
National Black Environmental Justice Network
P.O. Box 14944
Detroit, MI 48214
Phone: 313-833-DWEJ (3935)
Fax: 313-833-3955
E-mail: paytonwilkins@yahoo.com
Web site: http://www.nbejn.org/index.html#

New Jersey Environmental Justice Alliance

The New Jersey Environmental Justice Alliance (NJEJA) is a statewide umbrella, all-volunteer organization comprised of nearly 40 groups (as of this writing) and individuals. NJEJA has three regional components organized geographically within the state—Northern, Central, and Southern—that encourage and support local struggles. NJEJA meets quarterly. The regional groups are encouraged to meet quarterly and more often, as necessary. There is an 11-member steering committee, which conducts business and makes recommendations to the alliance between quarterly meetings.

Nicky Sheats
Director
New Jersey Environmental Justice Alliance
Thomas Edison State College
Center for the Urban Environment
John S. Watson Institute for Public Policy
101 West State Street
Trenton, NJ 08608-1176
E-mail: newbian8@verizon.net
Web site: http://www.njeja.org

New York City Environmental Justice Alliance

The New York City Environmental Justice Alliance (NYCEJA) is a citywide network that links grassroots organizations with low-income neighborhoods and communities of color in their struggle for environmental justice. NYCEJA is an umbrella organization comprised of member groups based in low-income communities throughout New York City. Founded in 1991 by environmental activists in New York's low-income communities of color, NYCEJA became a 501(c)(3) corporation in 1995. NYCEJA co-powers its member organizations to fight against environmental injustice by the coordination of citywide campaigns.

ShaKing Alston
Executive Director
New York City Environmental Justice Alliance
115 West 30th Street, Suite 1110B
New York, NY 10001
Phone: 212-239-8882
Fax: 212-239-2838
E-mail: shaking@nyceja.org
Web site: http://www.nyceja.org

North Carolina Environmental Justice Network

The North Carolina Environmental Justice Network works to empower affected communities through organized forums, conferences, and the support of member advocates on issues relevant to environmental disasters which negatively impact their health and quality of life.

Gary R. Grant
Cochair
North Carolina Environmental Justice Network
P.O. Box 61
Tillery, NC 27887
Phone: 252-826-3017
Fax: 252-826-3244
E-mail: tillery@aol.com
Web page: http://www.ncejn.org

Louisiana Environmental Action Network

The Louisiana Environmental Action Network (LEAN) was founded to help Louisiana citizens change the balance of power and challenge the continued economic and ecological destruction that had become institutionalized in the state. By empowering more than 100 grassroots, community organizations, and countless individuals, LEAN has already helped in gaining a tremendous foothold in the war to make Louisiana's communities safer, healthier places to live. LEAN's expanded efforts will allow the progress that has already been made to continue.

MaryLee Orr
Executive Director
Louisiana Environmental Action Network
P.O. Box 66323
Baton Rouge, LA 70896
Phone: 225-928-1315
E-mail: contact@leanweb.org
Web site: http://leanweb.org

Southeast Regional Economic Justice Network

The Southeast Regional Economic Justice Network (REJN) is a member-driven, movement-building network of the working poor. Based in Durham, North Carolina, REJN is made up of culturally and racially diverse organizations from across the South and eight nations in the Americas. Its members are low-wage workers, women, and youths—those who have borne the brunt of deeper economic dislocation and social crisis ushered in by globalization.

Leah Wise
Executive Director
Southeast Regional Economic Justice Network

P.O. Box 240
Durham, NC 27702-0240
Phone: 919-403-4310
Fax: 919-403-4302
E-mail: leah.wise@rejn.org
Web site: http://www.rejn.org

Southwest Network for Environmental and Economic Justice

The Southwest Network for Environmental and Economic Justice is an inter-generational, multi-issue, regional, binational organization of people of color comprised of 60 grassroots community-based, native, labor, youth, and student groups and organizations working for environmental and economic justice in the southwestern and western United States and Northern Mexico.

Richard E. Moore
Southwest Network for Environmental and Economic Justice
P.O. Box 7399
Albuquerque, NM 87194
Phone: 505-242-0416
Fax: 505-242-5609
E-mail: richardm@sneej.org
Web site: http://www.sneej.org

Youth Environmental Justice Groups
Boston Youth Environmental Network

The Boston Youth Environmental Network (BYEN) is a group of public and private sector organizations and professionals in the environmental education, park stewardship, youth development, and job training fields that aim to increase green youth employment and environmental educational opportunities both in and out of school settings. As a network, BYEN works to connect young people to both short-term environmental learning experiences and long-term environmental careers. Points of connection include network meetings, professional development, youth events, the BYEN Web site, and numerous collaborations.

Environmental Network Coordinator
Boston Youth Environmental Network
89 South Street, Suite 601
Boston, MA 02111

Phone: 617-345-5322, ext. 110
E-mail: dchavez@environetwork.org.
Web site: http://www.environetwork.org/aboutben/default.aspx

Literacy for Environmental Justice

Founded in 1998 by a coalition of youths, educators, and community leaders, Literacy for Environmental Justice addresses the ecological and health concerns of Bayview Hunters Point and the surrounding communities of Southeast San Francisco.

Literacy for Environmental Justice
800 Innes Avenue, Suite 11
San Francisco, CA 94124
Phone: 415-282-6840
Fax: 415-282-6839
E-mail: info@lejyouth.org
Web site: http://www.lejyouth.org

Environmental Justice Youth Advocates Program

The Community Coalition for Environmental Justice's Environmental Justice Youth Advocates Program has been instrumental in involving youths in community outreach and advocacy on environmental justice issues. To date, youths have done presentations, door knocking, outreach, a community survey, and organized a "toxic tour."

Community Coalition for Environmental Justice
1620 18th Avenue, Suite 10
Seattle, WA 98122
Phone: 206-720-0285
Fax: 206-720-5241
E-mail: justice@ccej.org
Web site: http://www.ccej.org/victories.html

Environmental Justice Youth Corps

The Duwamish River Cleanup Coalition's Urban Environmental Justice Youth Corps is a bilingual (English/Spanish) after-school and weekend service-learning program for high school students in South Seattle. The free program teaches young people about environmental health and justice issues, and blends community service and field trips with social and environmental issues in South Park and nearby neighborhoods.

Duwamish River Cleanup Coalition
1620 18th Avenue, Suite 10
Seattle, WA 98122
Phone: 206-954-0218
E-mail: contact@duwamishcleanup.org
Web site: http://www.duwamishcleanup.org/programs.html#justiceyouthcorps

Pacoima Beautiful Youth Environmentalists

Pacoima Beautiful Youth Environmentalists is a youth leadership and environmental education program for community youths ages 14 to 18 years. There are two parts to the program: the Environmental Justice and Education College Institute and the campus-based Youth Leadership and Environmental Awareness clubs. The Environmental Justice and Education College Institute works in collaboration with Project GRAD Los Angeles at San Fernando High School and Discovery Charter Preparatory Academy to reach more than 130 students yearly. The campus-based Youth Leadership and Environmental Awareness Club is a student-run organization at San Fernando High School.

Nury Martinez
Executive Director
Pacoima Beautiful
11243 Glenoaks Boulevard, Suite 1
Pacoima, CA 91331
Phone: 818-899-2454, ext.100
E-mail: nmartinez@pacoimabeautiful.org
Web site: http://www.pacoimabeautiful.org

The Point Community Development Corporation

The mission of The Point Community Development Corporation (The Point CDC) is to encourage youth development and the cultural and economic revitalization of the Hunts Point section of the South Bronx. They work with their neighbors to celebrate the life and art of their community, an area traditionally defined solely in terms of its poverty, crime rate, poor schools, and substandard housing. The Point CDC believes that residents' talents and aspirations are Hunts Point's greatest assets. Its mission is to encourage the arts, local enterprise, responsible ecology, and self-investment in the Hunts Point community.

The Point CDC
940 Garrison Avenue

Bronx, NY 10474
Phone: 718-542-4139
Fax: 718-542-4988
E-mail: thepointcdc@hotmail.com
Web site: http://www.thepoint.org

Roxbury Environmental Empowerment Project

Through Alternatives for Community & Environment (ACE's) Roxbury Environmental Empowerment Project (REEP), youth develop leadership in their home neighborhood through an environmental justice curriculum, leadership program, and youth-led organizing projects. REEP strives to ignite the spark of hope and passion that they believe exists in every young person and to fan that spark into a flame. Using an environmental justice framework, REEP helps young people understand that the appearance of and the problems in their communities are not their fault, they have the power to fight back, and they are not alone in their struggle for clean, healthy neighborhoods. Environmental justice gives a name to the oppression young people see in their community every day. REEP gives them the tools and skills they need to challenge that oppression and achieve improvements in the quality of life of their community.

ACE
2181 Washington Street, Suite 301
Roxbury, MA 02119
Phone: 617-442-3343
Fax: 617-442-2425
E-mail: info@ace-ej.org
Web site: http://www.ace-ej.org/reep

South Valley Environmental Justice Youth Media Project

The South Valley Environmental Justice Youth Media Project began in 2002 as a model to educate youths about environmental and health issues. The project facilitates youths involvement in the resolution of these issues from their perspective by engaging their participation in designing and implementing effective media outreach and education tools for public awareness.

Kalpulli Izkalli
1028 Ann Avenue Southwest
Albuquerque, NM 87105

Phone: 505-452-9208
E-mail: izkalli@comcast.net
Web site: http://www.kalpulliizkalli.org/svejymp.htm

Young Activists Organizing as Today's Leaders

Young Activists Organizing as Today's Leaders operates under the umbrella of the Little Village Environmental Justice Organization. The group works on issues ranging from fighting for cleaner air and space to immigration rights, but also completes fun, artistic projects like painting a mural and producing its own newsletter, *El Cilantro*. Participants can gain new leadership skills, learn about opportunities to get involved with their community, and receive help with college applications and scholarships.

Young Activists Organizing as Today's Leaders
Little Village Environmental Justice Organization
2856 South Millard Avenue
Chicago, IL 60623
Phone: 773-762-6991
Fax: 773-762-6993
E-mail: info@lvejo.org
Web site: http://www.lvejo.org

Youth for Environmental Justice

Youth for Environmental Justice (Youth-EJ) is a youth component of Communities for a Better Environment, a statewide organization working toward environmental health and justice. The group educates others as well as Youth-EJ members about racism and the many problems faced in their communities. Youth-EJ takes action to end these problems by developing campaigns and by supporting other organizations working to make their communities a better place to live.

Youth-EJ
Communities for a Better Environment
1440 Broadway, Suite 701
Oakland, CA 94612
Phone: 510-302-0430
Fax: 510-302-0437
E-mail: nmalloy@cbecal.org
Web site: http://cbecal.org/youth/index.html

Youth Ministries for Peace and Justice

Founded in 1994, Youth Ministries for Peace and Justice (YMPJ) works in the Bronx River, Bruckner, and Soundview neighborhoods in the South Bronx. YMPJ is a center for urban ministry dedicated to fostering peace and justice through youth and community organization and development. At the heart of YMPJ's mission is a framework which defines young people by their potential to effect social change. YMPJ promotes the development of indigenous leadership by mobilizing the already existing capacities of young people to reconstruct and sustain their community.

Youth Ministries for Peace and Justice
1384 Stratford Avenue
Bronx, NY 10472
Phone: 718-328-5622
Fax: 718-328-5630
E-mail: info@ympj.org
Web site: http://www.ympj.org

Youth United for Community Action

Youth United for Community Action, a grassroots community organization that was created by and is still led by young people of color (the majority from low-income communities), provides a safe space for young people to empower themselves and work on environmental and social justice issues to establish positive systemic change.

Youth United for Community Action
2135 Clarke Avenue
East Palo Alto, CA 94303
Phone: 650-322-9165
Fax: 650-322-1820
E-mail: epayuca@earthlink.net
Web site: http://www.youthunited.net/yucadwpgs/yucamain.htm

7

Funding Trends, Challenges, and Opportunities

NO SOCIAL MOVEMENT CAN sustain itself without funding. Foundation support is needed to provide the long-term systemic change necessary to address critical environmental problems in low-income communities and communities of color. According to Daniel R. Faber and Deborah McCarthy, authors of the 2001 *Green of Another Color: Building Effective Partnerships Between Foundations and the Environmental Justice Movement* Report, "the Environmental Justice Movement may be the most underfunded social movement in the United States. While funding for environmental justice has increased, it still represents less than 5 percent of all environmental funding given nationwide."[1]

The authors of *Green of Another Color* also point out that from 1996 to 1999, foundations provided an estimated $169.9 million in funding, an average of only $42.5 million per year for the entire environmental justice movement. They estimate that during that period, only two tenths of 1% of all foundation grants were dedicated to the environmental justice movement and only 4.3% of all environment-related grants were dedicated to environmental justice.

Writing in the 2007 *Toxic Wastes and Race at Twenty: 1987–2007* report, Michelle DePass, a former program officer at the Ford Foundation, summed up foundation funding support for environmental justice:

> As Executive Director, I saw what impact the UCC report had on the funding world as well. Foundations with program officers such as Dana Allston at the Public Welfare Foundation, Vic De Luca at the Jessie Smith Noyes Foundation, Stacey Cummberbatch at the Joyce Mertz Gilmore Foundation, and Anita Nager at the New York Community

Trust were compensating for the dearth of funding for issues of environment and race and class. They funded the environmental justice movement and provided support above and beyond financial resources.

Today, these foundations are still funding environmental justice as are several others, including the Ford Foundation—which established its Environmental Justice and Healthy Communities portfolio in 2000. However, the amount of foundation support for environmental justice research, advocacy and organizing is shrinking. Fewer and fewer organizations are able to find the type of sustainable funding to support their being a catalyst for systemic change in the environmental world. If we are ever to reverse the statistics of *Toxic Wastes and Race*, communities, environmentalists and workers must join forces to combat the root causes of pollution and environmental degradation in our communities. We also must provide financial resources and support for the innovative and creative initiatives that enhance the building of healthy, sustainable and just communities. Continued philanthropic support for community-based organizations and academic research and training centers working in the organizing and policy arena also is critical to this equation.[2]

Since the publication of *Green of Another Color*, some private foundations have dropped environmental justice funding and a few have entered the field with designated funding for environmental justice research, advocacy, and organizing. The number of foundations that have designated environmental justice programs has been shrinking in recent years. Funding support has been piecemeal—making it difficult for "building organizational infrastructure, community organizing, leadership development and participating effectively at the policy table."[3] Most environmental justice organizations are small, with fewer than five paid employees. The vast majority of these groups operate primarily as volunteer organizations.[4]

The larger environmental justice movement has message and image problems. It has been easier for some individual organizations, compared with the collective movement, to shake the narrow designation and expand their funding base by articulating a proactive, solution-oriented vision; "re-inventing" themselves; and merging and broadening their missions and agendas. As detailed in the 2007 *Growing Smarter: Achieving Livable Communities, Environmental Justice, and Regional Equity* anthology, the most successful environmental justice organizations have broadened and deepened their work to include such areas as smart growth, transportation equity, clean and renewable energy, green jobs, chemical policy reform, green chemistry, green products, parks and green access, green buildings, healthy schools, food security and food justice, sustainable agriculture, sustainable communities, equitable development, brownfields redevelopment, worker safety, health disparities, reproductive health and justice, immigrant rights, human rights, disaster response, regionalism and regional equity, climate change, and climate justice—all of which fall under the environmental justice umbrella.[5]

Recent funding gains appear to have benefited individual organizations more than advancing the larger movement. Nevertheless, some foundations understand and support the need for environmental justice research, advocacy, and organizing, while many others are unfamiliar with the broader scope of environmental justice. Program officers at foundations interested in environmental justice and health equity work should reach out to environmental justice groups and other organizations and develop plans to establish working relationships.

Why are foundations funding environmental justice? This question was partially answered in a 2008 report, *Environmental Health and Justice Scoping Report: Assessing the State of the Field and Opportunities for Philanthropic Investment in Environmental Health Through A Racial Justice Lens*, commissioned by the Health and Environmental Funders Network (HEFN): "Recognizing that EJ work is currently a hotbed of innovation in areas that the environmental and environmental health movements could benefit from including civic engagement and political base-building, green jobs, and the development of youth/next generation leadership"[6] has contributed to explaining the link between race, environmental protection, health, and sustainable development.

There are some hopeful signs regarding funding that connects environmental health with a racial justice framework. Some foundations are funding environmental justice work (though not officially labeled "environmental justice") even without having designated environmental justice portfolio. According to Kathy Sessions, executive director of HEFN, "there are some foundations that are funding environmental justice but not specifically through an EJ lens. It may be coming via a portfolio on health, environmental health, reproductive health, reproductive justice, transportation, climate, sustainable agriculture, sustainability, smart growth, immigrant rights, [or] civic engagement" (Kathy Sessions, Executive Director, Health and Environmental Funders Network;

e-mail, "Information on EJ Grantmaking," August 19, 2009). For example, HEFN collected 2007 data on grants from about 40 foundations doing grant-making related to health work and the environment. Of the $65 million grants awarded by the 40 foundations in 2007, $21 million or 32% went to broad categories of environmental justice.

Nongovernmental organizations seeking environmental justice in the twenty-first century will need to re-invent themselves, refine their message, and articulate the broad and diverse scope of work that falls under the environmental justice umbrella to attract foundation funding. This entails improved messaging to combat the stereotypes and perceptions that the environmental justice movement is so "fragmented, parochial, and dominated by single-issue approaches that its capacity to champion the types of fundamental social and institutional changes required to solve the ecological crisis is greatly diminished."[7]

Many environmental justice organizations have superb leadership, administrative, technical, training, organizing, policy advocacy, and legal skills but lack ample resources to develop their power base or attend important foundation briefings to promote their organization. According to Tina Eshaghpour, "These leaders cannot fulfill their potential or play a wider role in the Movement so long as funding is scarce or limited to a specific slice of an issue or community. Many groups lack the infrastructure to grow and become visible to the funding community."[8]

Environmental Protection Agency

The U.S. Environmental Protection Agency (EPA) was the first federal agency to award designated funding for environmental justice through its small grant program, which provided eligible organizations the financial assistance to build collaborative partnerships, identify the local environmental or public health issues, and envision solutions and empower the community through education, training, and outreach. Since its inception in 1994, the program has awarded more than $20 million in funding to 1,130 community-based organizations and local and tribal organizations working with communities that are facing environmental justice issues.[9] In 1995, more than 170 grants totaling $3 million were awarded. In 2008–2009, the number of grants was down to 40 worth $800,000. The number of grants in 2010 grew to 76, at a price tag of $1.9 million.

In 1995, the EPA established the Community/University Partnerships (CUP) grants program to help community groups efficiently address local environmental justice issues through active partnerships with institutions of higher education.[10] The program provided funding up to $300,000 for partnerships over 4 years. A total of 27 partnership grants worth $6.7 million were awarded from 1995 to 1998. The grant program was suspended in 1998.

In 1998 and 1999, the EPA funded the States and Tribal Environmental Justice Grants Pilot Program. The program sought to help states and tribes effectively implement their environmental programs.[11] For the 1998 fiscal year, the EPA awarded five grants, at $100,000 each, to four states (Vermont, New Jersey, Tennessee, and Texas) and one tribe (Kalispel Tribe of Indians, Washington State). In the 1999 fiscal year, the EPA awarded another five grants, at $100,000 each, to four states (Connecticut, New York, Indiana, and Minnesota) and one tribe (Maniilaq Association—11 Tribes of Northwest Arctic Region, Alaska).

In 2003, the EPA launched the Environmental Justice Collaborative Problem-Solving Cooperative Agreement program.[12] The grant program provided financial assistance to organizations working on or planning to work on projects to address local environmental or public health issues in their communities, using the EPA's "Environmental Justice Collaborative Problem-Solving Model." The program excluded colleges and universities. In May 2007, the EPA awarded $1 million in grants under this program to ten organizations (one grant per region) to work on improving the environment in low-income communities.[13]

In 2005, the EPA created the Community Action for a Renewed Environment (CARE) grant program.[14] The CARE program is designed to reduce pollution at the local level through a community-based program that works with county and local governments, tribes, nonprofit organizations, and universities to help the public understand and reduce toxic risks from numerous sources. The cooperative agreements are awarded in two levels. Level I awards range from $75,000 to $100,000 and help establish community-based partnerships to develop local environmental priorities. Level II awards, ranging from $150,000 to $300,000 each, support communities that have established broad-based partnerships, identified the priority toxic risks in the community, and are prepared to measure results, implement risk-reduction activities, and become self-sustaining.

In 2009, the EPA's CARE program distributed $2 million to nine communities. Since 2005, the grants have reached 68 communities in 34 states and territories. A recent evaluation by the National Association of Public Administrators recognized the CARE program as a solid tested framework for engaging communities and other stakeholders.[15]

In 2009, the EPA selected five state projects (in Alaska, California, Illinois, Pennsylvania, and South Carolina) to receive funding up to $160,000 each, totaling $800,000, under its State Environmental Justice Cooperative Agreement (SEJCA). The SEJCA grants provide funding so that states may work collaboratively with affected communities to understand, promote, and integrate approaches to provide meaningful and measurable improvements to the public health or environment in the communities.[16]

National Institute of Environmental Health Sciences

After prodding from environmental justice leaders, the National Institute of Environmental Health Sciences (NIEHS) held the "Health and Research Needs to Ensure Environmental Justice Symposium" in Arlington, Virginia, from February 10 through 12, 1994. During that same year, NIEHS launched the Environmental Justice: Partnerships for Communication Program.[17] The purpose of the program was to enable community residents to more actively participate in the full spectrum of research. To achieve this goal, the program sought to bring together three partners: a community organization, an environmental health researcher, and a health care professional to develop models and approaches to building communication, trust, and capacity, with the final goal of increasing community participation in the research process. A total of 33 grants were funded under this program.

Since 2002, NIEHS and the National Institute for Occupational Health and Safety have been working closely to address some occupational health issues in the context of environmental justice. NIEHS soon developed complementary extramural programs designed to increase community awareness of environmental health through outreach and science education. In addition, NIEHS established collaborative education and training programs for workers with the EPA to address environmental health issues resulting from hazardous waste contamination. Since 1995, NIEHS has funded the Minority Worker Training Program and the

Brownfields Worker Training Program that create lifelong work experience and jobs for African American and Latinos, who often get left behind economically.

In 2007, NIEHS initiated the Partnerships for Environmental Public Health Program (PEPH) to provide a structure to coordinate and support a variety of research and dissemination activities over 10 years.[18] Initiatives under the umbrella of PEPH are also designed to provide grant support in five major categories: research, communication and dissemination research, training and education, coordination, and evaluation. PEPH was conceived as an umbrella program that would bring scientists, community members, educators, health care providers, public health officials, and policymakers together in the shared goal of advancing the impact of science-based inquiries of environmental health threats of concern to communities on local, regional, and national levels. PEPH's emphasis is on protecting the health of groups that are disadvantaged by exposure to occupational or environmental hazards.

Partnerships to Address the Inner-City Asthma Epidemic

From 1998 to 2002, NIEHS and the U.S. Department of Housing and Urban Development conducted the National Survey of Lead and Allergens in Housing study.[19] The survey found that more than 46% of the participating homes had levels of dust mite high enough to produce allergic reactions, while nearly a quarter of the homes had allergen levels high enough to trigger asthma symptoms in genetically susceptible individuals.

Because of the rising incidence of asthma among inner-city children, NIEHS teamed with the National Institute of Allergy and Infectious Disease (NIAID) in 1991 to conduct the National Cooperative Inner-City Asthma Study, which was followed by the Inner-City Asthma Study, a long-term initiative that included seven asthma study centers across the country.[20] The goal of the study was to develop and implement a comprehensive, cost-effective intervention program aimed at reducing the incidence of childhood asthma in low-income areas. In November 2009, NIAID renewed the contract to continue studying asthma in children living in lower-income, inner-city communities. The new $56 million, 5-year award will support eight clinical and two basic research sites nationwide in the new Inner-City Asthma Consortium.[21]

Since 1998, the EPA and NIEHS have jointly funded 14 children's health research centers in universities around the United States that are investigating how asthma develops in children, which individuals may be most susceptible (including genetic factors), what environmental triggers may lead to asthma attacks, and how interventions can reduce the severity of asthma symptoms.[22] The centers comprise a national network of scientific and community leaders, health care providers, and government officials, with common goals of preventing and reducing childhood diseases in the research areas under study and translating the findings to the affected communities and the broader public.

In January 2009, NIEHS and the EPA announced plans to award a total of up to $9 million each year for 5 years to fund up to five Children's Environmental Health and Disease Prevention Centers and award a total of up to $3 million each year for 3 years to support up to four Formative Centers. Formative Centers are designed to foster and stimulate new research ideas in children's environmental health that are in the early phase of scientific inquiry and where the preliminary data or support or partnerships may be limited.

In 1999, the Robert Wood Johnson Foundation (RWJF) entered the pediatric asthma field. A 1999 staff paper provided the justification for the foundation entering the childhood asthma arena,[23] and soon after, the foundation funded a broad range of programs to complement the pediatric asthma work carried out by the federal government and by nongovernmental organizations. RWJF's initiative had six related components, each focusing on a different aspect of improving pediatric asthma treatment and management: addressing policy issues, training providers, examining barriers to financing and treatment, supporting community-based approaches to pediatric asthma management, testing new methods of providing emergency department–based care, and testing models of treating high-risk children in Medicaid managed-care settings. The RWJF pediatric asthma program included three national programs and three single-site programs.

National Programs

- Allies Against Asthma: A Program to Combine Clinical and Public Health Approaches to Chronic Illness. This 8-year, $12.5 million program, housed at the University of Michigan School of Public Health's Center for Managing Chronic Disease, supported seven local coalitions and their efforts to improve the prevention and management of asthma in their communities. This program was built on a belief within RWJF that local coalitions were an effective way of combating social and health issues in the community.

- Improving Asthma Care for Children. This $3.25 million program, housed at the Center for Health Care Strategies, whose offices are currently located in Hamilton, New Jersey, tested innovative approaches to managing asthma in children receiving care in five Medicaid managed-care settings.

- Managing Pediatric Asthma: Emergency Department Demonstration Program. This component attempted to find ways in which emergency physicians and nurses could educate and assist patients and their parents to better manage the illness and to direct them to community resources that could help them prevent or manage future attacks. The American Academy of Allergy, Asthma & Immunology served as the National Program Office for this 6-year, $3.5 million project that took place at four locations.

Single-Site Programs

- Policy Options to Improve Pediatric Asthma Outcomes in the United States. The policy component was carried out by the RAND Corporation, which received a grant of $228,000 from RWJF to develop a Blueprint for Policy Action calling for the creation of "asthma-friendly" communities, which are communities in which children with asthma are diagnosed quickly and receive appropriate treatment; health care facilities, schools, and social agencies are equipped to meet the needs of children with asthma and their families; and children are safe from the physical, social, and environment risks that exacerbate asthma.

- Physician Asthma Care Education. To improve the capacity of physicians to recognize and treat asthma, RWJF awarded $2.4 million to the University of Michigan School of Public Health to develop the Physician Asthma Care Education project, a multifaceted educational program to improve physician awareness, attitudes, ability, and the application of communication and therapeutic skills for asthma.

- Exploring Barriers to Financing and Treating Pediatric Asthma. The Center for Health Care Strategies received $500,000 to identify limits on financing and treatment for pediatric asthma and to disseminate its findings by means of a conference and publications.[24]

Although the RWJF asthma initiative was short lived—running from October 1999 through June 2005—it achieved some positive results: the demonstration sites achieved varying levels of success, but all five reported significant improvement in at least one area of childhood asthma management. The projects as a group demonstrated that Medicaid managed-care organizations can develop and implement interventions that have a favorable impact on the health care of children with asthma and on the cost of asthma care. In addition, the grantee organizations integrated a number of their projects' administrative and policy changes and clinical care delivery improvements into their routine practices and procedures.[25]

Progress and Prospects

Despite significant improvements in environmental protection over the past several decades, millions of Americans continue to live in unsafe and unhealthy physical environments. Pollution and environmental health threats are not randomly distributed across U.S. society. Predictably, lower-income and lower-wealth individuals and people of color are exposed to greater health hazards in their homes, neighborhoods, workplaces, schools, and playgrounds compared with the rest of society. Hardly a day passes without the media discovering some community or neighborhood fighting a landfill, incinerator, chemical plant, or some other polluting industry.

During its 40-year history, the EPA has not always recognized that many government and industry practices (whether intended or unintended) have adversely and disproportionately impacted poor people and people of color. It took decades for the government to acknowledge this fact and to begin implementing equal protection and dismantling institutional racism. The EPA is mandated to enforce the nation's environmental laws and regulations equally. It is required to protect all Americans—not just individuals or communities who have money to hire lawyers, lobbyists, scientists, and experts.

The right to a healthy and clean environment is a basic human right, but the nation is not color-blind. Because of the persistent challenges created by institutionalized racism, environmental justice advocates use a racial equity lens—applied to public health; exposure to harmful chemicals; pesticides; toxins in homes, schools, neighborhoods, and workplaces; faulty assumptions in calculating, assessing, and managing risks; zoning and land-use practices; and exclusionary policies and practices that limit participation in decision-making—to create environmental justice strategies. Many of these problems could be eliminated if the existing environmental, health, housing, and civil rights laws were vigorously enforced in a nondiscriminatory way.

The environmental justice movement has always emphasized prevention and precaution. The framework expanded the concept of environment to include where we live, work, play, and learn as well as the physical and natural world. The movement served to make vulnerable and marginalized communities visible, vocal, and empowered. Because of persistent societal inequities, the movement is as relevant and needed today as it was when founded nearly three decades ago.

The movement was founded by people of color in response to environmental injustice—largely toxics and environmental health threats in communities of color. Unlike the mainstream environmental and conservation movement, the environmental justice movement has never been exclusionary. Over the years, the movement expanded to become a multiethnic, multi-issue movement. However, even with an expanding base, it has held to the core founding principle of "people must speak for themselves," which has aided the movement in cultivating new leaders from communities most impacted by pollution and environmental threats.

The U.S. Environmental Protection Agency was created in December 1970 under a Republican president, Richard M. Nixon. Environmental justice was first elevated to the EPA under a Republican president—George H. Bush—and later expanded under President William J. Clinton, proving environmental justice is not a Republican or Democratic issue, but an American issue. In 2009, President Barack H. Obama made a bold move in selecting Lisa P. Jackson, the first African American to head the EPA. Having Jackson, an African American woman who grew up in New Orleans, Louisiana, at the helm of the EPA is historic. However, this progress is not sufficient.

The current environmental protection apparatus and land-use planning models, including zoning, underprotect some populations and some communities. Too often these systems manage, regulate, and distribute risks so that low-income households and families and children of color bear the brunt of health and environmental risks that other members of our society escape because of their economic resources, political clout, and the physical location of their neighborhoods.

The question of environmental justice is not anchored in a debate about whether planners and decision-makers should tinker with risk assessment and risk management. Environmental justice rests squarely on developing tools and strategies to eliminate unfair, unjust, and inequitable conditions and decisions that create, maintain, and exacerbate environmental, health, and racial disparities. This framework also attempts to uncover the underlying assumptions that may contribute to and produce differential exposure and unequal protection and bring to the surface the ethical and political questions of who gets what, when, why, and how much. This is the heart and soul of environmental justice.

For the past three decades, the movement has emphasized pollution prevention, waste minimization, and cleaner production techniques as strategies to achieve environmental justice for all Americans without regard to race, color, national origin, or income. The nation is not color-blind—and it never has been. And because of the persistent challenges created by institutionalized racism, environmental justice advocates set their strategies using a racial equity lens—applied to public health: exposure to harmful chemicals; pesticides; toxins in the homes, schools, neighborhoods, and workplaces; faulty assumptions in calculating, assessing, and managing risks; zoning and land-use practices; and exclusionary policies and practices that limit participation in decision-making. Many of these problems could be eliminated if the existing environmental, health, housing, and civil rights laws were vigorously enforced in a nondiscriminatory way.

Environmental justice leaders are demanding that no community, rich or poor, urban, suburban, or rural, Black, brown, yellow, red, or White, should be allowed to become a dumping grounds. They are also pressing federal, state, regional, and local governments to live up to their mandate of protecting public health and the environment. The legacy of environmental injustice remains a major barrier that impedes millions of Americans from achieving healthy, livable, and sustainable communities. It is unlikely that we as a nation can achieve the goals of sustainability until we address these issues, including that of racial equity.

Growing a Movement Built on Racial Equity

The following 20 recommendations emerged from a review and synthesis of the research, practice, and policy currently in place. They are offered in an effort to support and strengthen the work around environmental justice, health, and racial equity into the future.

Strategy 1

Support efforts of the larger environmental justice movement and its member organizations to "re-invent" themselves, refine their message, and articulate a proactive vision. Environmental justice organizations, networks, and university-based centers and programs need to better articulate their broad and diverse scope of work that falls under the environmental justice umbrella. Reinvention alone is not enough as long as institutionalized racism remains ingrained in the fabric of American society. Unfortunately, the environmental justice movement and individual environmental justice organizations in the twenty-first century must still combat stereotypes and artificial barriers that block opportunity.

Strategy 2

Assist organizations to build economically vibrant and socially just communities with an emphasis on health and well-being of families and children. Build networks, partnerships, and collaboratives that create trusting and nurturing relationships. Influence public policies that support safe, healthy, sustainable, and socially just communities. Support launching initiatives to clean up and develop degraded and vacant land exemplified by the following: use economic incentives to attract clean technology businesses; support job training and re-training the workforce that develops and produces "green jobs" for clean technologies; use zoning ordinances and other land-use tools to ensure healthy housing, adequate green space, and access to healthy foods and quality health care; and support transportation equity that ensures efficient and health-enhancing transit, safe biking, and walking routes.

Strategy 3

Support programs and strategies that strengthen the capacity of organizations to analyze and solve place-focused problems at the national, regional, statewide, and local community level. Nongovernmental organizations need support to grow a movement and leaders that emphasize solution-oriented, place-based strategies and approaches such as "Sustainable Development Zones," "Green Impact Zones," and "Health Impact Zones" to transform dying, redlined, and burdened neighborhoods into thriving centers of social connection, economic activity, and health-enhancing environments.

Strategy 4

Foster strong collaborations, alliances, and multigenerational networking. Assist with multigenerational, multidisciplinary, cross-issue collaboration, networking, and training opportunities for young people and emerging leaders who are transitioning to greater leadership roles. Broaden support for organizations that are in the process of leadership transition and expansion and collaborate with organizations to access organizational development consultants, researchers, scientists, educators, health professionals, and other "experts" with specialized training.

Strategy 5

Support youth and student work that intersects with a broad range of organizing areas across the broader environmental, health, and racial equity fields. Investing in youth and student organizing around environment, health, and racial equity provides an opportunity to connect youth leadership and young people to the broader goals of social change. Every successful social movement in the United States has had an active and informed youth and student component. Community-based organizations and university-based programs provide an important training ground for future leaders, technical experts, and professionals.

Strategy 6

Invest in work that intersects environmental health and reproductive health. Encourage multisector approaches that seek to change policies and practices designed to reduce toxic exposure and environmental degradation on women, children, and families. A number of groups are working on campaigns to regulate, disclose, and ultimately eliminate toxic ingredients in consumer products, including cosmetics, cleaning and household products, and toys and other products for infants and children. Groups are also calling for the elimination of toxic chemicals from consumer goods because of their long-term, cumulative impacts on human health and reproduction.

Strategy 7

Invest in long-term campaigns and programming. Demonstrating improvement in health outcomes takes time. A long-term commitment is necessary to change the conditions in underserved and environmentally burdened communities. Long-term campaigns, organizing, education and training, community-based participatory research, and policy infrastructure must be supported to enhance networking and collaborations with nongovernmental organizations within the environmental justice movement and with other organization allies working on similar topics and initiatives.

Strategy 8

Broaden the base of foundations and government funding of environmental justice and health equity work that extends beyond funding "silos." Environmental justice is integrative and holistic in its approach—encompassing a broad array of solution-driven protocols, including "anti-toxic" campaigns, pollution prevention, the Precautionary Principle, chemical reform, green chemistry, green products, food security, green jobs, green economy, and so forth. Incentives are needed to promote investment in clean technologies and healthy products, including renewable and nonpolluting energy, safer chemicals and materials, organic and sustainable agriculture, and sustainable fish harvesting, by using revenues from taxes levied on especially damaging consumer products and technologies.

Strategy 9

Help local governments, particularly public health departments, build and prioritize healthy community initiatives. Cities and counties must reorient their planning and operations to establish new methods of collaborating across sectors, and focus much more on prevention. Public health, medical, and social scientific research should continue to establish the link between health and community conditions, assess the effectiveness of existing policies, and help identify the priorities within and across communities.

Strategy 10

Strengthen the collaborative work on climate justice, public health, and vulnerable communities. Climate justice looms as a major environmental justice issue. Investments are needed in the growing climate justice movement, since the most vulnerable populations will suffer the earliest and most damaging setbacks because of where they live, their limited income and economic means, and their lack of access to health care. Yet low-income people and people of color contribute least to global warming. Unless appropriate actions are taken to mitigate its effects or adapt to them, climate change will worsen existing equity issues within the United States.

Strategy 11

Leverage public and private resources to support translations of environmental health and racial equity research. Information is power. Translation of research and technical reports and documents to highlight the link between community conditions and individual health and to provide insights about the effectiveness of different approaches must be fostered. Getting "community-friendly" research materials in the hands of local leaders can sometimes make the difference between a victory and a loss.

Strategy 12

Increase organization capacity and access to scientific data, policy analysis, and communications expertise. Translation of on-the-ground experiences of communities working on an array of campaigns must be supported. Nongovernmental organizations that represent low-income communities and people of color need rigorous research and scientific data, economic analysis, and the ability to communicate their work to constituencies in larger policy arenas.

Strategy 13

Document and disseminate "success stories." Environmental justice leaders have always subscribed to the principle that "people must speak for themselves" and "tell their own stories." In order to be authentic, "success stories" need to be told through the voices of the individuals who produced the successes. Vulnerable and environmentally burdened communities need to sense that change is possible in their lifetimes. Stories about advocacy and policy change need to highlight how change can happen and the ways it can make a difference.

Strategy 14

Help frame proactive communications and media campaigns. Stories about environmental, health, and racial equity need to emphasize communities, organizations, and people "overcoming" challenges and creating change. They also need to highlight the connection between health and protective factors in social, physical, and economic environments. Media stories need to provide possibilities for replication and attest that the broader movement can make a difference in communities across the country.

Strategy 15

Maintain a focus on racial equity and eliminating environmental and health disparities. Apply a racial equity lens to grant making. Achieving racial equity remains a core tenet of the environmental justice movement. Community advocates need to be involved in decision-making about the specific environmental and health challenges confronting their communities, the approaches to address them, and broader societal issues to ensure that new policies and practices are equitable and overcome previous barriers to full inclusion and participation.

Strategy 16

Help align formal and informal systems that support environmental justice, healthy communities, and racial equity and promote optimal health outcomes for vulnerable families and children. Innovative education, training and learning partnerships between schools, families, grassroots groups, communities, government, and the business community should be built that strengthen the conditions for healthy communities. Programs should be relevant to community needs, support community change agendas, be designed to document and better understand local issues, and provide diverse stakeholders with information needed to bolster efforts seeking policy change.

Strategy 17

Support movement for "toxic-free" neighborhoods and healthy schools. Healthy people and healthy environments are related. Advocates are fighting to get access to affordable housing in "toxic-free" neighborhoods and healthy schools. They are working on strategies to address the root causes of environmental risks, eliminate racial and ethnic disparities within geographic areas, and increase public sector investments in prevention and health promotion.

Strategy 18

Increase the percentage of grant dollars devoted to advocacy, community organizing, and civic engagement. Nongovernmental organizations need sustained resources to respond effectively to current challenges. They also need funds to plan for the future, capitalize on the philanthropic initiatives already underway, and leverage access to government benefit programs that support safe, healthy, and socially just communities.

Strategy 19

Increase general operating support and multiyear grants. The vast majority of environmental justice and health equity work is cross-disciplinary, holistic, and in most instances fit into several categorical program areas. In general, organizations prefer multiyear, reliable core support to project support, where the strategic goals of the funder and the nonprofit organization are substantially aligned. Reliable, predictable, and flexible multiyear core support allows organizations to carry out their mission and respond to new challenges and opportunities.

Strategy 20

Invest in community–university partnerships that advance the new "corporate environmental justice performance scorecard" and related Health Impact Assessment tools that assess the potential human health risk of toxic emissions at industrial sites. The time is right for achieving the goal of clean and safe environments for all Americans. More community–university partnerships are needed to support the health and racial equity goals of the environmental justice movement. There is a need to use health impact assessments to evaluate objectively the potential health effects of a project or policy before it is built or implemented. Health impact assessments should also be used to provide recommendations to increase positive health outcomes and minimize adverse health outcomes. More emphasis should be on planning for good health rather than managing risks. Since communities of color are on the frontline of chemical assault, we can reduce environmental health threats and racial disparities through defending and extending the right-to-know, linking modeling and monitoring, shifting pollution standards to assess cumulative impacts, and encouraging community, shareholder, and consumer activism.

Given the changing demographics in the United States, with people of color projected to become the majority by 2050, eliminating environmental and health inequality is not something that can be ignored or placed at the margins without dire consequences. By mid-century, Whites are expected to make up 49.9% of the U.S. population, Blacks 12.2%, Asians 4.4%, and Hispanics 28%. Children of color are expected to make up a majority of the children in the U.S. population in 2031.[26] Shifts in demographics also represent changing cultural values and political priorities. Beyond political imperatives, there are also moral and ethical grounds for remedying environmental and health disparities. To ignore or marginalize these historic trends and their potential impact is not in the best interest of keeping the United States competitive in the world. The question is, will adequate resources be committed to erasing the glaring environmental and health disparities that currently exist in the nation?

References

1. Environmental Justice and Health Union, http://www.ejhu.org/funding.html; Daniel R. Faber and Deborah McCarthy, *Green of Another Color: Building Effective Partnerships Between Foundations and the Environmental Justice Movement* (Washington, DC: Aspen Institute, 2001); and Elly Kugler, "Whose Environment Will Be Funded? Balance Popular Appeal and Community Accountability in Workplace Fundraising," *Responsive Philanthropy* (Summer 2006): 10–13.

2. Michelle DePass, "Funding Environmental Justice Work," in Robert D. Bullard, Paul Mohai, Robin Saha, and Beverly Wright, eds., *Toxic Wastes and Race at Twenty: 1987–2007* (Cleveland, OH: United Church of Christ Witness & Justice Ministries, 2007), p. 109.

3. Tina Eshaghpour, Environmental Health and Justice Scoping Report: Assessing the State of the Field and Opportunities for Philanthropic Investment in Environmental Health Through A Racial Justice Lens (Bethesda, MD: Health and Environmental Funders Network, 2008), p. 12.

4. Robert D. Bullard, People of Color Environmental Groups Directory, C.S. Mott Foundation (Flint, MI, 2000); and Angela Park, Everybody's Movement: Environmental Justice and Climate Change (Washington, DC: Environmental Support Center, 2009), p. 37.

5. Robert D. Bullard. Growing Smarter: Achieving Livable Communities, Environmental Justice, and Regional Equity (Cambridge, MA: MIT Press, 2007).

6. Tina Eshaghpour, *Environmental Health and Justice Scoping Report*, p. 9.

7. Daniel R. Faber and Deborah McCarthy, *Green of Another Color: Building Effective Partnerships Between Foundations and The Environmental Justice Movement*, Report by the Philanthropy and Environmental Justice Research Project (Boston, MA: Northeastern University, 2001), p. 11.

8. Tina Eshaghpour, *Environmental Health and Justice Scoping Report*, p. 28.

9. U.S. Environmental Protection Agency, "Environmental Justice Small Grants Fact Sheet," October 2009, http://www.epa.gov/oecaerth/resources/publications/ej/factsheets/fact-sheet-ej-small-grant-10-2009.pdf (accessed December 21, 2009).

10. U.S. Environmental Protection Agency, "Environmental Justice Fact Sheet: Community/University Partnership (CUP) Grants Program–1995–98," January 1998, http://www.epa.gov/compliance/resources/publications/ej/factsheets/fact_sheet_cup_grants_98.pdf (accessed December 21, 2009).

11. U.S. Environmental Protection Agency, "States and Tribal Environmental Justice (STEJ) Grants Program," November 1999, http://www.epa.gov/compliance/resources/publications/ej/factsheets/fact_sheet_stej_grants_99.pdf (accessed December 21, 2009).

12. U.S. Environmental Protection Agency, "Environmental Justice Collaborative Problem-Solving Cooperative Agreement Program: Fact Sheet," June 2006, http://www.epa.gov/oecaerth/resources/publications/ej/factsheets/fact-sheet-ej-cps-grants-6-13-06.pdf (accessed December 21, 2009).

13. Ibid., p. 2.

14. U.S. Environmental Protection Agency, "Community Action for a Renewed Environment: Basic Information," http://www.epa.gov/air/care/basic.htm (accessed December 21, 2009).

15. National Academy of Public Administration, "Putting Community First: A Promising Approach to Federal Collaboration for Environmental Improvement," May 2009, http://www.napawash.org/wp-content/uploads/2009/09-06.pdf (accessed November 29, 2010).

16. U.S. Environmental Protection Agency, "Environmental Justice Cooperative Agreements Fact Sheet," October 2009, http://www.epa.gov/oecaerth/resources/publications/ej/factsheets/fact-sheet-ej-sejca-grants-2009.pdf (accessed December 21, 2009).

17. National Institute of Environmental Health Sciences, "Environmental Justice and Community-Based Participatory Research," http://www.niehs.nih.gov/research/supported/programs/justice (accessed December 21, 2009).

18. National Institute of Environmental Health Sciences, "Partnerships for Environmental Public Health," http://www.niehs.nih.gov/research/supported/programs/peph/about/index.cfm (accessed December 21, 2009).

19. Patrick J. Vojta, Warren Friedman, David A. Marker, et al., "First National Survey of Lead and Allergens in Housing: Survey Design and Methods for the Allergen and Endotoxin Components," *Environmental Health Perspectives* 110 (2002): 527–532.

20. National Institute of Environmental Health Sciences, "Asthma and Its Environmental Triggers," May 2006, http://www.niehs.nih.gov/health/topics/conditions/asthma/docs/FactsheetAsthmaandItsEnvironmentalTriggers.pdf (accessed December 5, 2009).

21. National Institutes of Health, "NIAID Awards Five-Year, $56 Million Contract to Continue Study of Asthma in Inner-City Children," *NIH News*, November 4, 2009, http://www.nih.gov/news/health/nov2009/niaid-04.htm (accessed December 22, 2009).

22. National Institute of Environmental Health Sciences, *Centers for Children's Environmental Health and Disease Prevention Research Program: Review Panel Report*, April 6, 2007, http://www.niehs.nih.gov/research/resources/reports/docs/reviewpanelreportvf040607.pdf (accessed December 6, 2009).

23. Alexis D. Levy, Chapter 9, "The Robert Wood Johnson Foundation's Effort to Address Pediatric Asthma," in *To Improve Health and Health Care*, vol. XII, ed. Stephen L. Isaacs and David C. Colby (New York, NY: Jossey-Bass, 2009) pp. 209–230.

24. Ibid., p. 215.

25. Robert Wood Johnson Foundation, "Improving Asthma Care for Children," *Grant Results Report*, 2006, http://www.rwjf.org/pr/product.jsp?id=16848 (accessed December 5, 2009).

26. Hope Yen. "White Americans' Majority to End by Mid-Century," *theGrio*, December 16, 2009, http://www.thegrio.com/news/white-americans-majority-to-end-by-mid-century.php (accessed November 29, 2010).

Selected Annotated Bibliography on Environment, Health, and Racial Equity

FOR YEARS, COMMUNITIES HAD very little information, reports, or studies to rely upon in support of their arguments of unequal protection. Intense pressure was directed at government to document and come up with solutions to environmental problems that adversely and disproportionately impact low-income communities and communities of color. Today, environmental justice is well established as a topic of publications covering a range of areas: toxics; children's health; occupational health and worker safety; industrial pollution; environmental policy; sustainable, healthy, and livable communities; globalization and human rights; regional equity; urban health and the environment; transportation equity; energy; and climate justice, just to name a few.

Hundreds of books, reports, and monographs now analyze environmental health through a racial equity lens. Many of these publications are used in academia, public policy arenas, and community networking and organizing. The government reports, nongovernmental reports, and books profiled below represent a core selection of environmental justice publications over the last decade. This review is not meant to be exhaustive. It is meant to give a sampling of the depth and breadth of areas subsumed under the umbrellas of environmental justice and health equity.

Government Reports

1999

National Environmental Justice Advisory Council, *Environmental Justice in the Permitting Process: A Report From the Public Meeting on Environmental Permitting Convened by the National Environmental Justice Advisory Council, Arlington, Virginia—November 30–December 2, 1999* (Washington, DC: U.S. Environmental Protection Agency, 1999), http://www.epa.gov/compliance/resources/publications/ej/nejac/permit-recom-report-0700.pdf.

The U.S. Environmental Protection Agency's (EPA's) 1997 Strategic Plan commits the agency to ensure that all Americans are protected from significant risk to human health and the environment where they live, learn, and work. Requirements for the siting of solid waste incinerators must minimize, on a site-specific basis and to the maximum extent practicable, potential risks to public health or the environment.

U.S. Environmental Protection Agency, *Final Guidance for Consideration of Environmental Justice in Clean Air Act Section 309 Review* (Washington, DC: U.S. Environmental Protection Agency, 1999).

This policy guidebook is intended to improve the internal management of the EPA's environmental justice programs as it relates to EPA reviews made under Section 309 of the Clean Air Act. It does not create any right, benefit, or trust obligation either substantive or procedural, enforceable by any person, or entity in any court against the agency, its officers, or any other person.

2000

National Environmental Justice Advisory Council, *Guide on Consultation and Collaboration With Indian Tribal Governments and the Public Participation of Indigenous Groups and Tribal Members in Environmental Decision Making* (Washington, DC: U.S. Environmental Protection Agency, 2000), http://www.epa.gov/compliance/resources/publications/ej/nejac/ips-consultation-guide.pdf.

This guide responds to testimony before the National Environmental Justice Advisory Council (NEJAC) that, in some instances, existing public participation processes have provided inadequate opportunities for tribal communities and tribal members to have meaningful involvement in environmental and public health decision-making processes. As citizens of the United States, tribal members (as individuals or representatives of indigenous organizations) have a right to environmental and public health protection under federal law comparable with that afforded to other citizens.

2001

National Environmental Justice Advisory Council, *Environmental Justice and Community-Based Health Model Discussion and Recommendation Report* (Washington, DC: U.S. Environmental Protection Agency, 2001), http://www.epa.gov/compliance/resources/publications/ej/nejac/health-report-cover.pdf.

This report concluded that protecting the health of all communities presents a formidable challenge for the EPA. This responsibility does not rest solely with the EPA, but is shared with other federal departments and agencies as well as state and local governments. Environmental programs at the EPA do not adequately address low-income and poor people of color's disproportionate exposures to pesticides, lead, or other toxic chemicals at home and on the job.

Maryland Commission on Environmental Justice and Sustainable Communities Report, Governor Paris N. Glendening and Lieutenant Governor Kathleen Kennedy Townsend (Baltimore: State of Maryland, Department of Environment, December 2001), http://www.mde.state.md.us/programs/ResearchCenter/Reports andPublications/GeneralPublications/Documents/www.mde.state.md.us/assets/ document/environmental_justice/ejreport01/ej_2001_Annual_Report_part1.pdf.

The commission made several recommendations that could result in the development of more sustainable communities. The commission recommended that state agencies develop plans using the Maryland Department of Environment's Strategic Environmental Justice Plan as a guideline for developing a comparable approach in achieving their own agency missions.

2002

U.S. Environmental Protection Agency, *Status Report. Environmental Justice Collaborative Model: A Framework to Ensure Local Problem-Solving*, developed by Federal Interagency Working Group on Environmental Justice (Washington, DC: U.S. Environmental Protection Agency, 2002), http://www.epa.gov/compliance/ ej/resources/publications/interagency/iwg-status-02042002.pdf.

This collaborative model is an effective method for comprehensively and pro-actively addressing the interrelated environmental, public health, economic, and social concerns collectively known as environmental justice issues. This report summarizes the "lessons learned" from the ongoing projects, identifies the elements of success, examines the emerging outline of a coherent collaborative problem-solving model, and describes efforts to evaluate the model and specific demonstration projects.

2003

U.S. Commission on Civil Rights, *Not in My Backyard: Executive Order 12898 and Title VI as Tools for Achieving Environmental Justice* (Washington, DC: U.S. Commission on Civil Rights, 2003), http://www.usccr.gov/pubs/envjust/ej0104.pdf.

This report, based on commission hearings, interviews, research, and a review of relevant literature, reveals that while there has been some limited success in implementing Executive Order 12898 and the principles of environmental justice, significant problems and shortcomings remain. The report recommends that federal agencies coordinate and promulgate clear regulations, guidelines, and procedures for investigating, reviewing, and deciding without unnecessary delay Title VI claims, and that federal agencies implement formal Title VI compliance review programs to ensure nondiscrimination in programs and activities receiving federal funding.

Environmental Justice Foundation, *What's Your Poison? Health Threats Posed by Pesticides in Developing* Countries (London, England: Environmental Justice Foundation, 2003), http://www.ejfoundation.org/pdf/whats_your_poison.pdf.

This report summarizes health risks associated with pesticide exposure, particularly under conditions of use in the developing world. The information is drawn from more than 50 nations; the findings are especially relevant to countries in Asia, Latin America, Africa, and the Middle East, where pesticide use poses serious health concerns.

2004

National Environmental Justice Advisory Council, *Environmental Justice and Federal Facilities: Recommendations for Improving Stakeholders Relations Between Federal Facilities and Environmental Justice Communities* (Washington, DC: U.S.

Environmental Protection Agency, 2004), http://www.epa.gov/compliance/ resources/publications/ej/nejac/ffwg-final-rpt-102504.pdf.

This report stressed that low-income communities and communities of people of color near contaminated federal facilities, like such communities elsewhere, tend to have greater health problems on average than the American population as a whole. Community members blame many medical conditions and diseases on exposures to facility contamination, regardless of whether or not there is a medically understood link with diseases.

New Mexico Environment Department, *A Report on Environmental Justice in New Mexico*, Contract No. 04-667-1000-0003 (Albuquerque: Alliance for Transportation Research Institute, University of New Mexico, 2004), http://www. nmenv.state.nm.us/justice/Reports/NMEDFinalReport-Dec07-04.pdf.

The New Mexico Environment Department conducted four "listening sessions" in an effort to highlight environmental justice concerns in New Mexico. The goal was to get an idea of the nature of environmental justice from a grass-roots perspective.

U.S. Environmental Protection Agency, *Evaluation Report: EPA Needs to Consistently Implement the Intent of the Executive Order on Environmental Justice*, Report No. 2004-P-00007 (Washington, DC: U.S. Environmental Protection Agency, 2004), http://www.epa.gov/oig/reports/2004/20040301-2004-P-00007.pdf.

The report recommends that the EPA establish specific time frames for the development of definitions, goals, and measurements. It also recommends that the EPA develop and articulate a clear vision on the agency's approach to environmental justice. This report contains findings that describe problems and corrective actions recommended by the Office of Inspector General (OIG). This report represents the opinion of the OIG, and the findings in this report do not necessarily represent the final EPA position.

U.S. Environmental Protection Agency, *OSWER Environmental Justice Success Stories Report. Partnerships for Environmental Justice* (Washington, DC: U.S. Environmental Protection Agency, 2004/2005), http://www.epa.gov/oswer/ej/ pdf/2006_0428_final-2005-ej-success-stories_508.pdf.

The goal of this project was to investigate common environmental justice issues and concerns, and develop recommendations to address environmental justice issues and improve community involvement programs nationwide. Five federal facilities in South Carolina, Tennessee, Texas, New Mexico, and Washington were used as case studies.

2005

U.S. Government Accountability Office, *Environmental Justice: EPA Should Devote More Attention to Environmental Justice When Developing Clean Air Rules,* report to the Ranking Member, Subcommittee on Environment and Hazardous Materials, Committee on Energy and Commerce, House of Representatives, GAO-05-289 (Washington, DC: U.S. Government Accountability Office, 2005), http://www.gao.gov/new.items/d05289.pdf.

The General Accountability Office (GAO) was asked to examine how the EPA considers environmental justice during two phases of developing clean air rules: (1) drafting the rule, including activities of the work group that considered regulatory options, the economic review of the rule's costs, and making the proposed rule available for public comment; and (2) finalizing the rule, including addressing public comments and revising the economic review.

2006

National Environmental Justice Advisory Council, *Future Mechanisms to Enhance Stakeholder Involvement and Engagement to Address Environmental Justice* (Washington, DC: U.S. Environmental Protection Agency, 2006), http://www.epa.gov/compliance/resources/publications/ej/nejac/stakeholder-involv-9-27-06.pdf.

This report responds to the EPA's request for advice and recommendations on the following questions: (1) What venues and mechanisms would be most effective for the EPA to use to obtain public policy advice regarding specific environmental justice issues and concerns? (2) What mechanisms would be most effective for the EPA to receive timely advice on specific environmental justice issues and concerns that require action or decision on short notice? (3) What are the best mechanisms to use to continue to build a collaborative problem-solving capacity to address environmental justice issues and concerns among the EPA's regulatory partners and other environmental justice stakeholders?

National Environmental Justice Advisory Council, *The 2005 Gulf Coast Hurricanes and Vulnerable Populations—Recommendations for Future Disaster Preparedness/Response* (Washington, DC: U.S. Environmental Protection Agency, 2006), http://www.epa.gov/compliance/resources/publications/ej/nejac/gulf-coast-recomm-9-27-06.pdf.

NEJAC recommends that the EPA should work with appropriate agencies to address issues such as mold, debris, and sediments, and assess whether a health survey of Gulf Coast residents impacted by Hurricanes Katrina and Rita is appropriate. It is everyone's collective hope that, in the aftermath of such disasters, we as a nation not only will be able to rebuild healthier, more sustainable communities, but also will be better prepared to respond to future such events and to prevent their negative consequences.

U.S. Environmental Protection Agency, *EPA Needs to Conduct Environmental Justice Reviews of Its Programs, Policies, and Activities,* evaluation report, Report No. 2006-P-00034 (Washington, DC: U.S. Environmental Protection Agency, 2006), http://www.epa.gov/oig/reports/2006/20060918-2006-P-00034.pdf.

The survey results showed that EPA senior management has not sufficiently directed program and regional offices to conduct environmental justice reviews in accordance with Executive Order 12898. The majority of respondents reported that their programs or offices have not performed environmental justice reviews. The respondents expressed a need for further guidance in conducting reviews, including protocols, a framework, or additional directions.

2007
Jennifer Pike, *Spending Federal Disaster Aid: Comparing the Process and Priorities in Louisiana and Mississippi in the Wake of Hurricanes Katrina and Rita* (New York: Nelson A. Rockefeller Institute of Government, 2007), http://www.rockinst.org/pdf/disaster_recovery/gulfgov/gulfgov_reports/2007-09-17-gulfgov_reports_spending_federal_disaster_aid_comparing_the_process_and_priorities_in_louisiana_and_mississippi_in_the_wake_of_hurricanes_katrina_and_rita.pdf.

The report highlights some of the roadblocks Louisiana and Mississippi have been grappling with as they steer these somewhat flexible funding sources to the areas in need. The author emphasizes that what is at stake is the hospital dispute regarding whether Louisiana should rebuild the centerpiece of what many critics contend is a failed health care system and many proponents argue is the only way the poor can have access to adequate health care.

National Commission on Environmental Justice on the Gulf Coast and Lawyer's Committee for Civil Rights Under Law, *Protecting Vulnerable Coastal Communities: Meaningful Political Action and Strategies for Environmental Justice After Hurricane Katrina and Rita* (Washington, DC: Lawyer's Committee for Civil Rights Under Law, 2007), http://www.lawyerscommittee.org/admin/environmental_justice/documents/files/0001.pdf.

This report documents environmental activism on behalf of minority and poor communities before and after Hurricanes Katrina and Rita, identifies continuing threats to these communities, and provides recommendations to federal and state agencies for achieving environmental equality as recovery goes forward. The report focuses on the right of people to equal protection under, and enforcement of, the law.

U.S. Environmental Protection Agency Office of the Inspector General, *Public Liaison Report. Environmental Justice Concerns and Communication Problems Complicated Cleaning Up Ringwood Mines/Landfill Site*, Report 2007-00016 (Washington, DC: U.S. Environmental Protection Agency, 2007), http://www.epa.gov/oig/reports/2007/20070402-2007-P-00016.pdf.

The report found that problems with communications and relationships impeded effective cooperation between the EPA and residents. The report indicated that the EPA did not find evidence to indicate that the U.S. (EPA's) actions or decision-making to investigate or remediate environmental conditions at the Ringwood Mines/Landfill site were affected by the area's racial, cultural, or socioeconomic status. Many of the residents believed their health was adversely affected by exposure to site contamination.

U.S. Environmental Protection Agency Office of Solid Waste, *An Assessment of Environmental Problems Associated With Recycling of Hazardous Secondary Materials* (Washington, DC: U.S. Environmental Protection Agency, 2007), http://www.earthjustice.org/library/references/2007-epa-report-summary-on-hazardous-waste-recycling-sites.pdf.

The study identifies and characterizes cases of environmental damage that have been attributed to some type of hazardous material recycling activity, and that are relevant for the purpose of this rule-making effort. The report is expected to assist the EPA in making decisions as to the scope and substance of these regulatory revisions.

U.S. Government Accountability Office, Report to Congressional Committees, *Hurricane Katrina: EPA's Current and Future Environmental Protection Efforts Could Be Enhanced by Addressing Issues and Challenges Faced on the Gulf Coast*, GAO-07-651 (Washington, DC: U.S. Government Accountability Office, 2007), http://www.gao.gov/new.items/d07651.pdf.

The GAO recommends that the EPA develop an asbestos air monitoring plan for New Orleans, improve its communications on environmental risks for future disasters, and take steps to address several challenges the EPA has faced.

U.S. Government Accountability Office, *Environmental Right-To-Know: EPA's Recent Rule Could Reduce Availability of Toxic Chemical Information Used to Assess Environmental Justice* (Washington, DC: U.S. Government Accountability Office, 2007), http://www.gao.gov/new.items/d08115t.pdf.

This report states that a change to Toxics Release Inventory (TRI) reporting requirements may not affect how much toxic waste is released to the environment, but it could affect how much information communities will know about those toxic releases. Also in this report, GAO made several recommendations to improve the EPA's adherence to environmental justice principles.

2008

Staff Report Subcommittee on Investigations and Oversight by Committee on Science and Technology for U.S. House of Representatives, *Toxic Trailers–Toxic Lethargy: How the Centers for Disease Control and Prevention Has Failed to Protect the Public Health* (Washington, DC: Committee on Science and Technology, 2008), http://democrats.science.house.gov/Media/File/Commdocs/ATSDR_Staff_Report_9.22.08.pdf.

The report provides a detailed examination of the Agency for Toxic Substances and Disease Registry's (ATSDR) response to the Federal Emergency Management Agency (FEMA) trailer/formaldehyde issue and the Agency's production, approval, and release of that health consultation. ATSDR failed to translate its scientific findings and facts into appropriate public health actions to properly inform and warn FEMA and the tens of thousands of Hurricanes Katrina and Rita survivors living in FEMA-provided trailers and mobile homes of the potential health risks they faced from exposure to formaldehyde.

2009

U.S. Environmental Protection Agency Pacific Southwest Region 9, *Environmental Justice Resource Guide: A Handbook for Communities and Decision-Makers* (Washington, DC: U.S. Environmental Protection Agency, 2009), http://www.epa.gov/region09/ej/ej-resource-guide-booklet.pdf.

This guide for community organizers and decision-makers includes information on agency funding sources, training opportunities, and technical and program assistance for minority and low-income communities disproportionately affected by environmental and public health impacts.

U.S. Government Accountability Office, *Hurricane Katrina: Barriers to Mental Health Services for Children in Greater New Orleans, Although Federal Grants Are Helping to Address Them* (Washington, DC: U.S. Government Accountability Office, 2009), http://www.gao.gov/new.items/d09563.pdf.

This report discusses how Hurricane Katrina devastated the health care system in the greater New Orleans area, resulting in the closure of many area hospitals and clinics, including Charity and University hospitals, which provided outpatient services through clinics in addition to inpatient services. These hospitals, which were part of the statewide Louisiana State University public hospital system, had been the main points of entry for many low-income and uninsured children and families to gain access to health care services.

Nongovernmental Organization Reports

1999

Robert D. Bullard, *Sprawl Atlanta: Social Equity Dimensions of Uneven Growth and Development* (Atlanta, GA: Environmental Justice Resource Center, 1999), http://www.ejrc.cau.edu/sprawl%20report.PDF.

The report includes an analysis of factors that contribute to urban sprawl and their consequences. It also outlines policy recommendations and an action agenda. An extensive use of geographic information system analysis is used in mapping and graphically illustrating the environmental consequences of sprawl on low-income communities and communities of color in the region.

Institute of Medicine, *Toward Environmental Justice: Research, Education, and Health Policy Needs* (Washington, DC: National Academy of Sciences, 1999), http://www.nap.edu/catalog.php?record_id=6034.

This report concluded that low-income communities and communities of color are exposed to higher levels of pollution (toxic waste, pesticide runoff, and other hazardous by-products) than is the rest of the nation, and that these same populations experience certain diseases in greater number than do more affluent White communities. The report explores how current fragmentation in health policy could be replaced with greater coordination among federal, state, and local parties.

Natural Resources Defense Council, *Paving Paradise: Sprawl and the Environment* (Washington, DC: Natural Resources Defense Council, 1999), http://www.nrdc.org/cities/smartGrowth/rpave.asp.

This report was adapted and condensed from the book *Once There Were Greenfields: How Urban Sprawl Is Undermining America's Environment, Economy and Social Fabric,* by F. Kaid Benfield, Matthew D. Raimi, and Donald Chen (New York: Natural Resources Defense Council, 1999). The report answers the following questions: Where will these new citizens live, work, and shop? How important is it that we, as environmentalists who care about sustainability, bring resources to bear on the shape of America's future urban development?

2000
Hillary Gross, Hannah Shafsky, and Kara Brown, *Environmental Justice: A Review of State Responses* (San Francisco, CA: Public Law Research Institute at Hastings College of Law, 2000), http://www.uchastings.edu/site_files/environjustice.pdf.

In an effort to provide guidance to the California Environmental Justice Work Group in implementing SB 115, this report provides a brief overview of the federal environmental justice framework and a more comprehensive look at state environmental justice programs. The report at the time was the most comprehensive survey of state practices, and presents a useful snapshot of this dynamic field.

National Academy of Public Administration, *Transforming Environmental Protection for the 21st Century* (Washington, DC: National Academy of Public Administration, 2000), http://www.epa.gov/oar/caaac/aqm/aqm-06-16-05-transform.pdf.

The report provides a strategy for reform at the federal, state, and local levels of government, as well as in the private sector. It concludes that the EPA and Congress should focus aggressively on reducing ground-level ozone and smog, using a combination of market-based tools to reduce emissions of several of its chemical precursors: nitrogen oxide particulates and, where adequate safeguards are in place, volatile organic compounds.

Robert D. Bullard, *People of Color Environmental Groups Directory 2000* (Flint, MI: C.S. Mott Foundation, 2000), http://www.ejrc.cau.edu/raceequitysmart growth.htm.

This report examines how urban sprawl impacts the daily lives of people of color. The report concludes that a national communication strategy is needed to disseminate the equity and smart growth message to people-of-color leaders, organizations, educational institutions, professional associations, fraternal orders, business associations, and other voluntary associations, such as church-based, civil rights, education, housing, community development, bankers, health care, and legal associations.

2001

Eric Mann, Barbara Lott Holland, Geoff Ray, and Kikanaza Ramsey, *An Environmental Justice Strategy for Urban Transportation in Atlanta* (Los Angeles, CA: Labor/Community Strategy Center, 2001), http://www.thestrategycenter. org/report/environmental-justice-strategy-urban-transportation-atlanta.

This report provides significant detail to show the structural similarities of Los Angeles and Atlanta and the direct relevant applications of the Los Angeles Bus Riders Union experience to the Atlanta transportation equity movement.

National Academy of Public Administration, *Environmental Justice in EPA Permitting: Reducing Pollution in High-Risk Communities Is Integral to the Agency's Mission* (Washington, DC: National Academy of Public Administration, 2001), http://

www.issuelab.org/research/environmental_justice_in_epa_permitting_reducing_
pollution_in_high_risk_communities_is_integral_to_the_agencys_mission.

This report is designed to help community members and other stakeholders gain a better understanding of how they can more effectively bring environmental justice concerns to the attention of the EPA's permitting programs.

National Academy of Public Administration, *Evaluating Environmental Progress: How EPA and the States Can Improve the Quality of Enforcement and Compliance Information* (Washington, DC: National Academy of Public Administration, 2001), http://www.napawash.org/pc_economy_environment/environmental.pdf.

This report evaluates federal and state enforcement data as requested by Congress, but it does so in the context of recommendations made by other National Academy of Public Administration panels during the past several years.

2002

Black Leadership Forum, Clear the Air, Georgia Coalition for the People's Agenda and The Southern Organizing Committee for Economic and Social Justice, *Air of Justice: African Americans & Power Plant Pollution* (Washington, DC: Pew Charitable Trusts, 2002), http://www.energyjustice.net/coal/Air_of_Injustice.pdf.

This report chronicles how African Americans are affected by the air pollution emitted by our nation's biggest polluters: coal-fired power plants. These plants release millions of pounds per year of a wide variety of chemicals to the air, water, and landfills. It also describes the relationship between power plant pollutants like sulfur dioxide, particulate matter, mercury, nitrogen oxides, and carbon dioxide and environmental health issues that have the most impact on African Americans: pediatric asthma, infant death rates, emergency room visits and hospitalizations, fish contamination, and climate change.

Elizabeth Crowe and Mike Schade, *Learning Not to Burn: A Primer for Citizens on Alternatives to Burning Hazardous Waste* (Berea, KY: Chemical Weapons Working Group, 2002), http://www.cwwg.org/learningnottoburn.pdf.

This primer is intended to fill a gap in information on nonincineration technologies for hazardous waste disposal and present strategies that can be used in parallel with clean production and zero waste efforts to bring about sustainable solutions and environmental justice.

National Academy of Public Administration, *Models for Change: Efforts by Four States to Address Environmental Justice* (Washington, DC: National Academy of Public Administration, 2002), http://www.issuelab.org/research/models_for_change_efforts_by_four_states_to_address_environmental_justice.

The report recommends that states articulate a clear commitment to environmental justice, conduct a comprehensive examination of applicable state constitutional provisions, eliminate backlogs for permit renewals, identify and reduce environmental hazards in communities with high exposure levels, and enhance public participation by training state staff to value and utilize local knowledge.

We Act for Environmental Justice, *Human Genetics, Environment, and Communities of Color: Ethical and Social Implications* (New York, NY: We Act for Environmental Justice, 2002), http://www.weact.org/Publications/OtherPublications/tabid/260/Default.aspx.

This report and conference proceedings provide rich information on environmental justice, environmental health, and genetics, as well as recommendations from community-based environmental justice groups.

2003
Eliot Allen and F. Kaid Benfield, *Environmental Characteristics of Smart Growth Neighborhoods Phase II: Two Nashville Neighborhoods* (Washington, DC: Natural Resources Defense Council, 2003), http://www.nrdc.org/cities/smartGrowth/char/charnash.pdf.

This report (also conducted for the National Resources Defense Council in cooperation with the EPA) continues previous research by comparing two neighborhoods in Nashville, Tennessee, and suggests that the combination of better transportation accessibility and a modest increase in land-use density can produce measurable benefits even when both sites are automobile-oriented and suburban in character.

National Academy of Public Administration, *Addressing Community Concerns: How Environmental Justice Relates to Land Use Planning and Zoning* (Washington,

DC: National Academy of Public Administration, 2003), http://www.issuelab. org/research/addressing_community_concerns_how_environmental_justice_ relates_to_land_use_planning_and_zoning.

This study is designed to help the public understand how land-use planning and zoning relate to environmental justice, both in terms of resolving current issues and preventing future problems. The study also highlights opportunities for engaging the public in the local planning and zoning decisions that affect their communities.

2004

Steven Bonorris, *Environmental Justice For All: A Fifty-State Survey of Legislation, Policies, and Initiatives* (San Francisco, CA: American Bar Association and Hastings College of Law, 2004), http://www.abanet.org/irr/committees/environ mental/statestudy.pdf.

The report identifies the statutes, policies, and initiatives that states have undertaken to give force of law and tangible meaning to the goal of environmental justice. The report finds that from the first policy issued in 1993 to the present, more than 30 states have expressly addressed environmental justice, demonstrating increased attention to the issue at a political level. The report includes Performance Partnership Agreements (PPAs) between the EPA regional offices and states, whether the PPA expressly references environmental justice.

Joint Center for Political and Economic Studies, *A Place for Healthier Living: Improving Access to Physical Activity and Healthy Foods* (Washington, DC: Joint Center for Political and Economic Studies, 2004), http://www.jointcenter.org/ publications_recent_publications/health/a_place_for_healthier_living_improving_ access_to_physical_activity_and_healthy_foods.

The report indicates that there are significant, persistent racial, ethnic, and income disparities in the prevalence and consequences of chronic illnesses (heart disease, stroke, type 2 diabetes, and cancer) that are linked not just to nutrition and physical activity directly, but also to the social, economic, and community-level conditions in which people live.

Joint Center for Political and Economic Studies and PolicyLink, *Building Stronger Communities for Better Health* (Washington, DC: Joint Center for

Political and Economic Studies, 2004), http://www.jointcenter.org/publications_recent_publications/health/building_stronger_communities_for_better_health.

This report presents a framework for understanding how community conditions affect individuals' health both directly and indirectly. It discusses how attention to these determinants of health requires a shift from a narrow focus on treatment to a broader approach that includes prevention and health promotion. The overarching roles that race, ethnicity, and socioeconomic status play in health status are explored within this context, and the case is made that the legacy of racism must be addressed if the continuing health disparities between White Americans and Latino and African Americans are to be eliminated.

Jonathan A. Patz, Patrick L. Kinney, Michelle L. Bell, et al., *Heat Advisory: How Global Warming Causes More Bad Air Days* (Washington, DC.: Natural Resources Defense Council, 2004), http://www.nrdc.org/globalWarming/heatadvisory/heatadvisory.pdf.

The analysis assesses how much smog levels could increase over the eastern United States because of global warming and what that could mean for public health. Smog is formed when pollutants from vehicles, factories, and other sources mix with sunlight and heat, which means key air quality measures are highly sensitive to temperature. Researchers project that, by mid-century, people living in 15 cities in the eastern United States could see a 60% increase, from 12 to almost 20 days per summer, in the average number of days exceeding the health-based 8-hour ozone standard established by the EPA.

Adrianna Quintero-Somaini and Mayra Quirindongo, *Hidden Danger: Environmental Health Threats in the Latino Community* (Washington, DC: Natural Resources Defense Council, 2004), http://www.nrdc.org/health/effects/latino/english/latino_en.pdf.

This report discusses hazards (air pollution, unsafe drinking water, pesticides, lead and mercury contamination) that can cause serious health problems, including an increased risk of asthma and cancer; waterborne diseases such as giardiasis, hepatitis, and cholera; and neurological and developmental problems. This report also underscores the urgent need for government action on these environmental health threats.

Redefining Progress and Congressional Black Caucus Foundation, *African Americans and Climate Change: An Unequal Burden* (Oakland, CA: Redefining Progress, 2004), http://www.rprogress.org/press/releases/040721_climate.htm.

The report forecasts a difference in the impact of climate change on people of various socioeconomic and racial groups. The report examines the relationship between energy policy, climate change, and the African American population to inform the growing policy discussion. The basic conclusions of this report are that there is a stark disparity in the United States between those who benefit from the causes of climate change and those who bear the costs of climate change.

Urban Habitat, "Reclaiming Our Resources: Imperialism and Environmental Justice," *Race, Poverty and Environment* (Oakland, CA : Urban Habitat, Summer 2004), http://urbanhabitat.org/11-1.

In this report, there is discussion of the importance of geographic location and the power of one place over another. The fight over space and place has characterized urban development throughout the United States. Historically, colonialism's impact on indigenous populations' space and place explains how exploitation of indigenous land and resources continues today.

Urban Habitat, "Burden of Proof: Using Research for Environmental Justice," *Race, Poverty, and Environment* (Oakland, CA: Urban Habitat, 2004/2005), http://urbanhabitat.org/11-2.

This report focuses on methods used to protect communities of color. The environmental justice movement must be engaged in the debate over environmental science and research and become active participants in shaping the decisions that affect the lives of people of color.

2005

Kaid Benfield, Sarah Chasis, David Doniger, et al., *After Katrina: New Solutions for Safe Communities and a Secure Energy Future* (Washington, DC: Natural Resources Defense Council, 2005), http://www.nrdc.org/legislation/hk/hk.pdf.

This report represents the combined efforts of experts on public health, toxic waste, urban design, coastal protection, energy security, and global warming to offer up a set of policies and practices to protect the safety and well-being of Gulf Coast residents and all Americans.

Jesse Clarke, "Moving the Movement: Transportation Justice," *Race, Poverty and Environment* (Oakland, CA: Urban Habitat, 2005/2006), http://urbanhabitat. org/moving.

This report reveals a transportation and land-use system that harms urban quality of life, damages the planetary environment, promotes wars for resource domination, and supports racism and class-based segregation. In every urban center in the country, there are organizations challenging unequal access to transportation, coalitions fighting the burdens which international goods movement places on poor communities, and groups struggling for systemic reforms.

Environmental Justice Coalition for Water, *Thirsty for Justice: A People's Blueprint for California Water and Community Perspectives Companion Piece* (Oakland, CA: Environmental Justice Coalition for Water, 2005), http://www.ejcw.org/Thirsty%20for%20Justice.pdf.

Access to clean, safe, and affordable water is a fundamental human right essential for a healthy population, environment, and economy. The report provides case studies on how community environmental and health problems related to water fit into a pattern of discrimination embedded within water policy and water management, and highlight some of the struggles, campaigns, and model projects communities are undertaking to address local water issues.

David Pace, "More Blacks Live With Pollution: AP Analysis of U.S. Research Shows Blacks More Likely to Live With Dangerous Pollution," Associated Press, December 13, 2005, http://www.blackherbals.com/more_blacks_live_with_pollution_.htm.

An Associated Press analysis of a little-known government research project shows that Blacks are 79% more likely than are Whites to live in neighborhoods where industrial pollution is suspected of posing the greatest health danger. Residents in neighborhoods with the highest pollution scores also tend to be poorer, less educated, and more often unemployed than are those elsewhere in the country.

Urban Habitat, *A Community Guide to Brownfields Redevelopment* (Oakland, CA: Urban Habitat, 2005), http://urbanhabitat.org/pubs/003.

This handbook describes community-based brownfields redevelopment, from initial site selection through project implementations, with emphasis on urban planning, transportation, legal, scientific, and toxics issues.

2006

Citizens for Environmental Justice, *Corpus Christi, Texas: Criminal Injustice in an All-American City: Toxic Crimes, Race Zoning and Oil Industry Pollution Cover Up* (Corpus Christi, TX: Citizens for Environmental Justice, 2006), http://www.citgojustice.org/GCMcorpus.pdf.

The report highlights actual race-zoning restriction documents from the 1940s. Failures by the city, state, federal, and oil industry to rectify the effects of race-zoning means that people still suffer today. The report includes profiles from local residents fighting for justice and discloses the misleading information the City of Corpus Christi, Texas, used that was a major factor in its receiving the "All America City" title.

Jesse Clark, "Getting Ready for Change: Green Economics and Climate Justice," *Race, Poverty and Environment* (Oakland, CA: Urban Habitat, 2006), http://urbanhabitat.org/rpe/13-1.

This report draws a picture of the imminent challenges we face from global warming and sketches some routes toward survival, justice, and health using the principles of green economics. Climate change threatens all forms of life on planet Earth, but when it comes to human life—it is the poor communities that will be hit first, and hardest.

Meena Palaniappan, Swati Prakash, and Diane Bailey, *Paying With Our Health: The Real Cost of Freight Transport in California* (Seattle, WA: Pacific Institute, 2006), http://www.pacinst.org/reports/freight_transport/PayingWithOurHealth_Web.pdf.

This report is an innovative and powerful culmination of a year's work by the Ditching Dirty Diesel Collaborative, the Pacific Institute, and the testimony of 14 authors who either live next door to or work in the state's highly polluting freight transportation industry. The main conclusion of the report is that the cost to clean up much of the pollution generated by freight transport through-out California is under a third of a penny per dollar of revenue raked in by companies that depend on this infrastructure.

Manuel Pastor, Robert D. Bullard, James K. Boyce, et al., *In the Wake of the Storm: Environment, Disaster, and Race After Katrina* (New York, NY: Russell Sage Foundation, 2006), http://www.dscej.org/pubs/In%20The%20Wake%20of%20 the%20Storm.pdf.

This report reviews the existing literature and research on the relationship between race, the environment, and large-scale disasters. It concludes by stressing that the focus of environmental justice on disparities in hazards and disamenities is but a starting point in the work.

Tides Foundation, *Changing the Social Climate: How Global Warming Affects Economic Justice, the Future of the Progressive Movement, and Whether Your Child Walks to School* (San Francisco, CA: Tides Foundation, 2006), http://www.tides. org/fileadmin/tf_pdfs/Changing-the-Social-Climate.pdf.

This report provides an extensive conversation with Michel Gelobter of Redefining Progress and Catherine Lerza of the Tides Foundation on global warming and its effects on economic justice` and health impacts on poor communities around the world.

Tides Foundation, *Sustainability: The Ties That Bind* (San Francisco, CA: Tides Foundation, 2006), http://www.tides.org/fileadmin/pdfs/SustainabilityBriefing.pdf.

This report discusses avenues for change that require organizations to mobilize individuals who are knowledgeable about problems, solutions, and where the power to change resides. Change requires strategic communications strategies that reach mainstream as well as niche media, civic engagement strategies, and long-term accountability strategies.

Tides Foundation, *Reproductive Justice: Choosing A Broader Movement* (San Francisco, CA: Tides Foundation, 2006), http://www.tides.org/fileadmin/pdfs/ ReproductiveJusticeBriefing.pdf.

This report discusses reproductive justice and education and information initiatives within organizations, such as labor unions, that have not historically focused on reproductive justice. It also discusses reproductive justice as it pertains to organizations that provide a variety of community-based organizations with the tools they need to talk to their specific constituency about reproductive justice.

Laurel Tumarkin, Daniel Browne, Dora Fisher, and WE ACT for Environmental Justice, *Unhealthy Exposure: Mold in New York Homes: A Report by Public Advocate Betsy Gotbaum* (New York, NY: WE ACT for Environmental Justice, 2006), http://www.weact.org/Portals/7/Unhealthy%20Exposure%20-%20Mold%20in%20NYC%20Homes.pdf.

This report confirmed that mold contamination—a severe asthma trigger—has been rising in New York City for the past 5 years. The study makes concrete suggestions for addressing the growing problem, especially important in communities like Central Harlem, where one in four children suffer from asthma.

2007

Apollo Alliance and Urban Habitat, *Community Jobs in the Green Economy* (Oakland, CA: Urban Habitat, 2007), http://urbanhabitat.org/files/Community-Jobs-in-the-Green-Economy-web.pdf.

This report is a collaborative effort between the Apollo Alliance and Urban Habitat that reflects their shared belief in the potential of the "green economy" to generate quality jobs in low-income communities and communities of color. Both organizations believe that the United States can move toward energy independence while simultaneously creating high-skill and high-wage jobs for residents of low-income urban communities.

Judith Bell and Victor Rubin, *Why Place Matters: Building a Movement for Healthy Communities* (Oakland, CA: PolicyLink, 2008), http://www.policy link.org/atf/cf/%7B97c6d565-bb43-406d-a6d5-eca3bbf35af0%7D/WHYPLACEMATTERS_FINAL.PDF.

The report provides a framework that helps us understand the relationship between community conditions and health, analyzes the connections among all the environmental factors that contribute to a healthy community, and identifies environmental effects on community health.

Angela Glover Blackwell, Robert D. Bullard, Deeohn Ferris, and john a. powell, *Regionalism: Growing Together to Expand Opportunity to All* (Cleveland, OH: Presidents' Council of Cleveland, 2007), http://www.thepresidentscouncil.com/www/docs/CleveReportMay2007.pdf.

The purpose of this report was to understand how regionalism could impact the African American community. The goal of the report was to identify equity-based regional policies that could improve conditions for the African American community and increase the social health and economic vitality of the entire Cleveland region, thereby providing benefits to all residents of the metropolitan region.

Robert D. Bullard, Paul Mohai, Robin Saha, and Beverly Wright, *Toxic Wastes and Race at Twenty: 1987–2007* (Cleveland, OH: United Church of Christ Justice & Witness Ministries, 2007), http://www.dscej.org/pubs/Toxic%20Waste%20and%20Race%20at%20Twenty.pdf.

This report found people of color to be more concentrated around commercial hazardous waste facilities than previously found in 1987 and 1994. People of color comprised more than 56% of the residents living within a 2-mile radius of commercial hazardous facilities in 2007. They made up more than two thirds, or 69%, of residents living near two or more facilities. Generally, polluting industries still follow the path of least resistance, among other findings.

Leslie Fields, Albert Huang, Gina Solomon, et al., 2007, *Katrina's Wake: Arsenic-Laced Schools and Playgrounds Put New Orleans Children at Risk* (Washington, DC: Natural Resources Defense Council, 2007), http://www.nrdc.org/health/effects/wake/wake.pdf.

This report discusses soil samples taken from schoolyards after Hurricane Katrina and the lack of government response to residents' concerns. It also details the collaboration between the National Resources Defense Council and grassroots advocates to make sure cleanups take place.

Marcheta Gillam, Steve Fischbach, Lynne Wolf, et al., eds., *After Katrina: Rebuilding a Healthy New Orleans*, Final Conference Report of the New Orleans Health Disparities Initiative, sponsored by Poverty & Race Research Action Council, Alliance for Healthy Homes, Center for Social Inclusion, and the

Healthy Policy Institute of the Joint Center for Political and Economic Studies (Washington, DC: Poverty & Race Research Action Council, 2007), http://www. prrac.org/pdf/rebuild_healthy_nola.pdf.

This report summarizes the June 12, 2006, presentations, discussions, and the advocacy agenda that came from the conference. Since the conference, many participants have continued to work on many issues, in different ways. Several members of the planning committee participated in the "Louisiana Health Care Redesign Collaborative," which met for 6 months to design a new Medicaid delivery system for the state. This report includes a chapter that gives an overview of the collaborative's recommendations and their likely impact on lower-income New Orleans residents.

David Hallowes and Victor Munnik, *Peak Poison: The Elite Energy Crisis and Environmental Justice* (Pietermaritzburg, South Africa: groundWork, 2007), http://www.groundwork.org.za/Peak%20Poison.pdf.

This report is about energy in the twenty-first century. Its main focus is to explore the implications of peak oil (the likelihood that global oil production has peaked or will peak soon) for environmental justice. It identifies three ways in which environmental injustice is imposed on people: (1) by polluting them, degrading their environments, and coercing labor to work for less than it costs to live (this is called *externalization* because corporations get a free ride by off-loading costs onto communities, workers, the public purse, and the environment); (2) by dispossessing them and by privatizing common or public goods (this is called *enclosure* because it eliminates or subordinates noncapitalist systems of production, ensuring that all escape routes are closed and people cannot survive without capitalism); and (3) by excluding them from the political and economic decisions that lead to their being polluted or dispossessed.

Kim Knowlton, Miriam Rotkin-Ellman, and Gina Solomon, *Sneezing and Wheezing: How Global Warming Could Increase Ragweed Allergies, Air Pollution, and Asthma* (Washington, DC: Natural Resources Defense Council, 2007), http://www.nrdc.org/globalWarming/sneezing/sneezing.pdf.

This report discusses how global warming isn't just making our planet hotter, but also less healthy. Scientific studies have also shown that our changing climate could mean more ozone pollution in some areas and an intensification of health problems stemming from allergenic pollen such as ragweed. This is bad news for allergy sufferers and asthmatics, because both ragweed and ozone have been linked to respiratory problems such as asthma and to allergic symptoms in adults and children, and studies show that people exposed to both ragweed and ozone are likely to become sicker than are people exposed to just one of these pollutants.

Amy Mall, *Protecting Western Communities From the Health and Environmental Effects of Oil and Gas Production* (Washington, DC: Natural Resources Defense Council, 2007), http://www.nrdc.org/land/use/down/down.pdf.

The report provides a comprehensive assessment of the loopholes that allow oil and gas companies to continue polluting despite the risks, and describes the available—often economical—solutions for using technology to reduce environmental contamination. Despite readily available technological solutions capable of controlling hazardous pollution, such as air emission controls and nontoxic or less-toxic chemical alternatives, the industry as a whole has failed to take reasonable steps needed to protect families, communities, and the environment.

Mossville Environmental Action Now, Wilma Subra, Subra Co., and Advocates for Environmental Human Rights, *Industrial Sources of Dioxin Poisoning in Mossville, Louisiana: A Report Based on the Government's Own Data* (West Lake, LA: Mossville, Louisiana, Environmental Action Now, 2007), http://www.corpo ratecrimereporter.com/documents/mossville.pdf.

This report provides recommendations for corrective governmental action that would protect the human right to a healthy environment which is being violated in Mossville and numerous communities across the United States that are severely burdened with toxic pollution.

Natural Resources Defense Council, *Heat Advisory: How Global Warming Causes More Bad Air Days* (Washington, DC: Natural Resources Defense Council, 2007), http://www.nrdc.org/globalWarming/heatadvisory/heatadvisory07.pdf.

This 2007 report is an expansion of the *Heat Advisory* report first issued by National Resources Defense Council in 2004; it profiles ten new cities in the southern and eastern regions of the United States that could experience more "red alert" smog days, which can predispose the public to health risks such as asthma attacks and hospitalization from lung damage. On such days, the public should not partake in usual summer outdoor activities. In order to protect public health, it is important that Congress address global warming through mandatory legislation that reduces global warming pollution on the order of 20% by 2020.

Manuel Pastor, James Sadd, and Rachel Morello-Frosch, *Still Toxic After All These Years: Air Quality and Environmental Justice in the San Francisco Bay Area* (Santa Cruz, CA: Center for Justice, Tolerance & Community, University of California–Santa Cruz, 2007), http://cjtc.ucsc.edu/docs/bay_final.pdf.

The results from this report are clear: environmental inequality is unfortunately alive and well in the Bay Area—a fact that threatens the wellness of the most affected communities. The issue, of course, is what should be done to reduce disparities and improve environmental quality for everyone in the Bay Area. The authors offer some policy directions, but these are only a start to a longer dialogue between community, business, and regulatory leaders.

PolicyLink, *The Impact of the Built Environment on Health* (Oakland, CA: PolicyLink, 2007), http://www.policylink.org/site/apps/nlnet/content2.aspx?c=lkIXLbMNJrE&b=5136581&ct=6997423.

The report provides both a framework for understanding the necessary elements for building a movement for policy change and better planning, as well as numerous illustrations of innovative practices, projects, and networks of advocates and professionals.

U.S. PIRG Education Fund, *Toxic Pollution and Health: An Analysis of Toxic Chemicals Released in Communities Across the United States* (Washington, DC, 2007), http://pirgim.org/MI.asp?id2=31661.

In 2006, the Bush administration limited the public's right-to-know about pollution by giving some polluters a free pass on reporting their toxic emissions. The EPA's Toxics Release Inventory (TRI) program is a critical tool for citizens, public health officials, and policymakers interested in identifying trends in toxic pollution at the local, state, and national levels. Using the latest available TRI data, U.S. PIRG examined the releases of chemicals known or suspected to cause serious health problems and identified by states and localities that are bearing the brunt of this pollution.

WE ACT for Environmental Justice and Environmental Defense, *Green Renaissance Guide to Healthy, Sustainable Urban Development: A View From Harlem* (New York, NY: WE ACT for Environmental Justice, 2007), http://www.weact.org/Portals/7/Green%20Renaissance.pdf.

WE ACT for Environmental Justice and Environmental Defense have come together to point the way toward true partnerships between developers and communities, so that urban redevelopment is healthy and sustainable. They do so through the lens of New York City and Harlem's 125th Street corridor, where new investment is spurring rapid change. This report presents a fresh vision for community development—one that brings investors and communities together in order to focus the best of local knowledge, environmental design, technologies, and ideas on creating a sustainable future.

WE ACT for Environmental Justice and Genetics Equity Network, *Genes and Justice—A Community Symposium on Health, Race, and Rights* (New York, NY: WE ACT for Environmental Justice, 2007), http://www.weact.org/Publications/OtherPublications/tabid/260/Default.aspx.

This resource guide and report is a rich primer authored by symposium participants and others with topics that include basic genetics, health and race, law and regulation, criminal justice, genetic ethics, and policy.

2008

David A. Bositis, *Joint Center National Survey Results: African Americans Respond to Global Warming* (Washington, DC: Joint Center for Political and Economic Studies, 2008), http://www.jointcenter.org/climate/pdf/Nat_Poll_2_Sided.pdf.

The report concludes that while most African Americans do not believe global warming is one of the most pressing national problems the United States confronts, there is widespread recognition of the problem of global warming among them, and a strong belief that the federal government should take steps to deal with it.

Marilyn A. Brown, Frank Southworth, and Andrea Sarzynski, *Shrinking the Carbon Footprint of Metropolitan America* (Washington, DC: Brookings Institution Metropolitan Policy Program, 2008), http://www.brookings.edu/~/

media/Files/rc/reports/2008/05_carbon_footprint_sarzynski/carbonfootprint_report.pdf.

This report quantifies transportation and residential carbon emissions for the 100 largest U.S. metropolitan areas, finding that metro area residents have smaller carbon footprints than do the average American, although metro footprints vary widely. Federal government action is needed to set standards that protect the health and welfare of Americans.

James H. Carr, H. Beth Marcus, Shehnaz Niki Jagpal, and Nandinee Kutty, *In the Wake of Katrina: The Continuing Saga of Housing and Rebuilding in New Orleans* (Washington, DC: Joint Center for Political and Economic Studies, 2008), http://www.jointcenter.org/publications_recent_publications/environmental_projects/in_the_wake_of_katrina_the_continuing_saga_of_housing_and_rebuilding_in_new_orleans.

This report provides a thorough examination of the many factors that have delayed or continue to serve as persistent barriers to rebuilding housing stock in New Orleans. The report also highlights racial disparities and the social determinants of displacement, inadequate housing, and poor health, both pre- and post-Katrina.

Dominique Duval-Diop and Kalima Rose, *Delivering Equitable Development to a Recovering Louisiana: A State Policy Guide for 2008 and Beyond* (Oakland, CA: PolicyLink, 2008), http://www.policylink.org/atf/cf/%7B97c6d565-bb43-406d-a6d5-eca3bbf35af0%7D/DELIVERINGEQUITABLERECOVERY-LOUISIANA_FINAL.PDF.

The report examines these four principles: the integration of strategies that support people while improving places; the reduction of disparities between neighborhoods, localities, and across regions; promotion of "double bottom-line" investments that offer financial return to investors and economic and social benefits to residents; and full and meaningful community voice, participation, and leadership.

Rebecca Flournoy, *Breathing Easy From Home to School: Fighting the Environmental Triggers of Childhood Asthma* (Oakland, CA: PolicyLink, 2008), http://www.policylink.org/atf/cf/%7B97c6d565-bb43-406d-a6d5-eca3bbf35af0%7D/BREATHINGEASYFROMHOMETOSCHOOL_FINAL.PDF.

This report is a compilation of experiences and policy approaches of those working to create healthier environments for children across the nation. It offers a blueprint for what we all can do to make our children's air safer and healthier. The report describes how environmental conditions in three arenas—outdoors, in homes, and schools—aggravate asthma and highlights the efforts of groups that are pursuing promising policies and programs to improve the lives of children with asthma.

Angela Glover Blackwell and Sarah Treuhaft, *Regional Equity and the Quest for Full Inclusion* (Oakland, CA: PolicyLink, 2008), http://www.policylink.org/atf/cf/%7B97c6d565-bb43-406d-a6d5-eca3bbf35af0%7D/REGIONALEQUITY-QUESTFOR%20INCLUSION_FINAL.PDF.

The report examines the history of equity in the United States and how national and global forces are creating unique challenges and opportunities. The report provides a vision of the future characterized by shared economic prosperity and true participatory democracy, in which everyone—including people of color and residents of low-income communities—can contribute and benefit.

J. Andrew Hoerner and Nia Robinson, *A Climate of Change: African Americans, Global Warming, and a Just Climate Policy for the U.S.* (Oakland, CA: Environmental Justice and Climate Change Initiative and Redefining Progress, July 2008), http://www.rprogress.org/publications/2008/climateofchange.pdf.

African Americans are disproportionately affected by climate change and will lose more economically from a bad economic policy and stand to gain more from a good policy. The findings from the report by the Environmental Justice and Climate Change Initiative and Redefining Progress are the result of in-depth analysis of the effects of rising temperatures, greater pollution levels, and a host of other harms from global warming. African Americans will suffer disproportionately from illness, heat deaths, economic loss, and from the cost of wars designed to protect the flow of oil to the United States as global warming amplifies nearly all existing inequalities.

Chris Kromm and Sue Sturgis, *Hurricane Katrina and the Guiding Principles on Internal Displacement: A Global Human Rights Perspective on a Natural Disaster*, Special Report, vol. 36, nos. 1 and 2 (Durham, NC: Institute for

Southern Studies, Southern Exposure, 2008), http://www.southernstudies.org/
ISSKatrinaHumanRightsJan08.pdf.

Hundreds of thousands of people were forced to flee their homes as Hurricane
Katrina made landfall and, a few hours later, as the levees of New Orleans were
breached. The report concludes that the government should review its policies to
ensure the full implementation of its obligations to protect life and the prohibi-
tion of discrimination in the area of disaster prevention.

Serena W. Lin, *Understanding Climate Change: An Equitable Framework*
(Oakland, CA: PolicyLink, 2008), http://www.community-wealth.org/_pdfs/
articles-publications/green/report-lin.pdf.

The author argues that we need to understand the issues associated with complex ecological transformations of climate change in the world. Climate change
is one of the most important social, economic, human rights, and community
health issues facing our nation and our world. An equitable framework and policies are needed to address climate change as it impacts those individuals who will
suffer the most from it.

Reilly Morse, *Environmental Justice Through the Eye of Hurricane Katrina* (Washington, DC: Joint Center for Political and Economic Studies Health Policy Institute,
2008), http://www.jointcenter.org/hpi/sites/all/files/EnvironmentalJustice.pdf.

This publication explores a range of underlying causes for the disparate outcomes suffered by African Americans and other people of color in the aftermath of Hurricane Katrina. The author offers analyses of the social conditions
that gave rise to Katrina's tragic outcomes, the reasons behind the grossly inadequate disaster responses at all levels of government, and possible strategies for
addressing the legacy of inequality and ensuring effective disaster preparedness
in the future.

PolicyLink, *Designed for Disease: The Link Between Local Food and Environments and Obesity and Diabetes* (Oakland, CA: PolicyLink, 2008), http://www.
policylink.org/atf/cf/%7B97c6d565-bb43-406d-a6d5-eca3bbf35af0%7D/
DESIGNEDFORDISEASE_FINAL.PDF.

The report demonstrates that people who live near an abundance of fast-
food restaurants and convenience stores compared with grocery stores

and fresh produce vendors have a significantly higher prevalence of obesity and diabetes.

Kalima Rose, Annie Clark, and Domique Duval-Dlop, *A Long Way Home: The State of Housing Recovery in Louisiana* (Oakland, CA: PolicyLink, 2008), http://www.policylink.org/atf/cf/%7B97c6d565-bb43-406d-a6d5-eca3bbf35af0%7D/EQUITYATLAS.PDF.

The report examines how renters and homeowners have fared since Hurricanes Katrina and Rita and subsequent floods destroyed hundreds of thousands of homes. Also, the report reviews the housing recovery progress made by the state of Louisiana to implement major, federally funded housing recovery programs to restore storm-damaged housing.

Miriam Rotkin-Ellman, Mayra Quirindongo, Jennifer Sass, and Gina Solomon, *Deepest Cuts: Repairing Health Monitoring Programs Slashed Under the Bush Administration* (Washington, DC: National Resources Defense Council, 2008), http://www.nrdc.org/health/deepestcuts/deepestcuts.pdf.

This report examines the legacy of the Bush administration on environmental and health protection. We rely on the government to monitor contaminants and hazardous residues to ensure that we know our food, water, air, communities, and consumer products are safe. For decades, federal agencies charged with safeguarding health and the environment have tracked pollution, required industry reporting, and monitored disease rates. These programs provide the foundation for all health and environmental protection.

Karen Rowley, *Three Years After Katrina and Rita, Challenges Remain* (Baton Rouge, LA: Public Affairs Research Council of Louisiana, GulfGov Reports, 2008), http://www.rockinst.org/pdf/disaster_recovery/gulfgov/gulfgov_reports/2008-12-08-gulfgov-three_years_after_katrina_and_rita_challenges_remain.pdf.

This report is a regional analysis of ongoing issues related to the recovery. The report focuses on some of the misconceptions that continue to come up 3 years after Hurricanes Katrina and Rita moved ashore. The misconceptions challenge state and local officials in the affected communities because they make it harder for them to combat the ongoing issues surrounding the hurricanes.

Chad Stone and Matt Fiedler, *The Effects of Climate-Change Policies on the Federal Budget and the Budgets of Low-Income Households: An Economic Analysis* (Washington, DC: Center on Budget and Policy Priorities, 2008), http://www.cbpp.org/files/10-24-07climate.pdf.

The report concluded that low- and moderate-income families would be affected disproportionately by higher energy prices because they spend a larger percentage of their budgets on energy than higher-income families do. Effective measures to reduce greenhouse gas emissions can be compatible with sound budgeting and the fair treatment of low-income consumers in designing the strong policies that are essential to address climate change. Policymakers should take into account the implications for family budgets as well as the federal budget.

Children's Health Fund, *Preventing Further Trauma for Children and Families Relocated From FEMA Trailer Parks* (New York, NY: Children's Health Fund, 2008), http://www.childrenshealthfund.org/sites/default/files/FEMA-Trailers-white-paper-final-0508.pdf.

The report indicates that somewhere between 46,000 and 64,000 children remain at risk for persistent health and mental health problems, as well as reduced school performance, as a result of their protracted dislocation and the painfully slow recovery after Hurricanes Katrina and Rita. For many of the children and families who lost their homes and communities in the hurricanes, the shelter provided by FEMA often amounted to trailers grouped together in isolated areas.

Karyn Trader-Leigh, *Understanding the Role of African American Churches and Clergy in Community Response* (Washington, DC: Joint Center for Political and Economic Studies, 2008), http://www.jointcenter.org/publications_recent_publications/environmental_projects/understanding_the_role_of_african_american_churches_and_clergy_in_community_crisis_response.

This report examines the Hurricane Katrina-related experiences of Black clergy and churches to ensure that lessons learned help inform future disaster preparedness planning efforts and policy reforms. The research methodology starts with an extensive search of the literature on the role churches and clergy have played in responding to natural or man-made catastrophes in domestic or international contexts.

Michael R. Wenger, *No More Katrinas: How Reducing Disparities Can Promote Disaster Preparedness* (Washington, DC: Joint Center for Political and Economic Studies, 2008), http://www.jointcenter.org/publications_recent_publications/environmental_projects/no_more_katrinas_how_reducing_disparities_can_promote_disaster_preparedness.

This report presents a synthesis of findings and themes from a set of background papers commissioned by the Joint Center for Political and Economic Studies, Health Policy Institute. This report also reflects input provided by California-based stakeholders convened for a meeting in Oakland, California, sponsored by the Joint Center, in conjunction with PolicyLink and the California Endowment. It concludes with a set of core principles that should form a framework for disaster preparedness planning in the future.

University of California Berkeley School of Public Health and Policy Link, *Promoting Healthy Public Policy Through Community-Based Participatory Research: Ten Case Studies* (Oakland, CA: PolicyLink, 2008), http://www.policylink.org/atf/cf/%7B97C6D565-BB43-406D-A6D5-ECA3BBF35AF0%7D/CBPR_PromotingHealthyPublicPolicy_final.pdf.

The case studies offer a window into the world of community, health department, and academic partnerships throughout the nation that are working to change policy to improve community health, reduce disparities, and foster equity. The report draws on data from dozens of in-depth interviews with partnership members, community focus groups, and policymakers, as well as document review and participant observation.

WE ACT for Environmental Justice, *Northern Manhattan and the Congestion Pricing Plan: A Comprehensive Look at the Citywide Plan From a Community Perspective* (New York, NY: WE ACT for Environmental Justice, 2008), http://www.weact.org/Portals/7/Northern%20Manhattan%20and%20the%20Congestion%20Pricing%20Plan.pdf.

This report explains how the congestion pricing plan brings a wide range of benefits to the city as a whole, and certain localized benefits to communities such as northern Manhattan that are outside the charging zone. Congestion pricing provides a dedicated revenue source that, when combined with other funding sources, will allow the Metropolitan Transportation Authority to fund the first wave of major expansions to New York's transit system in over half a century.

2009

Tom Adams, *Communities Tackle Global Warming: A Guide to California's SB 375* (Washington, DC: Natural Resources Defense Council, 2009), http://www.nrdc. org/globalWarming/sb375/files/sb375.pdf.

This report examines California's Sustainable Communities and Climate Protection Act, or SB 375, the nation's first legislation to link transportation and land-use planning with global warming. SB 375 is an important step toward a cleaner, healthier, and more prosperous California. This groundbreaking measure shows us that where we live and how we get to work, go about our daily business, and take our kids to school matter a great deal in the fight against climate change.

Michael Ash, James K. Boyce, Grace Chang, et al., *Justice in the Air: Tracking Toxic Pollution From America's Industries and Companies to Our States, Cities, and Neighborhoods* (Los Angeles, CA: USC Center for Sustainable Cities, 2009), http://college.usc.edu/geography/ESPE/documents/justice_in_the_air_web.pdf.

This report has gathered information that will guide us toward positive solutions for addressing air pollution. One of the first efforts is based on a new database on industrially generated toxic air, with attempts to find solutions to air pollution. The authors examine not only the level of pollution but also who is being polluted. The problems of environmental hazards and air pollution are disproportionately borne by low-income communities of color.

David S. Beckman, *A Clear Blue Future: How Greening California Cities Can Address Water Resources and Climate Challenges in the 21st Century* (Washington, DC: Natural Resources Defense Council, 2009), http://www.nrdc.org/water/lid/ files/lid.pdf.

This report discusses low impact development (LID) and how it provides new ways to adapt to and mitigate serious challenges to our water supply posed by global warming. The study indicates that rainwater harvesting through use of LID can be of considerable help to California—and at bargain prices. LID can play a significant role in addressing water supply and global warming challenges throughout California and the southwestern United States.

Judith Bell and Larry Cohen, *The Transportation Prescription: Bold New Ideas for Healthy, Equitable Transportation Reform in America* (Oakland, CA: Policy Link, 2009), http://www.convergencepartnership.org/atf/cf/%7b245a9b44-6ded-4abd-a392-ae583809e350%7d/TRANSPORTATIONRX.PDF?tr=y&auid=5099518.

This report is a vision of transportation as more than a means to move people and goods, but also as a way to build healthy, opportunity-rich communities. The report describes policy proposals, including prioritizing investments in public transportation and bicycle and pedestrian infrastructure, encouraging equitable transit-oriented development through incentives for integrating land-use and transportation planning, targeting transportation investments to vulnerable communities, and supporting the development of cleaner bus and truck fleets.

Steven Bonorris, ed., University of California Hastings College of Law Public Law Research Institute, *Environmental Justice for All: A Fifty State Survey of Legislation, Policies and Cases*, 4th ed. (Chicago, IL: American Bar Association, 2009).

This report represents the collaboration between the University of California Hastings College of Law and the American Bar Association to maintain a comprehensive and up-to-date survey of state environmental justice laws, policies, and cases. Their goal was to present community members, environmental law practitioners, industry leaders, regulators, academics, and others with the breadth of regulatory and policy techniques that the 50 states and the District of Columbia have developed to pursue environmental justice.

Liisa Ecola and Thomas Light, *Equity and Congestion Pricing: A Review of the Evidence* (Santa, Monica, CA: Rand Corp., 2009), http://www.edf.org/documents/9876_Rand_TR680_.pdf.

This report examines the equity issues associated with congestion pricing. Because of the growing focus on congestion pricing, concern is increasing over whether congestion-based charging policies can be designed in an equitable way. The authors conclude that equity assessments need to become more sophisticated so that they can characterize equity impacts in specific locations.

Nicole Eng, *Clean Air Economic Justice Plan* (Los Angeles: Labor/Community Strategy Center, 2009), http://www.thestrategycenter.org/report/clean-air-economic-justice-plan.

This report discusses the Bus Riders Union plan that is needed for economic relief for Los Angeles County's low- and very low-income transit-dependent population. The plan will create an efficient, affordable system that can attract thousands of new riders. The plan also addresses the twin economic and environmental crises—generating thousands of well-paying green jobs while reducing automobile emissions that fuel global warming and toxic air pollution.

Environmental Working Group, *Pollution in People: Cord Blood Contaminants in Minority Newborns* (Washington, DC: Environmental Working Group, 2009), http://www.scribd.com/doc/23503846/EWG-2009-Minority-Cord-Blood-Report.

The Environmental Working Group found up to 232 toxic chemicals, including bisphenol A (BPA) and perchlorate, in the umbilical cord blood of ten babies from racial and ethnic minority groups. The findings constitute hard evidence that each child was exposed to a host of dangerous substances while still in his or her mother's womb. The contaminants found in these children are from unintended exposures to some of the most problematic consumer products and commercial chemicals ever put on the market. Scientists know very little about the health threats posed by exposure to toxic chemicals in the womb.

Radhika Fox and Solana Rice, *An Engine of Opportunity: A User's Guide to Advocate for Transportation Equity in the 2009 Recovery Act* (Oakland, CA: PolicyLink, 2009), http://www.policylink.org/atf/cf/%7B97C6D565-BB43-406D-A6D5-ECA3BBF35AF0%7D/Engine%20of%20Opportunity_final.pdf.

The report shows advocates how they can persuade local, state, and federal leaders to make fair and just transportation investments in low-income communities and communities of color. Transportation policy, planning, and investments have traditionally put lower-income people and communities of color in the slow lane, leaving economically distressed neighborhoods with few avenues to prosperity.

Radhika Fox, Jason Walsh, and Shawn Fremstad, *Bringing Home the Green Recovery: A User's Guide to the 2009 American Recovery and Reinvestment Act* (Oakland, CA: PolicyLink, 2009), http://www.policylink.org/atf/cf/%7B97C6D565-BB43-406D-A6D5-ECA3BBF35AF0%7D/BringingHometheGreenRecovery.pdf.

This report will assist local and state advocates, nonprofit organizations, public agencies, and policymakers in making the best use of recovery dollars. It offers tangible, up-to-date information and ideas for using and securing recovery dollars to help expand opportunity in low-income communities and communities of color.

Rachel Morello-Frosch, Manuel Pastor, Jim Sadd, and Seth Shonkoff, *The Climate Gap: Inequalities in How Climate Change Hurts Americans and How to Close the Gap* (Los Angeles: University of Southern California Center for Sustainable Cities, 2009), http://college.usc.edu/geography/ESPE/documents/ClimateGapReport_full_report_web.pdf.

The report assists in documenting the climate gap by connecting the dots between research on heat waves, air quality, and other challenges associated with climate change. The report explores how we might best combine efforts to both solve climate change and close the climate gap.

Wilhelmina A. Leigh and Anna L. Wheatley, *Trends in Child Health 1997–2006: Assessing Racial/Ethnic Disparities in Activity Limitation* (Washington, DC: Joint Center for Political and Economic Studies, 2009), http://www.jointcenter.org/publications_recent_publications/health/trends_in_child_health_1997_2006_assessing_racial_ethnic_disparities_in_activity_limitation.

This report examines disparities in the prevalence of an activity limitation of any type among children under the age of 18 years who are African American, Hispanic, or White. Comparisons of the prevalence of any activity limitation are made between the racial/ethnic groups of children overall and between children of various racial/ethnic groups in families with comparable sociodemographic characteristics (such as family type, educational attainment of householder, employment status of household, poverty status, and health insurance coverage).

Lowell Center for Sustainable Production, University of Massachusetts–Lowell, *A Common Agenda for Health and Environment: Goals for the Next Generation and Steps to Get There* (Lowell: University of Massachusetts, 2009), http://www.towardtomorrow.org/documents/CommonAgenda.pdf.

The general principle of this project is that healthy people and a healthy environment are achievable but require fundamental shifts in attitudes and practices. The main goal of the project is for all involved to make it their responsibility to call on community, civic and professional organizations, businesses, unions, students and scholars, health care providers, elected officials, and public institutions to use this agenda as context for reaching out to people and organizations they have not worked with before, as a standard for proposed policies and programs, and as a tool for tracking progress and holding everyone accountable to choices that lead to a healthy future for our children.

Richard P. Nathan and Marc Landy, *Who's in Charge? Who Should Be? The Role of the Federal Government in Megadisasters: Based on Lessons From Hurricane Katrina* (New York: Nelson A. Rockefeller Institute of Government, 2009), http://www.rockinst.org/pdf/disaster_recovery/gulfgov/gulfgov_reports/2009-06-02-Whos_in_Charge.PDF.

This report focuses on possible national legislation amending the Stafford Act by authorizing the appointment by the president of the United States of an officer-in-charge with preauthorized discretionary funding. This officer would be empowered to assemble and deploy experts, including experts seconded from federal agencies, and to recommend and obtain expedited consideration of a national action program if such a program is determined to be appropriate when megadisasters like Hurricane Katrina occur.

Angela Park, *Everybody's Movement: Environmental Justice and Climate Change* (Washington, DC: Environmental Support Center, 2009), http://envsc.org/esc-publications/ESC%20everybody%20s%20movement.pdf.

This report features the perspectives of 23 activists and funders who are engaged in or supporting work to connect environmental justice and climate change. The report also discusses how the environmental justice movement can be strengthened by better integrating climate issues into the content of environmental justice. It is important to know that environmental justice constituencies and strategies are underutilized assets in the work to build a movement in which everyone sees the relevance of climate, and sees the truth that our climate impacts nearly every facet of our lives.

PolicyLink, *Ensuring Equity and Inclusion Through the Surface Transportation Authorization Act of 2009: Analysis and Recommendations* (Oakland, CA: PolicyLink, 2009), http://transportationequity.org/index.php?option=com_cont ent&task=view&id=107&Itemid=1.

In this report, PolicyLink, the Transportation Equity Network, and the Gamaliel Foundation call on the House Transportation and Infrastructure Committee to ensure real benefits for lower-income people and communities of color in the Surface Transportation Authorization Act of 2009.

PolicyLink, *Health Food for All! Building Equitable and Sustainable Food Systems in Detroit and Oakland* (Oakland, CA: PolicyLink, 2009), http://www.poli- cylink.org/atf/cf/%7B97C6D565-BB43-406D-A6D5-ECA3BBF35AF0%7D/ Healthy%20Food%20For%20All-8-19-09-FINAL.pdf.

This report assists community organizations and leaders and the funding community to make more effective decisions about future projects and programs that address food equity and sustainability.

Victor Rubin, *All Aboard! Making Equity and Inclusion Central to Federal Transportation Policy* (Oakland, CA: Policy Link, 2009), http://www.policylink.org/ atf/cf/%7B97C6D565-BB43-406D-A6D5-ECA3BBF35AF0%7D/all_aboard.pdf.

This report addresses the key issues that comprise the quest for equitable transportation policies in three broad categories: shaping communities, power- ing the economy, and influencing health. It also summarizes recommendations for future federal transportation authorizations organized around the broader equity questions: Who benefits? Who pays? Who decides?

Ryan Snyder, *The Bus Riders Union Transit Model: Why a Bus-Centered System Will Best Serve U.S. Cities* (Los Angeles, CA: Labor/Community Strategy Center, 2009), http://www.thestrategycenter.org/report/bus-riders-union-transit-model.

The report concludes that if rail fails to meet the most basic planning thresh- olds to warrant its construction in Los Angeles—the most auto-centered, sprawl- ing city in the nation—then it cannot work in any other similar urban setting.

Midge Taylor, *Environmental Justice Needs Assessment Report. Report on the Organizational Needs of Environmental Organizations in the United States*

(Washington, DC: Environmental Support Center, 2009), http://envsc.org/2009-publications/EnvironmentalJusticeNeeds.pdf.

This report examines how the Environmental Support Center might better support environmental justice efforts around the country, particularly those groups with limited resources. The groups interviewed work in 21 states around the United States. The report found out that environmental justice groups are maturing in their appraisal of the environmental conditions they face, their role in how to effect change, and their refusal to be victims. Also, the groups measure themselves by what they have succeeded in doing programmatically, and not by internal capacity.

Kristen Zimmerman and Vera Miao, *Fertile Ground: Women Organizing at the Intersection of Environmental and Reproductive Justice* (Oakland, CA: Movement Strategy Center, 2009), http://www.movementstrategy.org/media/docs/1422_FertileGround.pdf.

This report discusses the powerful contributions environmental justice and reproductive justice (EJ/RJ) groups are making to secure safer, healthier environments for all women, children, and communities. The work of these groups demonstrates how an intersectional approach to organizing and movement building can lead to more powerful outcomes at all levels. Leadership by women of color has been critical to EJ/RJ work. Their perspectives and lived experiences deeply inform the intersectional analysis and pragmatic approach of EJ/RJ groups.

2010

Alternatives for Community & Environment, *Environmental Justice and the Green Economy: A Vision Statement and Case Studies for Just and Sustainable Solutions* (Roxbury, MA: Alternatives for Community & Environment, 2010), http://www.weact.org/Portals/7/Publications/EJGE_Report_English.pdf.

This report highlights the work of community-based environmental justice groups that manifest the ideals of the "vision statement." These case studies are only a sample of the breadth and depth of the work in the field. They are also works in progress, snapshots of partial successes which may grow into long-term, fuller successes with the support of stronger, more connected networks of like-minded leaders, advocates, and concerned community members.

Lawyers' Committee for Civil Rights Under Law, *Now Is the Time: Environmental Injustice in the U.S. and Recommendations for Eliminating Disparities* (Washington, DC: Lawyers' Committee, June 2010), http://www. lawyerscommittee.org/projects/environmental_justice/clips?id=0153.

The purpose of this report, presented to the Obama administration and its various agencies, including the EPA and the Department of Justice, outlines recommendations on how the administration can effectively utilize existing law to eliminate disparities in environmental protection and how the various agencies can fulfill their responsibilities under Executive Order 12898, "Federal Actions to Address Environmental Justice in Minority Populations and Low-Income Populations." It is far-reaching and incorporates the work of the environmental justice community during the past 10 years.

University of California Hastings College of Law Public Law Research Institute, *Environmental Justice for All: A Fifty State Survey of Legislation, Policies and Cases*, 4th ed. (San Francisco: University of California, 2010), http://www.abanet. org/environ/highlights/docs/Environmental_Justice_for_All.pdf.

This fourth edition identifies the statutes, policies, initiatives, or other commitments that states have undertaken to give force of law or tangible meaning to the goal of environmental justice. It also finds that from the first policy issued in 1993 to the present, more than 30 states have expressly addressed environmental justice, demonstrating increased attention to the issue at a political level. The report's improved index and innovative keyword classification system enables researchers to compare initiatives across states with ease.

Books

1999

Winona LaDuke, *All Our Relations: Native American Struggles for Land and Life* (Boston, MA: South End Press, 1999).

This work discusses the concerns of Native American activists, hundreds of years of violence against them, and their cultures' forced removal from their land. The "voices" of these women and men link their struggles to environmental degradation and their struggles for land rights, self-determination, and community health.

David Schlosberg, *Environmental Justice and the New Pluralism: The Challenge of Difference for Environmentalism* (New York, NY: Oxford University Press, 1999).

The author argues that the environmental justice movement and new pluralist theories now represent a considerable challenge to both conventional pluralist thought and the practices of the major groups in the U.S. environmental movement. This book demonstrates the development of a new form of critical pluralism, in both theory and practice.

Institute of Medicine, *Toward Environmental Justice: Research, Education, and Health Policy Needs* (Washington, DC: National Academies Press, 1999).

Driven by community-based organizations and supported by a growing body of literature, the environmental justice movement contends that poor and minority populations are burdened with more than their share of toxic waste, pesticide runoff, and other hazardous by-products of our modern economic life. Is environmental degradation worse in poor and minority communities? Do these communities suffer more adverse health effects as a result? This book addresses these questions and explores how current fragmentation in health policy could be replaced with greater coordination among federal, state, and local parties. The book is highlighted with case studies from five locations to which the committee traveled to hear citizen and researcher testimony.

2000

Robert D. Bullard, *Dumping in Dixie: Race, Class and Environmental Quality*, 3rd ed. (Boulder, CO: Westview Press, 2000).

This book explores the barriers to environmental and social justice experienced by African Americans and lays the foundation for understanding the factors that contribute to environmental conflicts, distributive impacts, and growing militancy among African American communities. The author chronicles the efforts of five African American communities empowered by the civil rights movement and their work to link environmentalism with issues of social justice.

Luke W. Cole and Sheila R. Foster, *From the Ground Up: Environmental Racism and the Rise of the Environmental Justice Movement* (New York, NY: New York University Press, 2000).

This book is about both the phenomenon of environmental racism and the movement that propelled environmental racism into national consciousness and forced action at the highest levels of government. The movement continues to shape environmental policy while creating increased opportunities for marginalized communities to talk about their own disenfranchisement and the social and economic policies that subject them to daily environmental hazards. The authors trace the movement's roots while illustrating the historical and contemporary causes of environmental racism.

Peter J. Dreier, J. Eugene Grigsby, III, Marta Lopez Garza, and Manuel Pastor, Jr. *Regions That Work: How Cities and Suburbs Can Grow Together* (Minneapolis, MN: University of Minnesota Press, 2000).

The book provides a history and critique of community-development corporations, a statistical analysis of the poverty–growth relationship in 74 metropolitan areas, a detailed study of three regions that have produced superior equity outcomes, and a provocative call for new policies. The authors make a case for emphasizing equity, arguing that metropolitan areas must reduce poverty in order to grow, and that low-income individuals must make regional connections in order to escape poverty.

Christopher H. Foreman, *The Promise and Peril of Environmental Justice* (Washington, DC: Brookings Institution Press, 2000).

The author argues that environmental justice has cleared significant political hurdles but displays substantial limitations and drawbacks. Yet, activism has yielded a presidential executive order (Executive Order 12898), management reforms at the EPA, and numerous local political victories. This book assesses the prospects and challenges of the environmental justice movement, which contends that low-income persons and communities of color bear a disproportionate burden when it comes to toxic waste sites, hazardous jobs, and polluted air and water.

Feng Liu, *Environmental Justice Analysis: Theories, Methods, and Practice* (Boca Raton, FL: CRC Press, 2000).

This text argues that it takes a multiperspective, multidisciplinary, and interdisciplinary approach to analyze environmental justice issues. He demonstrates how cutting-edge technologies and methods such as the Internet, geographic information systems, and modeling tools can contribute to better equity analysis and policy evaluations. The author focuses on the various methods of environmental justice research, providing an integrated framework for conducting rigorous equity analysis.

Patrick Novotny, *Where We Live, Work, and Play: The Environmental Justice Movement and the Struggle for a New Environmentalism* (Santa Barbara, CA: Praeger, 2000).

The author uses the concept of framing, combined with four case studies of poor and working-class people's resistance to environmental hazards, to argue that the success of the environmental justice movement depends on the movement's leaders' ability to frame environmental issues within historical concerns of poverty, health, civil rights, and workers' rights. The author examines how groups and leaders construct and promote organization development and action through language and activities that reflect current conflicts and realities, as well as interpolate shared cultural and historical experiences.

2001

Joni Adamson, *American Indian Literature, Environmental Justice, and Ecocriticism: The Middle Place* (Tucson, AZ: University of Arizona Press, 2001).

Adamson explores why what counts as "nature" is often very different for multicultural writers and activist groups than it is for mainstream environmentalists. This book is one of the first to examine the intersections between literature and the environment from the perspective of the oppressions of race, class, gender, and nature, and the first to review American Indian literature from the standpoint of environmental justice and ecocriticism. The author searches for ways to understand our cultural and historical differences and similarities in order to arrive at a better agreement of what the human role in nature is and should be.

William M. Bowen, *Environmental Justice Through Research-Based Decision-Making* (New York, NY: Routledge, 2001).

The author indicates that a fairly large and growing body of literature today presupposes that there are substantial public health costs borne primarily by minority, low-income, and other disadvantaged populations specifically because of their differential exposure to environmental hazards. Environmental justice, a newer arm of environmental concern and law, addresses poorer populations believed to be disproportionately exposed to environmental hazards. The author condemns the "poor and sloppy" science now promulgated by environmental justice advocates, calling for better and more scientific study so that environmental justice advocates joined with scientists can better make their points on critical environmental justice issues.

Al Gedicks, *Resource Rebels: Native Challenges to Mining and Oil Corporations* (Boston, MA: South End Press, 2001).

The author describes how native peoples in general are facing extinction as a result of the greed of mining and oil companies. In Mexico, the Philippines, Colombia, Ecuador, Nigeria, West Papua, Canada, and the United States, indigenous peoples are working with environmentalists and antiracists to stop corporate and state takeovers of their traditional lands and waters. He argues that building a multiracial, transnational movement to drastically limit resource extraction and create a new environmental ethic is badly needed. The author documents how a growing transnational environmental and human rights network has come to the assistance of native communities under siege by mining and oil companies.

J. Timmons Roberts and Melissa M. Toffolon-Weiss, *Chronicles From the Environmental Justice Frontline* (New York, NY: Cambridge University Press, 2001).

The authors place environmental justice struggles in the historical context of inequality and race relations in the U.S. South and apply social science theory to reveal how situations of environmental injustice are created, how they are resolved, and what accounts for their success or failure. The book describes how and why conflicts over environmental injustice are created and eventually resolved. The authors describe four cases in Louisiana in which residents were locked in struggles with industry and government representatives over issues of environmental injustice. They explain how, at the end of the twentieth century, situations of environmental injustice were created and eventually resolved.

2002

Joni Adamson, Mei Mei Evans, and Rachel Stein, *The Environmental Justice Reader: Politics, Poetics, and Pedagogy* (Tucson, AZ: University of Arizona Press, 2002).

This book examines environmental justice in its social, economic, political, and cultural dimensions in both local and global contexts, with special attention paid to intersections of race, gender, and class inequality. It is the first work to link political studies, literary analysis, and teaching strategies all in one work while combining perspectives from various organizations that deal with environmental justice issues. The book is divided into sections on politics (i.e., public policy), poetics (literature analysis), and pedagogy (how to teach environmental justice). The book's 19 chapters try to counter fear and uncertainty as they relate to environmental justice issues.

John Byrne, Leigh Glover, and Cecilia Martinez, *Environmental Justice: International Discourses in Political Economy, Energy, and Environmental Policy* (Edison, NJ: Transaction Publishers, 2002).

Global forces of technology and the development of global markets are transforming social life and the natural order. The authors consider the links between expanded patterns of environmental injustice and the structures and forces underlying and shaping the political international economy. In this book, the authors discuss how environmental injustice is examined across a variety of cultures in the developed and developing world. The use of case studies of climate colonialism, revolutionary ecology, and environmental commodification as well as the global and local dimensions of these problems are presented to the reader.

Richard Hofrichter, *Toxic Struggles: The Theory and Practice of Environmental Justice* (Salt Lake City, UT: University of Utah Press, 2002).

Hofrichter proposes that environmental injustices experienced disproportionately by poor minorities are inseparable from broader problems affecting their quality of life. The 23 chapters in the book document the fast-growing environmental justice movement as led by the people who suffer most from corporate ecological devastation. The book discusses how grassroots organizations are reshaping the environmental movement by forcing it to incorporate social justice issues such as racism, class, gender, antimilitarism, and poverty.

David A. McDonald, *Environmental Justice in South Africa* (Athens, OH: Ohio University Press, 2002).

McDonald critically examines the first decade of environmental activism in South Africa after the dismantling of apartheid, explicating some of the environmental justice movement's victories and contemplating future courses of action. The chapters are a crucial addition to the body of literature dealing with South Africa's transition from an apartheid regime to a full-fledged democracy capable of meeting all its citizens' most basic needs. The organizational structure of the book is in three parts: theory, practice, and narrative.

David Schlosberg, *Environmental Justice and the New Pluralism: The Challenge of Difference for Environmentalism* (New York, NY: Oxford University Press, 2002).

The author demonstrates the development of a new form of "critical" pluralism in both theory and practice. The environmental justice movement, with its base in diversity, its networked structure, and its communicative practices and demands, exemplifies the attempt to design political practices beyond those one would expect from a standard interest group in the conventional pluralist model. The author presents a challenge to both conventional pluralist thought and the practices of the major groups in the U.S. environmental movement.

2003

Julian Agyeman, Robert D. Bullard, and Bob Evans, *Just Sustainabilities: Development in an Unequal World* (Cambridge, MA: MIT Press, 2003).

The book is organized into four sections: (1) Theories and Concepts, in which the authors lay theoretical and conceptual ground for the foundation of the book; (2) Challenges by the authors to Andrew Dobson's theory that social justice and environmental sustainability are politically incompatible; (3) Cities, Communities, and Social and Environmental Justice, in which communities from the village to the U.S. state level are considered; and (4) Selected Regional Perspectives on Sustainability and Environmental Justice, in which the authors reflect on practical issues in a wide range of regional, national, and subnational contexts. The book addresses many aspects of the links between environmental quality and human equality and between sustainability and environmental justice, more generally.

Thomas H. Fletcher, *From Love Canal to Environmental Justice: The Politics of Hazardous Waste on the Canada-U.S. Border* (Peterborough, ON: Broadview Press, 2003).

The author deals with two major issues: (1) links between hazardous waste issues, primarily but not exclusively hazardous waste facility siting, and the larger issue of environmental justice; and (2) a comparison of the evolution of hazardous waste regulation in the United States and Canada. The book is a detailed analysis of ten case studies of siting disputes along the Canada–United States border. The comprehensiveness of the case studies is enhanced by the utilization of hearing transcripts, evidence submitted to governments, government agency decisions, and interviews with stakeholders and public officials.

2004

Ruchi Anand, *International Environmental Justice: A North-South Dimension* (Aldershot, England: Ashgate Publishing, 2004).

The author examines the question, Is the theory of environmental justice, as has been used at the U.S. level, a useful theoretical tool to analyze and inform the North-South schism in global environmental politics? Using three international environmental case studies, it extends the theory of environmental justice, commonly used in domestic settings, to the international arena of environmental law, policy, and politics. The author examines how the developed countries of the global North have an obligation to take action on environmental problems before developing countries are required to do so. Rich countries should aid poor countries in carrying out environmental protection measures.

Karen Lucas, *Running on Empty: Transport, Social Exclusion and Environmental Justice* (Bristol, England: Policy Press, 2004).

The author argues that past failure to address fundamental inequalities in the ability of low-income households to access adequate transport has undermined effective delivery of welfare policies in the United States and United Kingdom. This book examines the delivery of transport from a social policy perspective to assist in a better understanding of transportation equity in the United States and the United Kingdom. The author describes the new policies and initiatives being developed to address transportation injustice in the United States and United Kingdom while using case study examples of practical initiatives from both sides of the Atlantic to draw lessons for future policy and practice.

David Naguib Pellow, *Garbage Wars: The Struggle for Environmental Justice in Chicago* (Cambridge, MA: MIT Press, 2004).

The book explores the life cycle of waste production, collection, processing, and disposal in Chicago over some 120 years. The author examines how poor neighborhoods come to be burdened with a disproportionate amount of pollution and garbage. His research shows how "environmentally friendly" technologies like recycling plants and waste-to-energy incinerators actually end up adding to the pollution in poor neighborhoods. The author integrates social, environmental, and business studies, and raises questions concerning American consumption patterns, past and present.

Rachel Stein, *New Perspectives on Environmental Justice: Gender, Sexuality, and Activism* (New Brunswick, NJ: Rutgers University Press, 2004).

This book is the first collection of essays to pay tribute to the enormous contributions women have made in grassroots movements. The author offers varied examples of environmental justice issues such as children's environmental health campaigns, cancer research, HIV/AIDS activism, the Environmental Genome Project, and popular culture. Each example focuses on gender and sexuality as crucial factors in women's or gay men's activism and applies environmental justice principles to related struggles for sexual justice. Feminist and womanist impulses shape and sustain environmental justice movements around the world, making an understanding of gender roles and differences crucial for the success of these efforts. The author discusses issues of gender equality and sexuality that have been embedded within the environmental justice literature to increase the visibility of the environmental justice movement.

Jennifer Wolch, Manuel Pastor, Jr., and Peter Dreier, *Up Against Sprawl: Public Policy and the Making of Southern California* (Minneapolis, MN: University of Minnesota Press, 2004).

Los Angeles, with its problems of traffic, pollution, and growing inequality, is often depicted as diverse, fragmented, polarized, and ungovernable, a city without a unifying geographic center or civic culture. The authors discuss how governmental policies and public agencies have dictated many aspects of the region's growth: infrastructure, transportation, housing, immigration, finances, civic and regional administration, and the environment. The authors explore counter-movements by progressive activists to use innovative policies from smart growth initiatives to the actions of living wage advocates for greater social, economic, and environmental justice.

2005

Julian Agyeman, *Sustainable Communities and the Challenge of Environmental Justice* (New York, NY: New York University Press, 2005).

The author argues that environmental justice and the sustainable communities movement are compatible in practical ways. He explores the ideological differences between these two groups and shows how they can work together to create healthy and sustainable communities. The book provides concrete examples of potential model organizations that employ the types of strategies he advocates. The author addresses many aspects of the links between environmental quality and human equality and between sustainability and environmental justice.

Robert D. Bullard, *The Quest for Environmental Justice: Human Rights and the Politics of Pollution* (San Francisco, CA: Sierra Club Books, 2005).

Over the course of two decades, the grassroots environmental movement has spread across the globe. This book is divided into four parts. Part I presents an overview of the early environmental justice movement and highlights key leadership roles assumed by women activists. Part II examines the lives of people living in "sacrifice zones"—toxic corridors (such as Louisiana's infamous "Cancer Alley") where high concentrations of polluting industries are found. Part III explores land use, land rights, resource extraction, and sustainable development conflicts, including Chicano struggles in the U.S. Southwest. Finally, Part IV examines human rights and global justice issues, including an analysis of South Africa's legacy of environmental racism and the corruption and continuing violence plaguing the oil-rich Niger Delta. The world is not a just place and it is becoming more unequal, inspiring an increased interest by many in the environmental justice movement.

David Naguib Pellow and Robert J. Brulle, *Power, Justice and the Environment: A Critical Appraisal of the Environmental Justice Movement* (Cambridge, MA: MIT Press, 2005).

This book provides a critical appraisal of the environmental justice movement while examining the environmental justice movement's tactics, strategies, rhetoric, organizational structure, and resource base. The authors book also examine the progress, failures, and successes of the environmental justice movement; they look at the development of new strategies and cultural perspectives that shape the mobilization and organizational structure of the movement. Lastly, the book looks at how the environmental justice movement can address transnational environmental injustices.

Devon G. Peña, *Mexican Americans and the Environment: Tierra y Vida* (Tucson: University of Arizona Press, 2005).

The book provides an environmental history from both sides of the border and shows how contemporary environmental justice struggles in Mexican American communities have challenged dominant concepts of environmentalism. The author examines the experiences of people from a variety of experiences in life such as activists, farmworkers, union organizers, land managers, educators, and so forth. These individuals provide an overview of ecological issues facing Mexican people today.

Kristin Shrader-Frechette, *Environmental Justice: Creating Equality, Reclaiming Democracy* (New York, NY: Oxford University Press, 2005).

The author argues that burdens like pollution and resource depletion need to be apportioned more equally, and that there are compelling ethical grounds for remedying our environmental problems. She also argues that those affected by environmental problems must be included in the process of remedying those problems; that all citizens have a duty to engage in activism on behalf of environmental justice; and that in a democracy it is the people, not the government, who are ultimately responsible for fair use of the environment. The author provides at least one case study per chapter exemplifying a particular type of environmental injustice.

2006

Tammy Cromer-Campbell, Phyllis Glazer, Roy Flukinger, et al., *Fruit of the Orchard: Environmental Justice in East Texas* (Denton, TX: University of North Texas Press, 2006).

This book discusses how residents in the Piney Woods neighborhood in Winona, Texas, noticed an increase in cancer and birth defect rates after a toxic waste facility opened in their community. Phyllis Glazer founded Mothers Organized to Stop Environmental Sins and worked tirelessly to publicize the problems in Winona. In this book, Glazer describes the history of Winona and the fight against the toxic facility; Roy Flukinger discusses Cromer-Campbell's striking photographic technique; Eugene Hargrove explores issues of environmental justice; and Marvin Legator elaborates on how industry and government discourage victims of chemical exposure from seeking or obtaining relief. The story of the injustices in this community have been featured in *People,* the *Houston Chronicle* magazine, and *The Dallas Observer,* which played an important role in the plants' closing in 1998 after operating for 16 years.

Susan L. Cutter, *Hazards, Vulnerability, and Environmental Justice* (London, England: Earthscan Publications, 2006).

The author examines the following events: the South Asian tsunami, human-induced atrocities, terrorist attacks, and climate change. The book includes 26 reprints of Susan Cutter's research on human-environment interaction from 1982 to 2003. She reveals a great deal about her interests and background on disaster management, early influences, and academic career path. She also discusses humanity's attempt to dominate rather than coexist with nature. The entire book is framed around social inequality and vulnerability.

Steve Lerner, *Diamond: A Struggle for Environmental Justice in Louisiana's Chemical Corridor* (Cambridge, MA: MIT Press, 2006).

This book chronicles how the people of Diamond, an African American subdivision sandwiched between a Shell chemical plant and a Motiva oil refinery in the town of Norco, Louisiana, lobbied Shell to pay for their relocation after decades of exposure to the plants' toxic emissions. Diamond residents argued that the Shell plants' pollution caused many problems, including kidney and nervous-system damage and lung cancer, while their White neighbors, who lived further from the plants' shadow, tended to dismiss such claims. The residents received support from Greenpeace and the Sierra Club to help them relocate from the toxic community.

Eric Mann, *Katrina's Legacy: White Racism and Black Reconstruction in New Orleans and the Gulf Coast* (Los Angeles, CA: Frontlines Press, 2006).

The book focuses on the centrality of the Black liberation movement in the United States while providing ways to support the reconstruction of New Orleans and the Gulf Coast. The author identifies the Black-led struggle of the Katrina disaster. He also discusses how capitalism, colonialism, and imperialism have devasted the environment, human lives, and oppressed people in our society. The author's argument throughout the book is that all New Orleanians have a right to return to a "Black Majority City." He stressed that there cannot be no rebuilding or justice for residents of New Orleans without a right for them to return home.

J. Timmons Roberts and Bradley C. Parks, A *Climate of Injustice: Global Inequality, North-South Politics, and Climate Policy* (Cambridge, MA: MIT Press, 2006).

In this book, the authors develop new measures of climate-related inequality, analyzing fatality and homelessness rates from hydrometeorological disasters, patterns of emissions inequality, and participation in international environmental governments. The authors argue that global inequality hurts global climate change efforts by reinforcing structuralist worldviews and causal beliefs common in many poor nations, eroding conditions of generalized trust, and promoting particularistic notions of fair solutions. As a result, poor nations fear limits on their efforts to grow economically and meet the needs of their own people, and powerful industrial nations will not reduce their own excesses unless developing countries make similar sacrifices.

Julie Sze, *Noxious New York: The Racial Politics of Urban Health and Environmental Justice* (Cambridge, MA: MIT Press, 2006).

The author analyzes the culture, politics, and history of environmental justice activism in New York City. She describes the emergence of local campaigns organized around issues of asthma, garbage collection, and energy systems, and how in each neighborhood, activists framed their arguments in the environmental justice framework. She analyzes the influence of race, family, and gender politics on asthma activism while examining the community activists' responses to garbage privatization and energy deregulation. The author looks at how activist groups have begun to shift from fighting particular siting and land-use decisions to engaging in a larger process of community planning and community-based research projects within the larger context of privatization, deregulation, and globalization.

2007

James K. Boyce, Sunita Narain, and Elizabeth Stanton, *Reclaiming Nature: Environmental Justice and Ecological Restoration* (New York, NY: Anthem Press, 2007).

The book explores the relationship between human activities and the natural world, which include community-based fisheries, forestry management, and strategies to fight global warming. The author makes a case for us to reclaim our relationship with nature and the struggle for social justice. Humans positively and negatively effect the environment, but all humans have an inalienable right to clean air, clean water, and a healthy environment. Low-income communities, despite their lack of resources, can provide adequate solutions for ecological restoration. People in cities around the world are creating a new form of environmentalism that is grounded in defending their livelihoods and communities.

Robert D. Bullard, *Growing Smarter: Achieving Livable Communities, Environmental Justice, and Regional Equity* (Cambridge, MA: MIT Press, 2007).

This book examines the impact of the built environment on access to economic opportunity and quality of life. It also explores the costs and consequences of uneven urban and regional growth patterns, suburban sprawl, transportation investments and economic development, and enduring inequalities of place, space, and race. The book answers a specific set of questions: What changes and new paradigms can be offered that will improve quality of life and create healthy and livable metropolitan regions for everyone? How does the built environment impact health? How do current trends in racial and income segregation in metropolitan areas affect the process of urban redevelopment?

David Naguib Pellow, *Resisting Global Toxics: Transnational Movements for Environmental Justice* (Cambridge, MA: MIT Press, 2007).

The author examines widespread ecosystem damage resulting from toxic waste and the emergence of transnational environmental justice movements to challenge and reduce toxic waste from the 1980s to the present day. He argues that waste dumping across national boundaries from rich to poor communities is a form of transnational environmental inequality.

Ronald Sandler and Phaedra C. Pezzullo, eds., *Environmental Justice and Environmentalism: The Social Justice Challenge to the Environmental Movement*, Urban and Industrial Environments Series (Cambridge, MA: MIT Press, 2007).

The authors examine the relationship between the two movements (environmental and environmental justice) in both conceptual and practical terms and explores the possibilities for future collaboration by these movements to successfully address climate change and globalization. They examine the possibility of one unified movement as opposed to two complementary ones by means of analyses and case studies, and believe that it is necessary to rethink the relationship between the movements while realizing the effectiveness of their alliances and the mission of both movements.

2008

David V. Carruthers, *Environmental Justice: Latin American Problems, Promise, and Practice* (Cambridge, MA: MIT Press, 2008).

The book examines environmental justice in Latin America and its emergence as a unique environmental justice movement. The chapters explore ecotourism, inequitable land distribution in Brazil, the ongoing struggle for justice and accountability over the former U.S. Navy bombing range in Vieques, Puerto Rico, and water policy in Chile, Bolivia, and Mexico. The chapters also focus on industrial development, concentrated industrial waste hazards, and power and politics in land development. Environmental justice provides a way for disenfranchised groups to deal with environmental inequities in their country.

Daniel Faber, *Capitalizing on Environmental Justice: The Polluter-Industrial Complex in the Age of Globalization* (Lanham, MD: Rowman & Littlefield, 2008).

The author examines the successes and challenges of the environmental justice movement. He discusses innovative methods of addressing environmental problems and shaping environmental policy.

Manuel Pastor, Jr., Chris Benner, and Martha Matsuoka, *This Could Be the Start of Something Big: How Social Movements for Regional Equity Are Reshaping Metropolitan America* (Ithaca, NY: Cornell University Press, 2008).

In the United States, urban coalitions, including labor, faith groups, and community-based organizations, have come together to support living wage laws and fight for transit policies that can move the needle on issues of working poverty. In places as diverse as Chicago, Atlanta, and San Jose, California, the usual business resistance to pro-equity policies has changed, particularly when it comes to issues like affordable housing and more efficient transportation systems. The authors offer their analysis on what has and has not worked in various campaigns to achieve regional equity. They conclude that social movement regionalism is needed to revitalize the United States.

Vandana Shiva, *Soil Not Oil: Environmental Justice in an Age of Climate Crisis* (Boston, MA: South End Press, 2008).

The author discusses the relationship between industrial agriculture and climate change. She emphasizes throughout the book that what we need most is sustainable, biologically diverse farms that are more resistant to disease, drought, and flood. She makes a strong case that the solution to climate change and poverty are the same: our world must move toward being less dependent on fossil fuels and globalization. Her analysis in this book focuses on creating a healthy environmental and "just" world based on sustainability and a world community that is beneficial for all of us.

Steve Vanderheiden, *Atmospheric Justice: A Political Theory of Climate Change* (New York, NY: Oxford University Press, 2008).

This book discusses ways to achieve social justice, environmental justice, equality, and responsibility by exploring how climate change raises issues of both international and intergenerational justice. It provides ways on how political theory can contribute to reaching a better understanding of the proper human response to climate change. The author presents the first principles for achieving environmental justice and shows how climate policy offers insights into resolving contemporary controversies within political theory.

Laura Westra, *Environmental Justice and the Rights of Urban and Future Generations: Law, Environmental Harm and the Right to Health* (London: Earthscan Publications, 2008).

The book delves into social justice cases in Bhopal and Chernobyl, among others, to show the impact of environmental harm on millions of people. It provides a broad view of the arguments over international legal instruments, key legal cases and examples including the Convention on the Rights of the Child, industrial disasters, clean water provision, diet, HIV/AIDS, environmental racism, and climate change.

2009

Julian Agyeman, *Speaking for Ourselves: Environmental Justice in Canada* (Vancouver, BC: University of British Columbia, 2009).

Speaking for Ourselves brings together Aboriginal and non-Aboriginal scholars and activists who propel equity issues to the forefront by considering environmental justice from multiple perspectives, specifically in Canadian contexts.

Robert D. Bullard and Beverly Wright, *Race, Place, and Environmental Justice After Hurricane Katrina: Struggles to Reclaim, Rebuild, and Revitalize New Orleans and the Gulf Coast* (Boulder, CO: Westview Press, 2009).

The authors provide a comprehensive analysis of how race and place impact the rebuilding and revitalization of New Orleans and the Gulf Coast states. Poor people and people of color tend to suffer more in the wake of natural disasters. The authors raise very important questions: What went wrong? Can it happen again? Is our government equipped to plan for, mitigate, respond to, and recover from natural and man-made disasters? Can the public trust government response to be fair? Does race matter? Racial disparities exist in disaster response, cleanup, rebuilding, reconstruction, and recovery. Displaced residents have a right to return, a right to rebuild, a right to work, a right to vote, and a right to recover from the hurricane.

Al Gedicks, *Dirty Gold: Indigenous Alliances to End Global Resource Colonialism* (Boston, MA: South End Press, 2009).

The author discusses how indigenous peoples are working together to assert their sovereignty, using the language of human rights and the political might of transnational solidarity networks to challenge resource colonialism and environmental racism. The book offers numerous examples of their successful strategies for sovereignty. In Wisconsin, an Ojibwe tribe waged a 28-year battle against some of the world's largest mining corporations to preserve their sacred rice beds from mining pollution and won. In Nigeria, indigenous women successfully shut down oil production as part of their fight to preserve their subsistence farming and fishing economy.

Michael B. Gerrard and Sheila Foster, *The Law of Environmental Justice: Theories and Procedures to Address Disproportionate Risk*, 2nd ed. (Chicago, IL: American Bar Association, 2009).

This book is a resource for environmental justice lawyers, grassroots organizations, governmental agencies, and environmental groups. The authors discuss the infamous *Alexander v. Sandoval* case and techniques used to analyze environmental justice issues.

Barry I. Hill, *Environmental Justice: Legal Theory and Practice* (Washington, DC: Environmental Law Institute, 2009).

This book examines how environmental risks and harms affect specific populations in our society. The environmental justice movement aims at having the public and private sectors address this disproportionate burden of risk and exposure to pollution in minority and poor communities. The author indicates that these individuals need to be part of the decision-making process on environmental degradation in their communities. The book also examines environmental laws and civil rights legal theories adopted in environmental justice litigation to address environmental injustices.

H. Patrick Hynes and Russell Lopez, *Urban Health: Readings in the Social, Built, and Physical Environments of U.S. Cities* (Sudbury, MA: Jones & Bartlett, 2009).

The authors provide a fresh examination of how the urban environment in the late twentieth and early twenty-first centuries responded to plans of addressing social inequalities, health, and environmental justice in the United States. Each chapter offers a paradigm of environment protection that is grounded in social and racial equality.

M. Paloma Pavel and Carl Anthony, *Breakthrough Communities: Sustainability and Justice in the Next American Metropolis* (Cambridge, MA: MIT Press, 2009).

This book describes current efforts to create sustainable communities with attention to the "triple bottom line"—economy, environment, and equity—and argues that these three interests are mutually reinforcing. The book reflects a new way to think about cities and discusses the importance of people organizing to improve their quality of life and make their neighborhoods more livable. It includes the voices of people of color, labor activists, and community organizers, and case studies of communities not often included in the debate about sustainability.

Phaedra C. Pezzullo, *Toxic Tourism: Rhetorics of Pollution, Travel, and Environmental Justice* (Tuscaloosa, AL: University of Alabama Press, 2009).

The author examines environmental justice toxic tours as a tactic of resistance and their potential in reducing the cultural and physical distance between hosts and visitors. Tourism is at once both a beloved pastime and a denigrated form of popular culture. The author uses participant observation, interviews, documentaries, and secondary accounts in popular media to assist the reader in understanding these toxic tours. She provides the reader with illustrations such as Louisiana's "Cancer Alley," California's San Francisco Bay Area, and the Mexican border town of Matamoros.

Clifford Rechtschaffen, Eileen Gauna, and Catherine O'Neill, *Environmental Justice: Law, Policy & Regulation*, 2nd ed. (Durham, NC: Carolina Academic Press, 2009).

The authors provide an accessible compilation of interdisciplinary materials for studying environmental justice, interspersed with extensive notes, questions, and a teacher's manual with practice exercises designed to facilitate classroom discussion. In this second edition, the authors include new chapters addressing climate change, international environmental justice, and a capstone case study.

There is also in-depth information on public health and environmental justice for American Indian peoples.

David Schlosberg, *Defining Environmental Justice Theories, Movements, and Nature* (New York, NY: Oxford University Press, 2009).

The author examines how "justice" is used in self-described environmental justice movements and in theories of environmental and ecological justice. Justice is discussed in an environmental and ecological framework to explain the relationship of humans in their environment. The book provides a multifaceted notion of justice that is applied to environmental risks and human communities.

Dorceta E. Taylor, *The Environment and the People in American Cities, 1600s–1900s: Disorder, Inequality, and Social Change* (Durham, NC: Duke University Press, 2009).

The author explores the centuries-old connections between racism and the environment in American cities. She provides an in-depth examination of the development of urban environments and urban environmentalism in the United States over four centuries. She also traces the progression of several major thrusts in urban environmental activism, including the alleviation of poverty; sanitary reform and public health; safe, affordable, and adequate housing; parks, playgrounds, and open space; occupational health and safety; consumer protection (food and product safety); and land-use and urban planning.

Filomina C. Steady, ed., *Environmental Justice in the New Millennium: Global Perspective on Race, Ethnicity, and Human Rights* (New York, NY: Palgrave Macmillan, 2009).

This book provides a variety of case studies that discuss historical and theoretical perspectives on environmental justice; the persistence of models of domination, exploitation, and discrimination; gender implications of environmental degradation; violence and militarization; and corporate globalization, climate change, and the tragedy of Hurricane Katrina. The environmental justice movement is one of the fastest-growing social movements in the United States. The environmental justice paradigm provides a human rights challenge to the dominant model of economic development that emphasizes limitless growth where millions of people are threatened by an unsafe environment. All individuals are entitled to a clean, safe, and healthy environment.

2010

Steve Lerner, *Sacrifice Zones: The Front Lines of Toxic Exposure in the United States* (Cambridge, MA: MIT Press, 2010).

This book tells the stories of 12 communities, from Brooklyn, New York to Pensacola, Florida, that rose up to fight the industries and military bases causing disproportionately high levels of chemical pollution. The author calls these low-income neighborhoods "sacrifice zones," repurposing a Cold War term coined by U.S. government officials to designate areas contaminated with radioactive pollutants during the manufacture of nuclear weapons. He also argues that residents of a new generation of sacrifice zones, tainted with chemical pollutants, need additional regulatory protections.

Appendix

The W.K. Kellogg Foundation acknowledges and extends its gratitude to the following participants at our Environmental Health and Racial Equity Meeting on February 9–10, 2010, in Atlanta, Georgia. Each individual provided valuable insights into shaping this book.

Adolph Falcon
National Alliance for Hispanic Health
Washington, District of Columbia

Andrea Sybinsky
Communications Consortium Media Center
Washington, District of Columbia

Angel Torres
Clark Atlanta University/Environmental Justice Resource Center
Atlanta, Georgia

Angela Bryant
VISIONS Inc.
Rocky Mount, North Carolina

Annie Loya
Youth United for Community Action
East Palo Alto, California

Barbara Davis
VISIONS Inc.
Rocky Mount, North Carolina

Barbara Ferrer
Boston Public Health Commission
Boston, Massachusetts

Ben Gramling
Sixteenth Street Community Health Center
Milwaukee, Wisconsin

Beverly Wright
Deep South Center for Environmental Justice
New Orleans, Louisiana

Bianca Encinias
Southwest Network for Environmental and Economic Justice
Albuquerque, New Mexico

Brad van Guilder
Ecology Center
Ann Arbor, Michigan

Brenda Salgado
Movement Strategy Center
Oakland, California

Brian Smedley
Joint Center For Political and Economic Studies
Washington, District of Columbia

Carolina Macias
Little Village Environmental Justice Organization
Chicago, Illinois

Caroline Farrell
Center on Race, Poverty & the Environment
Delano, California

Carolyn Bell
Community Health Resources and Coalition of Black Trade Unionists
Memphis, Tennessee

Cecil Corbin Mark
WEACT for Environmental Justice
New York, New York

Claire Barnett
Healthy Schools Network
Albany, New York

Darryl Molina
Communities for a Better Environment
Huntington Park, California

Dave Jenkins
Alternatives for Community and Environment
Roxbury, Massachusetts

Diane Takvorian
Environmental Health Coalition
National City, California

Donele Wilkins
Detroiters Working for Environmental Justice
Detroit, Michigan

Elizabeth Tan
Urban Habitat
Oakland, California

Gail Christopher
W.K. Kellogg Foundation
Battle Creek, Michigan

Genaro Lopez-Rendon
Southwest Workers Union
San Antonio, Texas

Giovanna Di Chiro
Nuestras Raices
Holyoke, Massachusetts

Glenn Johnson
Clark Atlanta University/Environmental Justice Resource Center
Atlanta, Georgia

Heetan Kalan
New World Foundation
New York, New York

Joanne Perodin
Children's Environmental Health Network
Washington, District of Columbia

Joel Lewis
VISIONS Inc.
Roxbury, Massachusetts

Jonnette Hawkins
US Department of Housing and Urban Development
Atlanta, Georgia

Jose Bravo
Just Transition Alliance
San Diego, California

Juliet Ellis
Urban Habitat
Oakland, California

Kalila Barnett
Alternatives for Community and Environment
Roxbury, Massachusetts

Kathy Sessions
Health and Environmental Funders Network
Bethesda, Maryland

Kimberly Wasserman
Little Village Environmental Justice Organization
Chicago, Illinois

Linda Jo Doctor
W.K. Kellogg Foundation
Battle Creek, Michigan

Lisa Sutton
Clark Atlanta University/Environmental Justice Resource Center
Atlanta, Georgia

Mark Mitchell
Connecticut Coalition for Environmental Justice
Hartford, Connecticut

Martha Soledad Vela Acosta
The Kresge Foundation
Troy, Michigan

Marva King
Environmental Protection Agency
Washington, District of Columbia

Melissa Chandler
Clark Atlanta University/Environmental Justice Resource Center
Atlanta, Georgia

Michael Sarmiento
Southwest Network for Environmental and Economic Justice
Albuquerque, New Mexico

Michelle Dawkins
Clark Atlanta University/Environmental Justice Resource Center
Atlanta, Georgia

Millie Buchanan
Jessie Smith Noyes Foundation
New York, New York

Miquela Craytor
Sustainable South Bronx
Bronx, New York

Neenah Estrella-Luna
Northeastern University
Boston, Massachusetts

Nikke Alex
Black Mesa Water Coalition
Flagstaff, Arizona

Nile Malloy
Communities for a Better Environment
Huntington Park, California

Pamela Miller
Alaska Community Action on Toxics
Anchorage, Alaska

Patrick MacRoy
Alliance for Healthy Homes
Washington, District of Columbia

Paul Mohai
University of Michigan
Ann Arbor, Michigan

Payton Wilkins
Detroiters Working for Environmental Justice
Detroit, Michigan

Peggy Shepard
WE ACT
New York, New York

Ramtin Arablouei
Health and Environmental Funders Network
Bethesda, Maryland

Richard Gragg
Florida A&M University
Tallahassee, Florida

Rick Pinderhughes
VISIONS Inc.
Roxbury, Massachusetts

Robby Rodriguez
SouthWest Organizing Project
Albuquerque, New Mexico

Robert Bullard
Clark Atlanta University/Environmental Justice Resource Center
Atlanta, Georgia

Roger Kim
Asian Pacific Environmental Network
Oakland, California

Susana Almanza
PODER
Austin, Texas

Tennie White
Coalition of Communities
Jackson, Mississippi

Tom Goldtooth
Indigenous Environmental Network
Bemidji, Minnesota

About the Authors

Robert D. Bullard, PhD, is the Edmund Asa Ware Distinguished Professor of Sociology and director of the Environmental Justice Resource Center at Clark Atlanta University. Professor Bullard is the author of 15 books. His award-winning book, *Dumping in Dixie: Race, Class, and Environmental Quality* (Westview Press 2000), is a standard text in the environmental justice field. Some of his other related titles include *Just Sustainabilities: Development in an Unequal World* (MIT Press 2003); *Highway Robbery: Transportation Racism and New Routes to Equity* (South End Press 2004); *The Quest for Environmental Justice: Human Rights and the Politics of Pollution* (Sierra Club Books 2005); *Growing Smarter: Achieving Livable Communities, Environmental Justice, and Regional Equity* (MIT Press 2007); and *The Black Metropolis in the Twenty-First Century: Race, Power, and the Politics of Place* (Rowman & Littlefield 2007). Professor Bullard is the coauthor of *Toxic Wastes and Race at Twenty: 1987–2007 Report* (United Church of Christ Witness & Justice Ministries 2007). His most recent book is *Race, Place and Environmental Justice After Hurricane Katrina: Struggles to Reclaim, Rebuild, and Revitalize New Orleans and the Gulf Coast* (Westview Press 2009).

    Glenn S. Johnson, PhD, is a research associate with the Environmental Justice Resource Center and an associate professor in the Department of Sociology and Criminal Justice at Clark Atlanta University. He coordinates several major research activities into topics including transportation racism, urban sprawl, smart growth, public involvement, facility siting, toxics, and regional equity. He is the coeditor of *Just Transportation: Dismantling Race and Class Barriers to Mobility* (New Society Publishers 1997); *Sprawl City: Race, Politics, and Planning in Atlanta* (Island Press 2000); and *Highway Robbery: Transportation Racism and New Routes to Equity* (South End Press 2004). Johnson received his BA (1987), MA

(1991), and PhD (1996) degrees in sociology from the University of Tennessee at Knoxville.

Angel O. Torres, MCP, is a geographic information system (GIS) training specialist with the Environmental Justice Resource Center at Clark Atlanta University. He is the coeditor of *Sprawl City: Race, Politics, and Planning in Atlanta* (Island Press 2000) and *Highway Robbery: Transportation Racism and New Routes to Equity* (South End Press 2004). Torres received his BS degree (1993) in mathematics from Clark Atlanta University and his Masters of City Planning (MCP) degree (1995) from Georgia Institute of Technology in Atlanta, Georgia.

Index